EXTENDING FINANCIAL INCLUSION IN AFRICA

EXTENDING FINANCIAL INCLUSION IN AFRICA

Edited by

DANIEL MAKINA

Professor of Finance, University of South Africa, Pretoria, South Africa

ACADEMIC PRESS

An imprint of Elsevier

Academic Press is an imprint of Elsevier
125 London Wall, London EC2Y 5AS, United Kingdom
525 B Street, Suite 1650, San Diego, CA 92101, United States
50 Hampshire Street, 5th Floor, Cambridge, MA 02139, United States
The Boulevard, Langford Lane, Kidlington, Oxford OX5 1GB, United Kingdom

Notices
Knowledge and best practice in this field are constantly changing. As new research and experience broaden our understanding, changes in research methods, professional practices, or medical treatment may become necessary.

Practitioners and researchers must always rely on their own experience and knowledge in evaluating and using any information, methods, compounds, or experiments described herein. In using such information or methods they should be mindful of their own safety and the safety of others, including parties for whom they have a professional responsibility.

To the fullest extent of the law, neither the Publisher nor the authors, contributors, or editors, assume any liability for any injury and/or damage to persons or property as a matter of products liability, negligence or otherwise, or from any use or operation of any methods, products, instructions, or ideas contained in the material herein.

Library of Congress Cataloging-in-Publication Data
A catalog record for this book is available from the Library of Congress

British Library Cataloguing-in-Publication Data
A catalogue record for this book is available from the British Library

ISBN: 978-0-12-814164-9

For information on all Academic Press publications visit our website at https://www.elsevier.com/books-and-journals

Publisher: Candice Janco
Acquisition Editor: J. Scott Bentley
Editorial Project Manager: Susan Ikeda
Production Project Manager: Sojan P. Pazhayattil
Cover Designer: Mark Rogers

Typeset by TNQ Technologies

Working together to grow libraries in developing countries

www.elsevier.com • www.bookaid.org

CONTENTS

Section 4 EMPIRICAL EVIDENCE FOCUSING ON AFRICA

Chapter 8 Macroeconomic Determinants of Financial Inclusion: Evidence Using Dynamic Panel Data Analysis

Kidanemariam Gebregziabher Gebrehiwot, Daniel Makina

Chapter 9 Financial Inclusion and Economic Growth: Evidence From a Panel of Selected African Countries

Daniel Makina, Yabibal M. Walle

LIST OF CONTRIBUTORS

Joshua Yindenaba Abor
Department of Finance, University of Ghana Business School, Accra, Ghana

Elikplimi Komla Agbloyor
Department of Finance, University of Ghana Business School, Accra, Ghana

Sydney Chikalipah
Department of Finance and Tax, University of Cape Town, Cape Town, South Africa

Ashenafi Beyene Fanta
University of Stellenbosch Business School, Cape Town, South Africa

Kidanemariam Gebregziabher Gebrehiwot
Department of Economics, Mekelle University, Ethiopia

Haruna Issahaku
Department of Economics and Entrepreneurship Development, University of Development Students, Ghana

Jammeh Kebba
Research Department, African Development Bank, Abidjan, Côte d'Ivoire

John Kuada
Department of Business and Management, Aalborg University, Aalborg, Denmark

Daniel Makina
Department of Finance, Risk Management and Banking, University of South Africa, Pretoria, South Africa

Sheilla Nyasha
Department of Economics, University of South Africa, Pretoria, South Africa

Nicholas M. Odhiambo
Department of Economics, University of South Africa, Pretoria, South Africa

Jacob Oduor
Research Department, African Development Bank, Abidjan, Côte d'Ivoire

Iwa Salami
Royal Docks School of Business and Law, University of East London, United Kingdom

Christian Tipoy
Department of Economics, University of KwaZulu-Natal, South Africa

Yabibal M. Walle
Department of Econometrics, Georg-August-University of Goettingen, Germany

Mulatu F. Zerihun
Department of Economics, Tshwane University of Technology, Pretoria, South Africa

INTRODUCTION

AN OVERVIEW OF FINANCIAL SERVICES ACCESS AND USAGE IN AFRICA

Daniel Makina

Department of Finance, Risk Management and Banking, University of South Africa, Pretoria, South Africa

CHAPTER OUTLINE

1. Introduction

The clarion call — *finance for all* — has likely been around from as far back as when people started using money. In one of its publications, the Consultative Group to Assist the Poor (CGAP, 2006) provides salient historical milestones. Informal savings and credit groups are reported to have operated across the world for centuries. In 1462, towards the end of the Middle Ages, an Italian monk created the first official pawn shop, which did not charge interest in an effort to stem the usurious practices of private moneylenders who lent money at extortionate rates. Predictably, such pawn shops were not sustainable, leading Pope Leon X in 1515 to authorize the charging of interest so that pawn shops could cover their operating costs. Then in the 18th century, an Irish national,

Extending Financial Inclusion in Africa. https://doi.org/10.1016/B978-0-12-814164-9.00001-3

Jonathan Swift, established the Irish Loan Funds system, which could be regarded as the first microcredit program, as it disbursed small loans to poor farmers without collateral. In the 19th century, Friedrich Wilhelm Raiffeisen conceived a credit co-operative in Germany, which concept spread rapidly to other European countries and North America, eventually taking root in developing countries during the colonial periods. Between 1950 and 1970, governments took keen interest in expanding access to agricultural credit. To this end, they set up subsidized state-owned development finance institutions that would disburse concessional loans to farmers and small entrepreneurs which proved to be unsustainable once again. In the early 1970s, microcredit programs emerged whereby small loans were extended to groups of poor women, the early pioneers being Grameen Bank in Bangladesh, ACCION International in Latin America and the Self-Employed Women's Association Bank in India.

By the beginning of the 1990s, the term 'microcredit' was replaced by the term 'microfinance' — the provision of a full set of financial services such as credit, savings, money transfers, insurance and other related services to the poor. Today microfinance is provided not only by specialized institutions but also by a range of providers that includes both financial and non-financial institutions, such as telecommunications companies. The term 'finance to all' has now crystallized into the common term 'financial inclusion', which the Global Partnership for Financial Inclusion defines as provision of financial services — such as deposit and savings accounts, payment services, loans, and insurance — that are readily available to consumers so that they can actively and effectively use them to meet their specific needs. The role of financial inclusion has since been acknowledged in the goal to achieve the 17 Sustainable Development Goals (SDGs) adopted by the United Nations on 25 September 2015. Though none of the SDGs explicitly target financial inclusion, it is recognized as an enabler for most of them.

2. The State of Financial Inclusion at a Glance

The World Bank Global Findex (2017) estimates that about 1.7 billion adults in the world are unbanked; that is, they are without an account at a financial institution or through a mobile money provider. The majority of these unbanked populations are in the developing world, and about half are concentrated in just seven countries: Bangladesh, China, India, Indonesia, Mexico,

Nigeria and Pakistan. There is also a gender dimension to financial exclusion, as 56% of all unbanked adults are women.

Africa is the world's least banked region, with an estimated 80% of its one billion people lacking access to formal banking services in a world where, on average, 69% of adults have an account. On average, the World Bank estimates that only 24.8% of adults in sub-Saharan Africa have a bank account, and only 14.8% of adults possess a debit card. Compared with other developing regions, these percentages are significantly lower; in Asia, the average percentages of ownership of a bank account and debit card are 53.2% and 32%, respectively; for the MENA region, 47.7% and 36%; for Latin America, 46.7% and 31.2%; and for emerging Europe, 58.1% and 43.2%. The situation also is not good in terms of overall access to banking services, as African countries have only about 7.5 bank branches and 13.3 ATMs per 100,000 people, compared with the global average of 18.9 bank branches and 48.3 ATMs per 100,000 people.

The World Bank considers account ownership a key indicator of financial inclusion, because having an account enables an individual to store money, build savings, make payments, send and receive remittances and access credit. Formal account ownership across African countries in 2017 is depicted in Table 1.1.

The majority of African countries belong to the low-income group and have the lowest level of financial inclusion, with average account ownership of 34%. The lower middle-income group countries have a slightly higher level of financial inclusion with average account ownership of 41%, and the few upper middle income countries – Algeria, Botswana, Gabon, Libya, Mauritius, Namibia and South Africa – have the highest average account ownership at 66%. It would appear that the level of financial inclusion is positively correlated with the level of income – the higher the income, the higher the level of financial inclusion. The gender gap across countries is generally country-specific, and religion seems to have a bearing on women's financial exclusion. It is more acute in countries with substantial Muslim populations, such as Algeria, Benin, Burkina Faso, Egypt, Mali, Mauritania, Morocco, Nigeria and Tunisia. Poor countries such as Chad, Liberia, Mozambique, Togo and Uganda also have relatively high gender gaps. The gender gap between the rich and poor shows no relationship to the level of financial inclusion, as low-income countries have an average gap of 15%, not very different from that of upper middle-income countries at 14%.

Noteworthy in the account ownership statistics is the influence of mobile money account ownership in elevating the level of financial inclusion in a number of countries. Despite Kenya

Table 1.1 Account Ownership of African Countries, 2017.

Country	Income Group	Adults With an Account (%)	Gap Between Men and Women (% Age Points)	Gap Between Richer and Poorer (% Age Points)
Benin	Low	38	20	11
Burkina Faso	Low	43	17	27
Central African Republic	Low	14	8	8
Chad	Low	22	14	13
Congo, Dem. Rep	Low	26	–	14
Ethiopia	Low	35	12	21
Guinea	Low	23	8	6
Liberia	Low	36	15	15
Madagascar	Low	18	–	9
Malawi	Low	34	8	21
Mali	Low	35	20	7
Mozambique	Low	42	18	25
Niger	Low	16	9	8
Rwanda	Low	50	11	19
Senegal	Low	42	8	13
Sierra Leone	Low	20	9	11
South Sudan	Low	9	8	8
Tanzania	Low	47	9	16
Togo	Low	45	15	18
Uganda	Low	59	13	20
Zimbabwe	Low	55	8	19
Cameron	Lower middle	35	9	16
Congo, Rep	Lower middle	26	10	13
Côte d'Ivoire	Lower middle	41	11	12
Egypt, Arab Rep	Lower middle	33	12	21
Ghana	Lower middle	58	8	16
Kenya	Lower middle	82	8	18
Lesotho	Lower middle	46	–	22
Mauritania	Lower middle	21	11	13
Morocco	Lower middle	29	25	16
Nigeria	Lower middle	40	24	25
Tunisia	Lower middle	37	17	26

Table 1.1 Account Ownership of African Countries, 2017.—*continued*

Country	Income Group	Adults With an Account (%)	Gap Between Men and Women (% Age Points)	Gap Between Richer and Poorer (% Age Points)
Zambia	Lower middle	46	11	24
Algeria	Upper middle	43	27	13
Botswana	Upper middle	51	9	27
Gabon	Upper middle	59	10	15
Libya	Upper middle	66	11	12
Mauritius	Upper middle	90	6	6
Namibia	Upper middle	81	–	17
South Africa	Upper middle	69	–	11

Source: The Global Findex Database, 2017.

being in the lower middle-income group, it has now a level of financial inclusion comparable to that of countries in the upper middle income because it has more people with mobile money accounts than those with bank accounts. Three low-income countries in East Africa – Rwanda, Tanzania and Uganda – have account ownership levels similar to those of lower middle-income countries because of their increased levels of mobile money accounts. In West Africa, low-income countries – Burkina Faso, Senegal and Togo – have similarly improved account ownership because of mobile money usage. In Togo, for example, account ownership rose from 18% in 2011 to 45% in 2017 to surpass that of Cote d'Ivoire, a lower middle-income country, because of subscriptions to mobile money. For the West African region as a whole, mobile money usage has resulted in account ownership by individuals almost doubling from 23% in 2011 to 43% in 2017.

Despite gains in financial inclusion since the first World Bank Global Findex survey in 2011, for sub-Saharan Africa the proportion of adults with an account in a financial institution has largely remained stagnant; it is the proportion of adults with a mobile money account, which had nearly doubled to 21% by 2017, that has driven financial inclusion to new heights. This has resulted in eight African countries having 20% or more of adults who only use a mobile money account, namely Burkina Faso, Gabon, Kenya, Senegal, Tanzania, Uganda and Zimbabwe. Notwithstanding this notable progress, Africa still lags behind all other developing regions in terms of financial inclusion.

According to BMI Research (2018), sub-Saharan Africa is the lowest scoring region in its Financial Barriers Index, with a score of 29.2 out 100, compared with Asia (48.7 out of 100), emerging Europe (56.3 out of 100), Latin America (55.7 out of 100) and the Middle East and North Africa (MENA − 40.8 out of 100). While financial barriers are observed to be acute in Central and West Africa, countries such as Botswana, Cote d'Ivoire, Ghana, Kenya, Mauritius, Nigeria, Rwanda and South Africa perform far better than their regional peers do. BMI Research attributes the weak performance of many African states to low levels of financial inclusion, high lending rates, limited financial market efficiency and trustworthiness, and notes that these factors pose significant barriers to inclusive growth and foreign portfolio investment growth.

3. Africas Institutional Environment

In order to understand why Africa lags behind other developing regions in financial inclusion, one must consider its institutional setting. Much of Africa could be said to be at the bottom of the economic pyramid (BOP). The BOP is a socio-economic concept that endeavours to group the world's poorest, who face a significant number of barriers to opportunity, which include, among others, access to financial services. The concept was popularized by Prahalad (2004), whose vision was to unleash the creative and productive potential of the poor in an inclusive capitalist system. Prahalad focused corporate attention on opportunities at the BOP observing that low-income markets could be best reached through a low-price, low-margin, high-volume model. However, other scholars such as Simanis (2012) noted that the model could only work if two conditions are satisfied: (1) if 'a company can leverage an existing infrastructure that serves wealthier customers to offer a product or service to poor consumers, and (2) the consumers already know how to buy and use the offering'.

According to the UNDP (2007), BOP economies comprise about four billion people (roughly two-thirds of the world population) who live on less than $1.25 per day. The characteristics of BOP economies include, among others, agrarian orientation, poverty, income inequality, poor education and health services, gender inequality, inadequate hard and soft infrastructure, low per-capita income and underdeveloped financial sectors. These socio-economic conditions arise from institutional voids — that is, 'where institutional arrangements that support markets are absent, weak, or fail to accomplish the role expected of them' (Mair & Marti, 2009, p. 419). Accordingly, Khanna, Palepu, and Sinha (2005) observe that these conditions substantially increase operating costs of firms operating at the BOP, which have to work around these institutional voids.

Many African countries have low levels of financial inclusion because they suffer from institutional voids. The growing microfinance sector is a response to fill in the institutional voids in financial services. The concept of microfinance is to reach out to the huge low-income market through provision of tiny loans and other financial services in high volumes so as to make it profitable or sustainable. The same principle is being applied in the provision of mobile money. Enabling mobile phones are filling the institutional void of weak infrastructure that has prevented traditional banks from reaching out to unbanked low-income communities.

4. Organization of the Book

The book is organized in five parts, of which this chapter is Part I — Introduction. Part II — Evolution of Financial Markets and Institutions — comprises chapters exploring the evolution of banks, the causal relationship between financial development and economic growth, and the role of finance in promoting the private sector. Part III — Geography of Financial Markets and Institutions — comprises chapters that scan the landscape of the financial sector in Africa. Part IV — Empirical Evidence Focusing on Africa — comprises chapters that examine empirical evidence on various issues regarding financial inclusion. Part V — The Trajectory of Future Developments — concludes with chapters that look at the trajectory of financial inclusion in Africa.

Snapshots of the contents of the book chapters follow.

4.1 Part II — Evolution of Financial Markets and Institutions

In Chapter 2, Daniel Makina traces the evolution of banks in Africa from pre-colonial to post-colonial periods. Crucially, post-colonial institutions are discussed in the context of differences arising from colonial origins and how they have since evolved in extending financial inclusion.

In Chapter 3, Nicholas Odhiambo, Sheilla Nyasha, Mulatu Zerihun and Christian Tipoy examine the dynamic causal relationship between financial development and economic growth in French- and English-speaking African countries during the 1990–2014 period. They use three macroeconomic proxies of financial development, namely liquid liabilities, deposit money bank assets and bank deposits, to examine this linkage. Their results show that the causality between financial development and economic growth differs significantly between English-speaking and French-speaking countries.

In Chapter 4, Joshua Yindenaba Abor, Haruna Issahaku, Agyapomaa Gyeke-Dako and Elikplimi Komla Agbloyor examine the role of finance in promoting private sector development in Africa, and discuss the constraints to extending financial inclusion. They conclude by advocating innovative funding sources such as remittances, crowdfunding, structured trade finance, private equity and venture capital, green bonds, leasing and factoring, mobile money services, and alternative capital markets for small and medium enterprises.

4.2 Part III — Geography of Financial Markets and Institutions

In Chapter 5, Sydney Chikalipah and Daniel Makina provide an overview of the geography of the financial sector in Africa. The landscape of financial markets and institutions explored includes banking institutions, capital markets, and the pension and insurance sectors. They further explore, in Chapter 6, the landscape of microfinance institutions and the informal finance sector as well as the growing microinsurance and mobile money sectors.

In Chapter 7, Jacob Oduor and Jammeh Kebba discuss the role of regulation and governance in either enhancing or limiting financial inclusion. Additionally, they examine the efficacy of prudential reforms implemented over the years, citing successes, failures, policy recommendations and trajectories for the future.

4.3 Part IV — Empirical Evidence Focusing on Africa

In Chapter 8, Kidanemariam Gebregziabher Gebrehiwot and Daniel Makina examine the macroeconomic determinants of financial inclusion across 27 African countries. Their results show that financial inclusion is significantly and positively related to its lagged value, GDP per capita and mobile infrastructure, and negatively related to government borrowing. The negative relationship between financial inclusion and government borrowing has important policy implications for African countries, which have a low ratio of private sector credit to GDP.

In Chapter 9, Daniel Makina and Yabibal Walle investigate the relationship between financial inclusion and macroeconomic growth in selected African countries against the odds of non-availability of long-dated time series data on indicators of financial inclusion. Despite data constraints, they find that financial inclusion − as measured by the dimension of access − has a significantly positive effect on economic growth in Africa.

In Chapter 10, Ashenafi Beyene Fanta and Daniel Makina investigate the relationship between financial inclusion and technology using cross-sectional data of 168 countries, of which 48 are African. They report a significant positive relationship between financial inclusion and technology proxied by internet and ATM access.

In Chapter 11, Ashenafi Beyene Fanta and Daniel Makina analyse unintended consequences of financial inclusion in the form of over-indebtedness and its links with poverty using FinScope survey data from selected African countries. Their results show that while over-indebtedness can be triggered by cross-borrowing and lack of credit literacy, it can be curbed by increased income and employment. They further find that over-indebtedness is likely to aggravate rather than alleviate poverty.

4.4 Part V − the Trajectory of Future Developments

In Chapter 12, John Kuada discusses the different ways in which financial inclusion can help achieve the UN's 17 SDGs for ending poverty, protecting the planet, and ensuring prosperity for all by 2030. He also provides pointers to some of the challenges that need to be addressed. A key message is that financial inclusion alone may not provide the poorest segments of African populations with the skills and competencies they need to find pathways out of poverty.

In Chapter 13, Iwa Salami observes that some emerging technology-enabled alternative financing approaches have cross-border dimensions. This therefore requires a coordinated approach to regulation, of which a regional regulatory approach is likely to play a prominent role. She discusses the feasibility of such an approach.

In Chapter 14, Daniel Makina examines the manner in which FinTech is breaking the barriers to financial inclusion. He first traces the history of FinTech and its evolution both globally and in Africa. Then he discusses the impact of selected FinTech products in the African context.

References

BMI Research. (2018). *Industry trend analysis —Index signals: SSA rising stars for financial sector development.* BMI Research, 24 April 2018.

CGAP. (2006). *Access for all: Building inclusive financial systems.* Washington DC: CGAP.

Khanna, T., Palepu, K. G., & Sinha, J. (2005). Strategies that fit emerging markets. *Harvard Business Review, 83,* 63–74.

Mair, J., & Marti, I. (2009). Entrepreneurship in and around institutional voids: A case study from Bangladesh. *Journal of Business Venturing, 55,* 819–850.

Prahalad, C. K. (2004). *The fortune at the bottom of the pyramid: Eradicating poverty through profits.* Wharton School Publishing, 2004.

Simanis, E. (2012). *Realty check at the bottom of the pyramid.* Harvard Business Review. June 2012 issue https://hbr.org/2012/06/reality-check-at-the-bottom-of-the-pyramid.

UNDP. (2007). *Human development report 2007/2008.* New York: United Nations Development Programme.

World Bank. (2017). *The global findex database: Measuring financial inclusion and the fintech revolution.* Washington DC: World Bank.

Further Reading

CGAP. (2016). *Achieving the sustainable development goals: The role of financial inclusion.* Washington DC: CGAP.

Cheston, S., & Kuhn, L. (2002). Empowering women through microfinance. In S. Daley-Harris (Ed.), *Pathways out of poverty: Innovations in microfinance for the poorest families: 167–228.* Bloomfield, CT: Kumarian Press.

GPFI. (2011). *Global standard-setting bodies and financial inclusion for the poor: Toward proportionate standards and guidance.* Washington DC: CGAP.

Varman, R., Skalen, P., & Belk, R. W. (2012). Conflicts at the bottom of the pyramid: Profitability, poverty alleviation, and neoliberal governmentality. *Journal of Public Policy and Marketing, 31,* 19–35.

2

EVOLUTION OF FINANCIAL MARKETS AND INSTITUTIONS

2

HOW DID BANKS EVOLVE IN AFRICA?

Daniel Makina
Department of Finance, Risk Management and Banking, University of South Africa, Pretoria, South Africa

1. Introduction

The contemporary view is that a competitive financial system that intermediates funds from those who save to those who consume and/or invest is the lifeblood of a healthy and vibrant economy. A financial system comprises financial intermediaries (banks, insurance companies and similar institutions) and financial markets (stock and bond markets) that play this intermediation role. When one looks at the proliferation of financial intermediaries and financial markets today, one is tempted to think they have existed from time immemorial. Just like human beings, financial institutions have evolved over time to become what they are today.

In ancient times, before the advent of money, trade among people was conducted through barter deals. A producer of cooking pots, for instance, would sell excess production to another for

Extending Financial Inclusion in Africa. https://doi.org/10.1016/B978-0-12-814164-9.00002-5

other goods such as, say, clothes he/she does not produce, and vice versa. The value of exchanged goods or services was determined through negotiation. For instance, by agreement a cooking pot could be exchanged for two pieces of cloth. Assuming ancient people were rational economic agents, value was determined taking account of (a) the effort or labour involved in producing the good or service and (b) the demand and supply of the good or service. However, in the absence of a medium of exchange, during this process the value of a good or service could change depending on what it was exchanged for. The cooking pot could be exchanged for one chicken, but this would not mean that the chicken is also worth two pieces of cloth. The chicken exchanged for one cooking pot could be worth three pieces of cloth in another exchange. In other words, there was no measure of value. Hence, the value of exchanged goods or services could be distorted because a barter exchange could only be possible when there was a 'double coincidence of wants' between two parties. Some other obvious limitations of barter trade include indivisibility of some goods, lack of standard for deferred payments and problems in storing wealth.

According to Adam Smith in his *Wealth of Nations*, the limitations of barter trade gave rise to money as a medium of exchange but did not eradicate the practice of barter trade. Davies (2002, p. 28) provides an all-embracing definition of money as 'anything that is widely used for making payments and accounting for debts and credits'. Thus it can be anything, but money is best defined by its functions as a unit of account, medium of exchange, means of payment, standard for deferred payments and store of value.

From ancient literature we are told that the concept and system of banking preceded that of money. Recorded history shows that the concept of banking originated in Ancient Mesopotamia.[1] During those times, royal palaces and temples were used as warehouses for grain and other valuable commodities. Receipts issued to depositors were transferable among both depositors and third parties, which practice was in essence a banking operation. Over time, some private houses got involved in these banking operations, which were regulated according to the Code of Hammurabi[2] (Dyneley, 1904).

---

[1]According to the *Ancient History Encyclopaedia*, Mesopotamia, which meant 'land of rivers', was a historical region situated within the Tigris–Euphrates river system that corresponds to most of Iraq, parts of Iran, Syria and Turkey.
[2]In recorded history, the Code of Hammurabi is one of the earliest surviving codes of law, named after Hammurabi, the sixth King of the First Babylonian Dynasty, who reigned from 1792 BC to 1750 BC.

In Ancient Egypt,[3] a system of banking developed from the practice of centralizing harvests in state warehouses. Farmers would deposit their grain in these state warehouses and receive deposit receipts reflecting their wealth, which they would use as one method of making payment of debts to third parties. In the aftermath of the metallic monetary system during the Hellenistic Era[4] (323–30 BC), precious metals commenced to be used as a store of value and medium of exchange, largely for external payments in Egypt, but grain banking continued to exist nevertheless. However, during the Roman Era (753 BC to CE 1453), the grain system was more or less displaced by the metallic monetary system that introduced coinage – that is, the use coins as a medium of exchange. During the same era, Armstrong (sa) narrates that something similar to today's offshore banking industry first emerged in the small and remotes island of Delos whose only greatest assets were the harbour and the wealthy temple of Apollo. By then, banking in Europe was conducted exclusively on a cash basis. However, in Delos cash transactions were replaced by a system of credit receipts and payments. Delos competed with a cash-based system conducted by Europe's main banking centres – Carthage and Corinth. Fortuitously, the rise of Rome disabled these centres, leaving the remote island of Delos to practise its model of banking, which the Romans subsequently copied during their reign.

The historian Ferris (1902) narrates that the Knights Templar[5] ran the earliest Europe-wide and Mideast banking from the 12th to 14th century. Then in 1397, the first modern bank in Europe, the Medici Bank of Florence, was established in Italy and operated until 1494. By the 17th century the banking system had become fairly developed, so that European countries that ventured into Africa from that period forward exported the system to the countries they colonized.

---

[3]According to Kitchen (1991), Ancient Egypt was a civilization that existed around 3150 BC in North Eastern Africa along the lower reaches of the Nile River, now known as Egypt.

[4]According to *Encyclopaedia Britannia*, this is the period between the death of Alexander the Great in 323 BC and the conquest of Egypt by Rome in 30 BC. The numerous kingdoms that resulted from the breakup of Alexander's empire spread the Greek (Hellenic) culture and fused it with the cultures of other populations.

[5]The *Oxford Dictionary* defines the Knights Templar as a religious and military order for the protection of pilgrims to the Holy Land, founded as the Poor Knights of Christ and the Temple of Solomon in 1118. Ferris (1902) reports that these soldiers of the Temple were pioneers in the development of credit and its instruments, as they handled capital in Europe and were expert accountants and judicious administrators.

Before colonization there was a rudimentary and unsophisticated banking system in the form of private banking and lending and rotating savings and credit associations (ROSCAS) across some parts of Africa. During colonization, these arrangements were either replaced by modern banks from Europe or existed side by side with the modern banks. Over time these indigenous forms of private banking and lending and ROSCAS became more sophisticated in the sense that they used banks rather than keeping their savings outside the banking system. It can be argued that indigenous private banking and lending as it existed in some parts of West Africa formed the foundation of modern microfinance institutions.

The modern banking system in post-independence Africa mirrors its colonial origin. The greater the economic power of the colonizer, the greater the development of banking systems in the former colonies. In this respect, Britain, whose economy was the biggest in Europe during colonial time, bequeathed its colonies with a more developed banking system than those of other European colonizers.

In what follows, the rest of this chapter is divided into four sections. Section 2 explores the nature of financial institutions in pre-colonial Africa. Section 3 discusses the colonial demarcation of Africa and the nature of colonial financial institutions. Section 4 examines how institutions have evolved post-colonially. Finally, Section 6 concludes by assessing the potential of post-colonial reforms in extending financial inclusion.

2. Financial Institutions in Pre-Colonial Africa

Because of scant studies on Africa, mainstream literature usually commences from the simple premise that financial systems evolved from pre-colonial indigenous barter trade-like structures. However, a historical evaluation of Ancient Egypt before it fell to the Romans shows that there was a monetary system that prevailed. Before the use of coinage, Meskell (2004) and Manuelian (1998) have observed that ancient Egyptians indeed had a money-barter system. The system involved the use of standard sacks of grain and the *deben*, which according to Bianchi (2004, p. 270) was unit of roughly 91 g or 3 ounces of copper or silver. Throughout Egypt prices were fixed and recorded using these units. Historians narrate that coined money was only introduced from abroad first as standardized pieces of precious metal during the 5th century BC in the Late Period (664–332 BC) of Ancient Egypt.[6] Historian Walbank (1984) narrates that in the centuries that followed, coinage became the acceptable medium of exchange by international traders.

Elsewhere in Africa, a pre-colonial system of money, credit and banking has been fairly recorded in West Africa. Economic historians such as Johnson (1968, 1970) have reported the use of cowrie shells obtained from the Indian and Pacific Oceans as money. Cowrie shells were polished, shiny egg-like sea snails that were of various types, colours and sizes. They were scarce, durable, countable, not easy to counterfeit and hence served as money in Africa and Asia. During the beginning of the 16th century, extensive use of cowries was reported by the Portuguese in West Africa. Johnson (1970, p.17) emphasized the usefulness of cowries as a means of exchange by stating: 'West African cowrie currencies ....[were] in no sense a "primitive" money, but a sophisticated form of currency capable of adaptation to the particular needs of West African trade'.

The oldest pre-colonial traditional savings, credit and banking institutions recorded in Africa were rotating credit associations that were believed to be of Yoruba (Nigeria) origin in which contributions were made in cowries. Crowther's Vocabulary of Yoruba Language published in 1843 provides details of small rotating credit associations among the Yoruba people meaning that they were in existence before 1843. The term 'rotating credit association' was coined by Geertz (1962, p. 243) who defined it as: 'The basic principle upon which the rotating credit association is founded is everywhere the same: a lump sum fund composed of fixed contributions from each member of the association is distributed, at fixed intervals and as a whole, to each member in turn'. However, scholars including Geertz found the definition to be too restrictive as contributions were not always fixed, the whole of the lump sum was not always received by a member and the word 'sum' did not accommodate contributions in kind which also could be made. To this end, Ardener (1964, p. 201) provides an all-embracing definition: 'An association formed upon a core of participants who agree to make regular contributions to a fund which is given, in whole or in part, to each contributor in rotation'.

---

[6]According to Mark (2016), the Late Period of Egypt refers to the final phase of an unbroken Egyptian artistic and cultural tradition dating back to the existence of the human species in the region.

The earliest rotating credit associations were not limited to the tribes of present Nigeria, and also included the tribes of present Benin, Cameroon, Egypt, Ghana, Sierra Leone, Sudan and some parts of Central Africa. In other parts of Africa, such associations have been observed during the colonial period, and their origins have been roughly dated as similar to those in West Africa.

Adebayo (1994) made a significant attempt to document the characteristics of the Yoruba savings and credit institutions before colonial rule. The Yoruba were observed to have had two basic institutions for saving and credit — *esusu* and *ajo*. *Esusu*, which was more developed, was a savings institution in the form of ROSCAS, while *ajo* was an institution that facilitated the process of accumulating money whereby an individual would enter into an agreement with a savings collector (the *alajo*) to pay a fixed sum of money at regular intervals and drew all his/her contribution at the end of an agreed period or on demand as needed. In essence the *alajo* operated like a mobile bank, pursuing his/her vocation either on a full-time or part-time basis, travelling from one client to another to collect their savings. A number of risks were inherent in the *ajo* institution. First, society then was illiterate, so that both the *alajo* and contributor relied on the power of the human memory, and hence cheating must have been common, especially by the *alajo*, the banker, whose accuracy of records was relied upon. Second, some unscrupulous *alajo* could simply disappear with contributors' savings, as there was no system of monitoring and regulating practices.

One main criticism of the *ajo* institution practiced in pre-colonial Yoruba is that the funds collected by the *alajo* were not lent out for investment, ostensibly because funds could be drawn on demand. Therefore, the *alajo* did not perform a maturity transformation function as in modern banking. However, it has been reported that there were instances when loans were made to the kingdom when the community was at war. Also, as society developed, the *alajo* extended credit to clients, thus forming the nucleus of the moneylending business as we know it today.

Bascom (1952) did a comprehensive study of *esusu* (a brand of ROSCAS), an ancient institution among the Yoruba. Although it has been difficult to pinpoint the exact date or period when *esusu* started, it is recorded that it was in existence during the cowrie currency period. Furthermore, Adebayo (1994) speculates that it could have preceded the introduction of cowrie currency judging from the similarity between *esusu* and mutual help associations.[7]

Thus, in pre-colonial Africa ROSCAS performed some of the functions that modern banks perform now. They assisted in capital formation. Savings were loaned out to those who needed them to expand their farms or businesses, or to pay for emergencies. The loans were restricted to the members of an association considered to be creditworthy by the group leader, and no security was required. In fact, all members would receive total funds as credit and would continue to repay the debt until the end of the cycle. In Yoruba society, interest was not charged on ROSCAS and was generally frowned upon. However, other cultures charged interest, as Ardener (1964) observed in ROSCAS in India.

By the beginning of the 19th century ROSCAS had increased in sophistication, had spread to most parts of Africa and were using modern money introduced by colonial governments. They were actually what we could term 'indigenous' financial institutions that colonial banks found in existence in Africa.

3. Colonial Demarcation of Africa and Financial Institutions

3.1 Colonial Demarcation

In order to understand how modern financial institutions evolved in Africa, one must account for the colonial structure of the continent. The colonial structure was laid out at the Berlin Conference in late 1884 and early 1885 that was chaired by Germany's chancellor, Otto von Bismarck. As Table 2.1 shows, the continent was carved out among seven European countries — Belgium, Britain, Germany, France, Italy, Portugal and Spain — according to spheres of influence that had been established through conquest. The British had most of East and Southern Africa carved out to it as well as a few countries in West Africa including Nigeria. The French had most of West Africa and a number of islands in both the Atlantic and Pacific Oceans. Belgium acquired the Congo, for which King Leopold II had financed its expeditions, and a small chunk of East Africa. Germany acquired four territories — Togo, Cameroon, German East Africa (present Tanzania, Burundi and Rwanda) and South West Africa (present Namibia).

---

[7]He cites *aro*, a mutual help association whereby a small group of friends or relations of between three and seven members form a club that would go to work in one member's farm in turns.

Table 2.1 Colonial Spheres of Influence After the Berlin Conference of 1884.

Colonial Power	Countries
Belgium	Belgian East Africa (Burundi and Rwanda)
	Belgian Congo (DRC)
Britain	Union of South Africa (South Africa)
	Basutoland (Lesotho)
	Swaziland
	Bechuanaland (Botswana)
	Southern Rhodesia (Zimbabwe)
	Northern Rhodesia (Zambia)
	Kenya
	Uganda
	British Somaliland (Somalia)
	Sudan
	Nigeria
	Gold Coast (Ghana)
	Sierra Leone
	Gambia
	Nyasaland (Malawi)
France	French Somaliland (Somalia)
	French Equatorial Africa (Congo, Gabon, Central African Republic and Chad)
	French West Africa (Senegal, Mauritania, Mali, Niger, Guinea, Benin and Burkina Faso)
	Algeria
	Morocco
	Tunisia
	Ivory Coast Cote d' Voire
Italy	Italian Somaliland (Somalia)
	Eritrea
	Libya
Portugal	Angola
	Mozambique
	Portuguese Guinea (Guinea Bissau)
	Cape Verde

Table 2.1 Colonial Spheres of Influence After the Berlin Conference of 1884.—*continued*

Colonial Power	Countries
Spain	Spanish Morocco (Morocco)
	Rio De Oro (Western Sahara)
	Rio Muni (Equatorial Guinea)
Germany	South-West Africa (Namibia)
	Tanganyika (Tanzania)
	Cameron
	Togo
Independent Nations	**Ethiopia and Liberia**

Source: Compiled from De Blij, H. J., & Muller, P. O. (2003). Geography: Realms, regions and concepts *(14th ed.). City: Wiley.*

Portugal acquired two colonies in Southern Africa, one inland West Africa and some small islands off West Africa. Italy acquired two colonies – Libya and a chunk of Somaliland. Spain took a small chunk of Morocco that was renamed Spanish Morocco. The only states not colonized were Liberia (created for freed and repatriated African slaves) and Ethiopia.

When Germany lost the First World War in 1918, its colonies were distributed to the alliance victors. Tanzania was distributed to the British, Togo and Cameron to the French, and South-West Africa (present-day Namibia) to South Africa and present-day Burundi and Rwanda to the Belgians. Considering that Germany joined the colonization spree late in the 1800s and lost the acquired colonies early in the 20th century, its influence in Africa with regard to the development of institutions was very limited.

Despite the disruption of traditional life and practices that accompanied colonialism, it served as an agent for the spread of Western civilization. One important feature of colonialism was the replacement of pre-colonial monies with European currencies. Local communities were forced to adopt the new currencies through imposition of taxes that had to be paid in the new currencies; in other words, they had to seek work from settlers and colonial firms to earn European currencies in order to pay the imposed taxes. Concomitantly, financial institutions in Africa evolved based on each country's links with the colonial authority. Trade and investment that took off in the colonies required financial services. In order to service the financial needs of colonial companies and settlers, British banks set up branches in the British Empire colonies; French banks set up branches in French colonies; Portuguese banks set up branches in Portuguese colonies; and likewise with German, Italian and Spanish banks.

The legal systems that guided the development of financial systems were exogenous in the sense that they were derived from the systems of the colonizers. Typically, British colonies adopted English common law, while French colonies adopted French civil law. According to the legal origins literature popularized by La Porta, Lopez-de-Silanes, Shleifer (2008), financial development (as measured by the ratio of equity market capitalization to GDP and the ratio of private credit to GDP) is influenced by legal origins. Klerman, Mahoney, Spamann, Weinstein (2011) have observed that legal origins literature found correlations between English common law and institutions such as financial markets and property rights, among others, to be conducive to growth. This observation was also the case in former French colonies but not in French civil law countries. Furthermore, their empirical study found that the identity of the colonizer is the better predictor of post-colonial growth rates than legal origins. In other words, colonial history mattered more than legal origins. This was consistent with the observations by Acemoglu, Johnson, and Robinson (2001) who argued that colonizers tended to build good institutions in environments hospitable to European settlements. Thus, generally, the nature of financial institutions that emerged in colonies was primarily meant to serve European settler societies.

3.2 Colonial Banks

3.2.1 British Colonial Banks

The banking system established by Britain in its colonies was typically the 'English model', now commonly known as the Anglo-Saxon model, which is essentially market-oriented whereby banking institutions primarily acted as deposit-taking institutions. Initially, the main role of these institutions was to mobilize savings, and only took on a stronger intermediation role at a later stage.

Economic historians have written substantially on the nature of colonial banking in British West Africa (BWA), which comprised what is now known the Gambia, Sierra Leone, Ghana, Nigeria and the Anglophone part of Cameron. Drawing from archival evidence and old literature, Austin and Uche (2007) explored the nature of colonial banking in BWA from 1916. They made several observations. First, they observed that during most of the colonial period, the banking industry was dominated by two banks — the Bank of British West Africa and the Colonial Bank that was later renamed Barclays in 1925. Second, these colonial banks colluded with each other to minimize competition. This enabled them to impose higher bank charges than they could in a competitive market and thus they were able to extract substantial economic rents. Third, the lack of competition reduced the incentive for the banks to innovate and perform direct lending to Africans. Also, the lucrative bank charges served as a disincentive for the banks to take an active role in lending to Africans.

Notwithstanding the observation that British colonial banking lacked competition, other researchers found otherwise. For instance, using archival sources, Capie and Billings (2004) examined data on interest rates charged and paid, rate spreads, profitability and expenses ratios of English colonial banks during the middle of the 20th century, when collusion was considered strongest, and came to a different conclusion. They concluded that the collusion could be described as 'soft' rather than 'hard'. That is to mean there were no strictly agreed output quotas and profits among members of a cartel; in other words, there was some modicum of competition among the banks.

3.2.2 Continental Colonial Banks

Continental colonial banks were those from mainland Europe, which had a different orientation from British colonial banks. British colonial banks had a deposit-taking orientation, and lending was mainly for short-term operations, whereas continental banks had a strong intermediation approach — lending both short-term and long-term to businesses in colonies. There were also differences in their respective sources of finance. The sources of finance of continental banks was largely mobilized from savers in Europe, whereas British colonial banks mobilized savings from colonies for short-term lending to businesses operating in the colonies, and the parent banks acted as lenders of last resort.

3.2.2.1 French Colonial Banks

France organized its colonial rule under the French West African federation. French banks set up branches in the colonies. In each colony, France issued currencies linked to the French Franc. The currencies of the different colonies were subsequently consolidated into one currency — La Franc des colonies Francaise d'Afrique. The idea was to have a broad Franc zone in the colonies with convertibility into the French Franc at fixed parity.

At the end of the Second World War, France renamed its colonial empire the French Union. In 1945 the common currency in the colonies was renamed the CFA franc. Then the CFA acronym meant Colonies Francaise Africaine (French colonies of Africa), but in 1958 the acronym was changed to mean Communaute Financiere Africaine (French Community of Africa). Initially, the CFA was issued by the Banque de France, which responsibility was transferred to regional currency-issuing banks created in 1955. These regional banks were consolidated in 1962 into two: the Banque Centrale des Etats de l'Afrique de l'Ouest (BCEAO) for the West African Zone and the Banque des Etats de l'Afrique Centrale (BEAC) for the Central African Zone. They were based in Paris until 1972 well after the colonies had gained independence. Over time they were given more autonomy and during the reforms of 1972 their headquarters were moved to Africa. The BCEAO which issues the Franc de la Communaute Financiere became headquartered in Dakar while the BEAC which issues the Franc de la Cooperation Financiere en Afrique Centrale became headquartered in Yaounde (Kirk & Bach, 1995). Despite the two official currencies being different and only legal tender in their respective zones, they are all referred to as the CFA Franc. Both CFA Francs are pegged to the Euro and convertibility is guaranteed by France. Countries in each currency zone pool their foreign currency reserves. Half of the reserves are deposited with the French Treasury. Table 2.2 shows the member countries that fall under each currency zone.

Despite the arrangement being a colonial legacy, it has brought financial stability in Francophone Africa as well as eliminating the risks of foreign exchange rate fluctuations in trading with Europe, the region's largest trading partner. The Economist (2018) provides evidence regarding stability by citing that over the past 50 years, inflation in Cote d'Ivoire averaged 6%, while that of neighbouring Ghana, a non-Francophone state, averaged 29%. However, critics of the system argue that the euro peg denies Francophone countries the opportunity to pursue flexible monetary policies.

3.2.2.2 Portuguese Colonial Banks

There is a paucity of studies on banking development in Portuguese colonial Africa. Nevertheless, two studies by Agur (2011) and Austin and Sugihara (1993) give some insights. Portugal regarded its colonies as overseas provinces. However, in the early

Table 2.2 Currency Zones and Members in Francophone Africa.

BCEAO CFA Franc Members in West Africa	BEAC CFA Franc Members in Central Africa
Benin	Cameroon
Burkina Faso	Central African Republic
Cote d'Ivoire	Congo Republic
Guinea Bissau	Gabon
Mali	Chad
Niger	Equatorial Guinea
Senegal	
Togo	

years of colonization, the colonies were not served by Portuguese banks. As a result, colonies had constraints in funding operations. They largely relied on private lenders who supplied credit to businesses and individuals. This distinguished Portugal from other colonizers in that, despite having a long colonial tradition, it did not promote or establish banking systems in their colonies as did the British and the French.

Portugal mooted the idea of having a bank to serve colonies in 1864 and established the Banco Nacional Ultramarino (BNU) for the purpose. The bank headquartered in Lisbon was promoted by private Portuguese capitalists with the support of government through the Minister of Marine and Overseas. It established branches in the major cities in Portugal and in the overseas colonies. Its functions in the colonies included issuing currency, provision of business credit, mortgages, agricultural credit and financing colonial government projects. Other Portuguese banks also followed the BNU in providing credit to African colonies without setting branches in the colonies. However, in the late 19th century several saving banks also opened branches in the colonies for purposes of mobilizing savings. In 1891 British banks, especially those operating in the colonies, were allowed to operate in Portuguese colonies. This saw the British Standard Bank that was operating in South Africa opening its first branch in Mozambique in 1894 and, subsequently, the National Bank of South African Republic (Transvaal) and Bank of Africa followed suit.

Similar to British and French colonial banks, the Portuguese colonial banks mainly served big businesses whose parents were headquartered in Europe. Such businesses were involved in plantations, agriculture and other different operations in the colonies. Like French colonial banks, Portuguese colonial banks had a strong intermediation role – lending short-term, medium-term and long-term, and a close association with the companies they lent to in the colonies. After all, they knew these companies from home. Mobilization of savings was not a primary operation as savings mobilized in Europe were the funds lent to the businesses overseas in the colonies. Even though over time some savings were mobilized in the colonies, the lending decisions were made in the banks' headquarters in Europe. As a result, the local and indigenous population that engaged in business in the colonies had no access to formal financial services except from locally established private moneylenders.

4. Financial Institutions in Post-Colonial Africa

In post-independence Africa, the financial sector continued to be dominated by colonial banks. By and large, these banks served the same clientele they served during colonial times, namely, multinational companies that continued their operations post-independence. The lending was largely short-term to finance foreign trade and working capital and not developmental. Post-independence African governments also provided the banks with a large chunk of risk-free business in the form of treasury bonds. In other words, the colonial foreign banks became the main source of loan finance for governments. Since governments could not raise loan finance from the general public, which was largely poor, they made banks their captive market by prescribing that they should hold a certain percentage of their assets in government bonds. The losers in this scheme were small domestic firms which, in addition to being crowded out by governments in the credit market, were shunned by banks with regard to access to credit. They had to resort to informal finance as they did in colonial times, thus perpetuating the colonial legacy. Banks had no appetite to lend to these risky customers and did not see the need to collect monitoring information on them when they could engage in the lucrative risk-free business of lending to governments. Naturally, over time the situation became politically unsustainable as it caused much discontent among the local populations.

In the first instance, the response of governments was to establish state banks either from scratch or by nationalizing foreign banks. This enabled governments to direct lending to specific sectors, including small-scale sectors they deemed beneficial to national development. This directed lending became characterized by financial repression, whereby nominal interest rates were kept artificially low, lending was subsidized for favoured borrowers, and exchange controls were put in place. Consistent with predictions of financial repression theory, these interventions did not result in the availability of credit to the underserved sectors of African economies. Since credit was not allocated using commercial criteria, defaults were common, so that state banks ended up being a drain on the national *fiscus* of many African countries. It is important to note that nationalized banks reinforced banks acting as captive markets for government borrowing. Nationalization also meant that governments could borrow beyond their prescribed asset limits from state banks.

In the 1980s it became clear that financial repression and misguided policies were not sustainable as they exacerbated economic crises emanating from both internal and external shocks. In response, many African countries adopted the Structural Adjustment Programmes recommended by the World Bank and the IMF that entailed implementing stabilization polices and market oriented reforms. The objective of these programmes was to reduce the scale of government intervention in the economy, including interventions in the financial markets via financial liberalization. Financial liberalization entailed abolishing government directed lending, allowing lending based on commercial criteria, privatizing state banks, opening up the banking sector to both domestic and foreign players, relaxing exchange controls, reforming prudential regulation and supervision, and encouraging the establishment of stock markets.

Focusing on selected former English colonies, Brownbridge and Harvey (1998) demonstrate that the prognosis in the first two decades (1980–2000) of reform was not encouraging for two reasons. Firstly, they observed that the financial sector had become distorted by government intervention, so that privatized banks lacked expertise in providing credit using commercial criteria. On the other hand, central banks lacked technical capacity in regulation and supervision. Secondly, by the time financial liberalization was implemented, the real sectors of African economies had already been weakened to such an extent that many borrowers were unable to repay bank loans.

Makina (2009) provides the example of Zimbabwe, which can be considered typical with regard to the outcomes of financial reforms in Africa. When the country implemented reforms in the 1990s, the financial sector initially grew at an average rate of 3% per annum when other sectors of the economy were contracting. New domestic banks entered the banking sector and competed with the dominant foreign banks. Despite creating a semblance of competition, the reforms did not address the structural causes of financial exclusion, as the banking sector continued to favour big prime clients. The majority of new domestic banks engaged in merchant and discount banking rather than commercial banking in order to take advantage of the lucrative business in risk-free government securities. Small businesses in which the majority of the population were engaged remained without access to finance. The government's response was to increase resources for subsidized schemes, which initiatives conflicted with the market orientation of the reforms. As with many other African countries, such schemes were not sustainable and became a drain on the *fiscus*, and access to subsidized credit became a privilege of the politically connected.

In postulating the financial repression theory, McKinnon (1973) had observed that long periods of financial repression can result in structural changes to economic activities that can make change very difficult. Makina (2009) observed this phenomenon in the Zimbabwe example. The small scale sector that could not obtain finance from commercial banks became increasingly reliant on government intervention and subsidies creating a more or less permanent dependency.

In contrast, Tanzania was a relative success story with regard to some aspects of financial liberalization. With the support of the IMF and other donors, Tanzania introduced reforms for its repressed and deteriorating state-controlled financial sector in 1991 whose objective was to develop a sound market-oriented financial system that is efficient in the mobilization and allocation of financial resources to support economic growth. According to the AfDB (2000), the most significant achievement was creating the enabling policy, legal and regulatory framework for a sound and competitive financial sector that enabled the entry of private banks and strengthened bank supervision. The reforms were however not very successful in restructuring existing banks.

Commenting on the overall results of financial reforms in Africa, Senbet and Otchere (2005) observe that they have not been wholly encouraging as issues of institutional development such as contractual and legal systems, accounting and disclosure rules, and regulatory and supervisory mechanisms were not adequately reformed. Furthermore, issues of access to credit and other financial services are yet to be addressed.

5. Commercial Bank Access Four Decades Post-Colonial

Having discussed post-colonial reforms, one would want to see an indication of the success of the reforms across the breadth of Africa. In 2004, roughly four decades after most colonies gained independence, the World Bank for the first time collected data that measured the number commercial bank branches per 100,000 adults for most African countries. This indicator is a rough measure of the availability of banking services to a population of a country. It is a rough measure because a higher number of bank branches is not synonymous with outreach in rural areas, where the majority of people live in Africa. Most bank branches in Africa are located in cities and not in rural areas which lack basic infrastructure. Notwithstanding the shortcomings of the measure, it can provide indications of relative financial development across countries. Moreover, it is one of the measures of financial inclusion for Sustainable Development Goal (SDG) sub-goal 8.10 that states: 'Strengthen the capacity of domestic financial institutions to encourage and expand access to banking, insurance and financial services for all'.

Table 2.3 below gives bank branches per 100,000 adults in 2004 of African countries as well as former colonizers and date of independence. Ethiopia, which was never colonized, is used as a benchmark against which to measure other countries' bank branch network. Roughly, a measure above that of Ethiopia is considered a colonial premium.

In general, countries that were former British colonies have performed better in bank penetration than those countries under other European colonizers. Measured against the Ethiopian benchmark, all former British colonies have higher bank branch networks than un-colonized Ethiopia. The worst performers are former Belgian colonies followed by former Portuguese colonies and then former French colonies.

6. Looking Ahead

As financial integration in Africa gathers steam in the 21st century, colonial delineations are disappearing. This is manifesting in several ways. Language barriers are being broken as English

Table 2.3 Commercial Bank Branches per 100,000 Adults of African Countries in 2004.

Country	Former Colonizer	Year of Independence	Commercial Bank Branches (per 100,000 adults), 2004	Branches Over-/ Under Ethiopia Not Colonized
Ethiopia	... ...	... ...	0.8	... ...
Burundi	Belgium	1962	1.5	0.7
Congo, Dem. Rep.	Belgium	1960	0.5	−0.3
Rwanda	Belgium	1962	0.4	−0.4
Botswana	Britain	1966	6.6	5.8
Egypt, Arab rep.	Britain	1953	3.9	3.1
Gambia, the	Britain	1965	4.3	3.5
Ghana	Britain	1957	3.1	2.3
Kenya	Britain	1963	2.7	1.9
Lesotho	Britain	1966	2.6	1.8
Malawi	Britain	1964	1.0	0.2
Mauritius	Britain	1968	18.0	17.2
Nigeria	Britain	1960	4.7	3.9
Seychelles	Britain	1976	42.0	41.2
Sierra Leone	Britain	1961	1.2	0.4
South Africa	Britain	1931	4.7	3.9
Sudan	Britain	1956	2.5	1.7
Swaziland	Britain	1968	5.9	5.1
Tanzania	Britain	1962	1.2	0.4
Uganda	Britain	1962	1.1	0.3
Zambia	Britain	1964	3.1	2.3
Zimbabwe	Britain	1980	2.7	1.9
Algeria	France	1962	4.6	3.8
Benin	France	1960	0.9	0.1
Burkina Faso	France	1960	1.2	0.4
Cameroon	France	1960	0.5	−0.3
Central Afri rep	France	1960	0.3	−0.5
Chad	France	1960	0.4	−0.4
Comoros	France	1975	0.6	−0.2
Congo, rep.	France	1960	0.7	−0.1
Cote d'Ivoire	France	1960	1.4	0.6
Djibouti	France	1977	2.1	1.3

Table 2.3 Commercial Bank Branches per 100,000 Adults of African Countries in 2004.—*continued*

Country	Former Colonizer	Year of Independence	Commercial Bank Branches (per 100,000 adults), 2004	Branches Over/-Under Ethiopia Not Colonized
Equatorial Guinea	Spain	1968	3.2	2.4
Gabon	France	1960	4.0	3.2
Guinea	France	1958	0.7	−0.1
Madagascar	France	1960	1.1	0.3
Mali	France	1960	2.6	1.8
Morocco	France	1956	10.0	9.2
Niger	France	1958	0.4	−0.4
Senegal	France	1960	2.0	1.2
Togo	France	1960	1.2	0.4
Tunisia	France	1956	12.0	11.2
Libya	Italy	1951	9.2	8.4
Angola	Portugal	1975	2.2	1.4
Cape Verde	Portugal	1975	15.7	14.9
Guinea-Bissau	Portugal	1974	0.1	−0.7
Mozambique	Portugal	1975	1.8	1.0
Sao Tome and Principe	Portugal	1975	4.7	3.9
Namibia	South Africa	1990	10.7	9.9

Source: World Development Indicators.

is increasingly becoming the main language of business across the continent. Operations of multinational banks and other financial institutions are now scattered throughout Africa irrespective of origin and language. More importantly, there has been a rise in pan-African financial institutions operating in all regions of the continent.

The role of financial development in economic development is now widely accepted. Hence, financial inclusiveness is acknowledged as a necessary ingredient for inclusive growth that allows low-income populations to participate in productive activities. Today, efforts to facilitate access to finance to those at the bottom of the economic pyramid are being pursued by both the traditional banking sector and specialized institutions such as microfinance institutions, credit unions, postal banks and lately telecommunications companies that solely or in collaboration with banks provide microfinance in the form of mobile money.

References

Acemoglu, D., Johnson, S., & Robinson, J. A. (2001). Colonial origins of comparative development: An empirical investigation. *The American Economic Review, 91,* 1369–1401.

Adebayo, A. G. (1994). Money, credit, and banking in precolonial Africa: The Yoruba experience. *Anthropos, 89*(4/6), 379–400.

AfDB. (2000). *Tanzania Financial Sector Adjustment Programme Project, Completion Report.* African Development Fund, AfDB: Abidjan.

Agur, S. (2011). *Banking and credit facilities in Portuguese Africa 1850–1910.* Paper for EH590 Workshop, November 2011 http://www.lse.ac.uk/economicHistory/seminars/EH590Workshop/2011papers/agur.pdf.

Ardener, S. (1964). The comparative study of rotating credit associations. *The Journal of the Royal Anthropological Institute, 94,* 201–229.

Armstrong, M. A. (n.d.). The origins of money, www.armstrongeconomics.com/research/monetary-history-of-the-world/historical-outline-origins-of-money/money-and-the-evolution-of-banking/ retrieved on 7 February 2017.

Austin, G., & Sugihara, K. (1993). *Local suppliers of credit in the third word, 1750–1960.* New York: Macmillan Press.

Austin, G., & Uche, C. U. (2007). Collusion and competition in colonial economies: Banking in British West Africa, 1916 – 1960. *Business History Review, 81,* 1–26.

Bascom, W. R. (1952). The *esusu*: A credit institution of the Yoruba. *The Journal of the Royal Anthropological Institute, 82,* 63–69.

Bianchi, R. S. (2004). *Daily life of the Nubians.* Greenwood Press.

Brownbridge, M., & Harvey, C. (1998). *Banking in Africa: The Impact of Financial Sector Reform since Independence.* James Currey Oxford.

Capie, F., & Billings, M. (2004). Evidence on competition in English commercial banking. *Financial History Review, 11,* 69–103.

Davies, G. (2002). *A history of money from ancient times to the present day* (3rd ed.). Cardiff: University of Wales Press.

De Blij, H. J., & Muller, P. O. (2003). *Geography: Realms, regions and concepts* (14th ed.). Hobeken, NJ: John Wiley & Sons, Inc.

Dyneley, P. J. (1904). Review: The code of Hammurabi. *The American Journal of Theology, 8*(3), 601–609.

Ferris, E. (1902). The financial relations of the knights Templars to the English crown. *The American Historical Review, 8*(1), 1–17.

Geertz, C. (1962). The rotating credit association: A 'middle rung' in development. *Economic Development and Cultural Change, 10,* 241–263.

Johnson, M. (1968). The nineteenth-century gold "mithqal" in West and North Africa. *The Journal of African History, 9,* 547–569.

Johnson, M. (1970). The cowrie currencies of West Africa. *The Journal of African History, 11*(17–49), 331–353.

Kirk, A., & Bach, D. (1995). *State and society in francophone Africa since independence.* London: Macmillan Press.

Kitchen, K. A. (1991). The chronology of ancient Egypt. *World Archaeology: Chronolog, 23,* 202.

Klerman, D. M., Mahoney, P. G., Spamann, H., & Weinstein, M. I. (2011). Legal origin or colonial history. *Journal of Legal Analysis, 3*(2), 379–409.

La Porta, R., Lopez-de-Silanes, F., & Shleifer, A. (2008). Economic consequences of legal origin. *Journal of Economic Literature, 46,* 285–332.

Makina, D. (2009). Recovery of the financial sector and building financial inclusiveness. In *Working paper 5, comprehensive economic recovery in Zimbabwe working paper series.* Harare: United Nations Development Programme.

Manuelian, P. D. (1998). *Egypt: The World of the pharaohs. Bonner straße.* Cologne Germany: Könemann Verlagsgesellschaft mbH.

Mark, J. J. (2016). *The Late Period of Egypt.* https://www.ancient.eu/Late_Period_of_Ancient_Egypt/.

McKinnon, R. I. (1973). *Money and capital in economic development.* Washington, DC: Brookings Institution.

Meskell, L. (2004). *Object worlds in ancient Egypt: Material biographies past and present (materializing culture).* Oxford, England: Berg Publishers.

Senbet, L. W., & Otchere, I. (2005). Financial sector reforms in Africa: Perspectives on issues and policies. In *Paper presented at the annual World Bank conference on development economics, Dakar, Senegal, January 2005.*

The Economist. (2018). Franc exchange. In *The economist January 27th – February 2nd, 2018.*

Walbank, F. W. (1984). *The Cambridge ancient history.* Cambridge, UK: Cambridge University Press.

Further Reading

Ajayi, S. I., & Ojo, O. (1981). *Money and banking: Analysis and policy in the Nigerian context.* London: G. Allen & Unwin.

Bascom, W. R. (1951). Social status, wealth, and individual differences among the Yoruba. *American Anthropologist, 53,* 490–505.

Chronology, Digital Egypt for Universities, University College London. <http://www.ucl.ac.uk/museums-static/digitalegypt/>retrieved 10 April 2017.

Del Mar, A. (1885). *History of money in ancient countries: From the earliest times to the present.* London: George Bell and Sons.

Graeber, D. (2011). *Debt: The first 5,000 years.* New York: Melville House.

Makina, D. (2017). Introduction to the financial services in Africa special issue. *African Journal of Economic and Management Studies, 8*(1), 2–7.

3

FINANCIAL DEVELOPMENT IN AFRICA: IS IT DEMAND-FOLLOWING OR SUPPLY-LEADING?

Nicholas M. Odhiambo,[1] **Sheilla Nyasha,**[1]
Mulatu F. Zerihun,[2] **Christian Tipoy**[3]

[1]*Department of Economics, University of South Africa, Pretoria, South Africa;*
[2]*Department of Economics, Tshwane University of Technology, Pretoria,*
South Africa; [3]*Department of Economics, University of KwaZulu-Natal,*
South Africa

1. Introduction

Financial development (i.e. financial depth) is measured by macroeconomic variables such as domestic credit to the private sector as a percentage of GDP, money supply measures, and

Extending Financial Inclusion in Africa. https://doi.org/10.1016/B978-0-12-814164-9.00003-7

stock market indicators. Alternatively, financial inclusion – its probable cousin – is measured by three qualitative dimensions recommended by the Group of 20 countries, namely (1) access to financial services; (2) usage of financial services; and (3) the quality of products and service delivery. It can be argued that financial development is a precursor of financial inclusion. Thus, there must be financial development in order for one to have access to financial services.

The causal relationship between financial development and economic growth has been a subject of interest among economists and policymakers alike during the past decades. It has also attracted a plethora of empirical studies from both developed and developing countries. To date, four different views have been advanced on the causal relationship between financial development and economic growth. The first view is commonly referred to as the supply-leading phenomenon response and is largely supported by neoclassical economists. According to this view, the financial sector precedes and induces real growth by channelling scarce resources from small savers to large investors according to the relative rate of return (see Jung, 1986). This view has been widely supported by McKinnon (1973), Shaw (1973) and King and Levine (1993), among others. The second view, popularly known as the demand-following response, is the converse of the first view. According to this view, it is economic growth that leads to financial development. This view can be traced back as far as 1952, when Robinson challenged the supply-leading wisdom that was dominant at that time. According to Robinson (1952), it is the development of the real sector of the economy (i.e. economic growth) that precedes the development of the financial sector. This is supported by her causality view, which suggests that "where enterprise leads finance follows" (Robinson, 1952, p. 86).

According to Patrick (1966), the direction of causality between financial development and economic growth changes over the course of development. A supply-leading response is usually expected to take place at the early stages of economic development, because financial development is expected to induce real innovation of investment before sustained modern economic growth gets underway. However, as modern economic growth occurs, the supply-leading impetus gradually becomes less and less important, while the demand-following response becomes dominant (Patrick, 1966, p. 177).

Between the supply-leading and demand-following views exists a middle-ground view that argues that both financial sector development and economic growth Granger-cause each other. In other words, this view maintains that there is bidirectional causality between financial development and economic growth. This view was strongly supported by Lewis (1955), who suggested a two-way relationship between financial development and economic growth, where financial markets develop as a consequence of economic growth and in turn act as a stimulus to real growth.

Contrary to these three views, which support a causal relationship between financial development and economic growth, is a fourth view that argues that these two macroeconomic variables are not causally related at all, and any causal relationship between them could be merely a coincidence rather than a causal linkage. Put slightly differently, this view asserts that financial development and economic growth are neutral with respect to each other, and hence neither has a significant effect on the other (see also Graff, 1999; Lucas, 1988).

Despite the numerous empirical studies that have been conducted on the finance—growth nexus, the direction of causality between these two policy variables remains unclear. Previous studies have shown that the causal relationship between financial development and economic growth differs from country to country and is time-dependent. Specifically, it has been found that the causal relationship between these variables is sensitive to a country's level of financial and economic development. Countries whose financial sectors are still at a developmental stage have been found by some studies to portray a finance-led growth response (i.e. supply-leading phenomenon), while countries whose financial systems are at an advanced stage have been found to support a demand-following response.

Although many empirical studies have been conducted on the causal relationship between financial development and economic growth involving a number of African countries, some of them suffer from a number of methodological deficiencies. Firstly, some previous studies over-relied on a bivariate causality model, which has been found to suffer from omission-of-variable bias. The introduction of one or more additional variables — affecting both financial development and economic growth in the bivariate-causality setting — may not only change the magnitude of the results but also alter the direction of causality between the two variables (see also Caporale & Pittis, 1997; Caporale, Howells, & Soliman, 2004; Odhiambo, 2008a). Secondly, some previous studies used cross-sectional data, which do not adequately address country-specific issues. As has been underlined in some previous studies, the traditional cross-sectional method, which simply groups together countries, cannot satisfactorily address the inherent country-specific effects that underlie the relationship between financial development and economic growth (see also Quah, 1993; Ghirmay, 2004; Odhiambo, 2008a; Odhiambo, 2009a). Thirdly, some previous studies used only a monetization variable to measure the level of financial development; yet it has been found that the relationship between financial development and economic growth may be sensitive to the proxy used to measure the level of financial development.

In order to fill this lacuna, the current study aims to examine the causal relationship between financial development and economic growth in African countries from 1990 to 2014 using a dynamic panel Granger-causality model. The main advantage of using a panel data technique is that it addresses the weaknesses of both time-series and cross-sectional data techniques. In order to address the omission-of-variable bias associated with a bivariate causality model, the current study uses a trivariate Granger-causality model that incorporates investment as a control variable between financial development and economic growth. Unlike some previous studies, the study uses three proxies of financial development: (1) liquid liabilities[1] (% of GDP); (2) money bank assets[2] (% of GDP); and (3) bank deposits[3] (% of GDP). The choice of these proxies was informed by the nature of financial development in many African countries. Indeed, the financial sectors in many developing countries are still at a developmental stage; hence, they are largely bank-based in nature. Very few countries have fully developed a market-based system. Finally, the study grouped the sample countries into English-speaking and French-speaking countries. To our knowledge, this may be the first study of its kind to independently examine the causal relationship between financial development and economic growth in English-speaking and French-speaking countries using a dynamic panel data analysis.

The rest of the chapter is organized as follows: Section 2 gives an overview of some previous studies on the causal relationship between financial development and economic growth in both African and non-African countries; Section 3 deals with the empirical model specification, estimation techniques and discussion of the results; and Section 4 concludes the study.

[1]Also known as broad money or M3.
[2]Total assets held by deposit money banks.
[3]Bank deposits consist of money placed into banking institutions for safekeeping.

2. Empirical Literature Review

Empirical evidence on the direction of causality between financial development and economic growth is varied. Although most studies support the supply-leading response, there is also evidence in support of the demand-following response, bidirectional response, and causality view.

Odhiambo (2009a), Nwosa, Agbeluyi, and Saibu (2011) and Osuala, Okereke, and Nwansi (2013) examined the causality between financial development and economic growth in Anglophone African countries and found evidence in support of the supply-leading hypothesis. Studies conducted in other African countries by Ghali (1999), Adjasi and Biekpe (2006), Akinlo and Akinlo (2009), Akinlo and Egbetunde (2010) and Ahmed and Wahid (2011) found support for the same hypothesis. In non-African countries, Arestis and Demetriades (1997), Ahmed and Ansari (1998), Rousseau and Wachtel (1998), Shan and Morris (2002), Choong, Yusop, Law, and Liew (2005), Majid (2008), Deb and Mukherjee (2008), Hussain and Chakraborty (2012), Bayar, Kaya, and Yildirim (2014) and Gokmenoglu, Amin, and Taspinar (2015) found evidence of unidirectional causality flowing from financial development to economic growth. In the same vein, results of similar research carried out in other countries by Jung (1986), King and Levine (1993), Beck, Levine, and Loayza (2000), Graff (2002), Jalilian and Kirkpatrick (2002), Christopoulos and Tsionas (2004), Arestis, Luintel, and Luintel (2005), Kar, Nazlioqlu, and Aqir (2011) and Omri, Daly, Rault, and Chaibi (2015) were consistent with the finance-led growth response.

Then, there is another scholarly group that argues the opposite — that economic growth leads to financial development. Thus, a number of studies on the finance—growth nexus support the demand-following hypothesis (see, among others, Odhiambo, 2004, 2008a, 2008b, 2009b, 2009c for the Anglophone countries). Although relevant studies covering Francophone countries were not found, a number of studies from African and non-African countries are consistent with the demand-following hypothesis (see Agbetsiafa, 2004; Akinlo & Akinlo, 2009; Akinlo & Egbetunde, 2010; Ang & McKibbin, 2007; Athanasios & Antonios, 2012; Guryay, Safakli, & Tuzel, 2007; Ho & Odhiambo, 2013; Rachdi & Mbarek, 2011; Shan, Morris, & Sun, 2001; Shan & Morris, 2002; Zang and Kim, 2007).

Despite the prodigious arguments in support of the supply-leading and demand-following hypotheses, a number of studies also provide evidence of bidirectional causality, where financial development and economic growth have been found to

Granger-cause each other (see Akinboade, 1998 for Anglophone countries). Several other studies covering African and non-African countries have concluded that financial development and economic growth are mutually causal. Such studies include those by Arestis and Demetriades (1997), Abu-Bader and Abu-Qarn (2008), Akinlo and Akinlo (2009), Akinlo and Egbetunde (2010), Jedidia, Boujelbène, and Helali (2014), Wood (1993), Shan et al. (2001), Shan and Morris (2002), Fase and Abma (2003), Hondroyiannis, Lolos, and Papapetrou (2005), Shan and Jianhong (2006), Deb and Mukherjee (2008), Carp (2012), Cheng (2012) and Marques, Fuinhas, and Marques (2013). Luintel and Khan (1999), Calderon and Liu (2003) and Masoud and Hardaker (2012) also found evidence consistent with the feedback hypothesis.

Lastly, there is the neutrality view, which is the fourth variant in the literature on the causal relationship between financial development and economic growth. According to this view, no causal relationship exists between the two variables. For Anglophone countries, see Nyasha and Odhiambo (2015); for non-African countries, see Shan et al. (2001). A summary of studies on the causality between bank-based financial development and economic growth is presented in Table 3.1.

3. Estimation Techniques and Empirical Analysis

3.1 Data and Empirical Model Specifications

3.1.1 Data

The dependent variable used in this study is GDP growth rate (YGR). The three proxies of financial development utilized in this study, one at a time, are: Liquid liabilities-to-GDP ratio (FD1); deposit money bank assets-to-GDP ratio (FD2); and bank deposits-to-GDP ratio (FD3). Additionally, one intermittent variable — gross fixed capital formation (GFCF) — is used between economic growth and financial development to create a trivariate causality model.

The selected African countries are organized into two panels, A and B. Panel A consists of French-speaking African countries, while Panel B is composed of English-speaking African countries. Each of the three models (Eqs. 3.1–3.3) is run for each panel (A and B). This study utilized panel data covering the period from 1990 to 2014. All data for this study were sourced from *World Bank Development Indicators* (World Bank, 2017a) and *Financial Development and Structure Dataset* (World Bank, 2017b).

Table 3.1 A Summary of Studies on the Causality Between Bank-Based Financial Development and Economic Growth.

Author(s)	Region/Country	Methodology	Direction of Causality
Unidirectional causality from finance to growth			
Odhiambo (2009a)	Zambia	— Annual time-series data — Cointegration-based error-correction model — Trivariate causality model	Finance → Growth
Nwosa et al. (2011)	Nigeria	— Error-correction model — Trivariate causality model	Finance → Growth
Osuala et al. (2013)	Nigeria	— Time-series — ARDL bounds-testing approach	Finance → Growth (causality only from total number of deals ratio to economic growth)
Ghali (1999)	Tunisia	— Annual time-series	Finance → Growth
Adjasi and Biekpe (2006)	14 African countries	Dynamic panel data modelling	Finance → Growth (upper middle income economies)
Akinlo and Akinlo (2009)	7 countries in sub-Saharan Africa	ARDL bounds test	Finance → Growth (in Egypt and South Africa)
Akinlo and Egbetunde (2010)	10 sub-Saharan African countries	— Multivariate cointegration analysis and error-correction modelling	Growth → Finance (for Zambia)
Ahmed and Wahid (2011)	7 African countries	— Panel cointegration analysis — Dynamic time series modelling	Finance → Growth
Arestis and Demetriades (1997)	South Korea, Germany and USA	— Johansen cointegration analysis	Finance → Growth (in Germany)
Ahmed and Ansari (1998)	South-Asia: India, Pakistan and Sri Lanka	— Cross-sectionally heteroscedastic, time-wise autoregressive model	Finance → Growth

Continued

Table 3.1 A Summary of Studies on the Causality Between Bank-Based Financial Development and Economic Growth.—*continued*

Author(s)	Region/Country	Methodology	Direction of Causality
Rousseau and Wachtel (1998)	5 countries (United States, United Kingdom, Canada, Norway and Sweden)	— Granger-causality in a VAR — Vector error-correction model	Finance → Growth
Shan and Morris (2002)	19 OECD countries and China	— Individual country time-series	Finance → Growth (for one country)
Choong et al. (2005)	Malaysia	— Time-series — Bounds-test approach — Granger-causality test within vector error-correction model	Finance → Growth
Majid (2008)	Malaysia	— Quarterly time-series data — ARDL approach — Vector error-correction model	Finance → Growth
Deb and Mukherjee (2008)	India	— Quarterly time-series — Granger non-causality test	Finance → Growth
Hussain and Chakraborty (2012)	An Indian State	— Time series techniques	Finance → Growth
Bayar et al. (2014)	Turkey	— Johansen—Juselius cointegration test	Finance → Growth
Gokmenoglu et al. (2015)	Pakistan	— Time series analysis — Granger causality test	Finance → Growth
Jung (1986)	56 Countries (19 of which are industrial)	— Cross-section	Finance → Growth (supply-leading pattern occurs more often than demand-following pattern in LDCs)
King and Levine (1993)	80 countries	— Cross-country analysis	Finance → Growth
Beck et al. (2000)	63 counties	— Cross-section and panel	Finance → Growth
Graff (2002)	93 countries	— Pooled cross-section	Finance → Growth (but unstable)

Table 3.1 A Summary of Studies on the Causality Between Bank-Based Financial Development and Economic Growth.—*continued*

Author(s)	Region/Country	Methodology	Direction of Causality
Jalilian and Kirkpatrick (2002)	42 countries (including 26 developing and 16 developed countries)	— Pooled panel data approach with both a time-series and cross-section dimension — Simple OLS, panel and two-stage least squares	Finance → Growth
Christopoulos and Tsionas (2004)	10 developing countries (Colombia, Paraguay, Peru, Mexico, Ecuador, Honduras, Kenya, Thailand, Dominican Republic and Jamaica)	— Panel unit root tests — Panel cointegration analysis — Dynamic panel data — estimation for a panel-based vector error-correction model — OLS	Finance → Growth
Beck and Levine (2004)	40 countries	— Panel data analysis — Generalised-method-of-moments (GMM) estimators	Finance → Growth
Arestis et al. (2005)	Developing countries (Greece, India, South Korea, the Philippines, South Africa and Taiwan)	— Time-series data and methods — Dynamic heterogeneous panel approach	Finance → Growth
Kar et al. (2011)	15 MENA countries	— Panel causality testing approach	Finance → Growth
Omri et al. (2015)	12 MENA countries	— Simultaneous-equation panel data modelling	Finance → Growth
Unidirectional causality from growth to finance			
Odhiambo (2004)	South Africa	— Johansen–Juselius cointegration technique and vector error-correction model	Growth → Finance
Odhiambo (2008a)	Kenya	— Cointegration and error-correction techniques — Trivariate causality model	Growth → Finance

Continued

Table 3.1 A Summary of Studies on the Causality Between Bank-Based Financial Development and Economic Growth.—*continued*

Author(s)	Region/Country	Methodology	Direction of Causality
Odhiambo (2008b)	Kenya	— Dynamic Granger-causality model	Growth → Finance
Odhiambo (2009b)	Kenya	— Annual time-series data — Cointegration and error-correction model within bivariate and trivariate causality systems	Growth → Finance
Odhiambo (2009c)	South Africa	— Annual time-series data — Trivariate causality model — Cointegration and error-correction models	Growth → Finance
Agbetsiafa (2004)	Sub-Saharan Africa	— Error-correction model	Growth → Finance
Akinlo and Akinlo (2009)	7 countries in sub-Saharan Africa	ARDL bounds test	Growth → Finance (Evidence of growth-led finance in Nigeria)
Akinlo and Egbetunde (2010)	10 sub-Saharan African countries	— Multivariate cointegration analysis and error-correction modelling	Growth → Finance (for Zambia)
Shan et al. (2001)	9 OECD countries and China	— Individual country time-series	Growth → Finance (for three countries)
Shan and Morris (2002)	19 OECD countries and China	— Individual country time-series	Growth → Finance (for 5 countries)
Ang and McKibbin (2007)	Malaysia	— Trivariate VAR models	Growth → Finance
Guryay et al. (2007)	Northern Cyprus	— Time series — Ordinary least squares techniques	Growth → Finance
Athanasios and Antonios (2012)	Greece	— Time-series — Vector error-correction model	Growth → Finance
Ho and Odhiambo (2013)	Hong Kong	— Time-series	Growth → Finance
Rachdi and Mbarek (2011)	10 countries	— Panel data cointegration and GMM system	Growth → Finance (for the MENA countries)

Table 3.1 A Summary of Studies on the Causality Between Bank-Based Financial Development and Economic Growth.—*continued*

Author(s)	Region/Country	Methodology	Direction of Causality
Bidirectional causality			
Akinboade (1998)	Botswana	— Annual time-series	Finance ↔ Growth
Arestis and Demetriades (1997)	South Korea, Germany and USA	Johansen cointegration analysis	Finance ↔ Growth (USA)
Abu-Bader and Abu-Qarn (2008)	Egypt	— Cointegration and vector error-correction methodology — Trivariate vector autoregressive framework	Finance ↔ Growth
Akinlo and Akinlo (2009)	7 countries in sub-Saharan Africa	ARDL bounds test	Finance ↔ Growth (in Cote DIvoire, Kenya, Morocco and Zimbabwe)
Akinlo and Egbetunde (2010)	10 sub-Saharan African countries	— Multivariate cointegration analysis and error-correction modelling	Finance ↔ Growth (for Chad, South Africa, Kenya, Sierra Leone and Swaziland)
Jedidia et al. (2014)	Tunisia	— ARDL bounds test	Finance ↔ Growth
Wood (1993)	Barbados	— Lag-length parameterization of individual time-series	Finance ↔ Growth
Shan et al. (2001)	9 OECD countries and China	Individual time-series	Finance ↔ Growth for five countries
Shan and Morris (2002)	19 OECD countries and China	Individual country time-series	Finance ↔ Growth for 4 countries
Fase and Abma (2003)	8 Asian countries	— Individual country time-series	Finance ↔ Growth
Hondroyiannis et al. (2005)	Greece	Time-series	Finance ↔ Growth
Shan and Jianhong (2006)	China	— Annual time-series data — Vector autoregression approach — Variance decomposition and impulse response function	Finance ↔ Growth

Continued

Table 3.1 A Summary of Studies on the Causality Between Bank-Based Financial Development and Economic Growth.—*continued*

Author(s)	Region/Country	Methodology	Direction of Causality
Deb and Mukherjee (2008)	India	— Quarterly time-series — Granger non-causality test	Finance ↔ Growth (between real market capitalisation ratio and economic growth)
Carp (2012)	Romania	Time-series	Finance ↔ Growth
Cheng (2012)	Taiwan	— Time-series — Vector autoregressive model	Finance ↔ Growth
Marques et al. (2013)	Portugal	Time-series	Finance ↔ Growth
Luintel and Khan (1999)	10 developing countries	— Multivariate time-series — VAR framework	Finance ↔ Growth
Calderon and Liu (2003)	109 developing and industrial countries	— Geweke decomposition test on pooled data	Finance ↔ Growth
Masoud and Hardaker (2012)	42 emerging market countries	Endogenous growth model	Finance ↔ Growth
No causality			
Nyasha and Odhiambo (2015)	South Africa	— ARDL bounds-test approach	Finance ≠ Growth (between bank-based financial development and economic growth)
Shan et al. (2001)	9 OECD countries and China	Individual time-series	Finance ≠ Growth (for two countries)

3.1.2 Trivariate Granger-Causality Model

To address the shortfalls of bivariate Granger-causality, this study utilizes a trivariate Granger-causality model within a panel data framework. Panel data techniques are employed in this study to analyse the causal relationship between financial development and economic growth in selected African countries. The use of this technique is deemed most suitable because of the various advantages it renders. First, it has the ability to test more complicated behavioural models than a single cross-sectional or time-series data set would allow. Second, it allows one to control for variables that cannot be observed or measured, or variables that change over time but not across entities, such as national policies, regulations and international agreements, thereby allowing for individual heterogeneity. Third, it allows for a more accurate inference of model parameters, since panel data usually contain more degrees of freedom and more sample variability than cross-sectional or time-series data (Hsiao, Mountain, & Ho-Illman, 1995). Fourth, it generates more accurate predictions for individual outcomes by pooling the data rather than generating predictions of individual outcomes using the data on the individual in question (Hsiao, Appelbe, & Dineen, 1989; 1993).

The Granger-causality model adopted in this study is expressed as follows:

Model 1:

$$\Delta YGR_{it} = \alpha_{0i} + \sum_{m=1}^{P} \alpha_{1im}\Delta YGR_{it-m} + \sum_{m=1}^{P} \alpha_{2im}\Delta FD1_{it-m}$$

$$+ \sum_{m=1}^{P} \alpha_{3im}\Delta GFCF_{it-m} + \alpha_4 ECT_{t-1} + \varepsilon_{it} \qquad (3.1)$$

$$\Delta FD1_{it} = \beta_{0i} + \sum_{m=1}^{P} \beta_{1im}\Delta FD1_{it-m} + \sum_{m=1}^{P} \beta_{2im}\Delta YGR_{it-m}$$

$$+ \sum_{m=1}^{P} \beta_{3im}\Delta GFCF_{it-m} + \beta_4 ECT_{t-1} + \varepsilon_{it} \qquad (3.2)$$

$$\Delta GFCF_{it} = \delta_{0i} + \sum_{m=1}^{P} \delta_{1im}\Delta GFCF_{it-m} + \sum_{m=1}^{P} \delta_{2im}\Delta YGR_{it-m}$$

$$+ \sum_{m=1}^{P} \delta_{3im}\Delta FD1_{it-m} + \delta_4 ECT_{t-1} + \varepsilon_{it} \qquad (3.3)$$

Model 2:

$$\Delta YGR_{it} = \alpha_{0i} + \sum_{m=1}^{P} \alpha_{1im}\Delta YGR_{it-m} + \sum_{m=1}^{P} \alpha_{2im}\Delta FD2_{it-m}$$

$$+ \sum_{m=1}^{P} \alpha_{3im}\Delta GFCF_{it-m} + \alpha_4 ECT_{t-1} + \varepsilon_{it} \qquad (3.4)$$

$$\Delta FD2_{it} = \beta_{0i} + \sum_{m=1}^{P} \beta_{1im}\Delta FD2_{it-m} + \sum_{m=1}^{P} \beta_{2im}\Delta YGR_{it-m}$$

$$+ \sum_{m=1}^{P} \beta_{3im}\Delta GFCF_{it-m} + \beta_4 ECT_{t-1} + \varepsilon_{it} \qquad (3.5)$$

$$\Delta GFCF_{it} = \delta_{0i} + \sum_{m=1}^{P} \delta_{1im} \Delta GFCF_{it-m} + \sum_{m=1}^{P} \delta_{2im} \Delta YGR_{it-m}$$

$$+ \sum_{m=1}^{P} \delta_{3im} \Delta FD2_{it-m} + \delta_4 ECT_{t-1} + \varepsilon_{it} \qquad (3.6)$$

Model 3:

$$\Delta YGR_{it} = \alpha_{0i} + \sum_{m=1}^{P} \alpha_{1im} \Delta YGR_{it-m} + \sum_{m=1}^{P} \alpha_{2im} \Delta FD3_{it-m}$$

$$+ \sum_{m=1}^{P} \alpha_{3im} \Delta GFCF_{it-m} + \alpha_4 ECT_{t-1} + \varepsilon_{it} \qquad (3.7)$$

$$\Delta FD3_{it} = \beta_{0i} + \sum_{m=1}^{P} \beta_{1im} \Delta FD3_{it-m} + \sum_{m=1}^{P} \beta_{2im} \Delta YGR_{it-m}$$

$$+ \sum_{m=1}^{P} \beta_{3im} \Delta GFCF_{it-m} + \beta_4 ECT_{t-1} + \varepsilon_{it} \qquad (3.8)$$

$$\Delta GFCF_{it} = \delta_{0i} + \sum_{m=1}^{P} \delta_{1im} \Delta GFCF_{it-m} + \sum_{m=1}^{P} \delta_{2im} \Delta YGR_{it-m}$$

$$+ \sum_{m=1}^{P} \delta_{3im} \Delta FD3_{it-m} + \delta_4 ECT_{t-1} + \varepsilon_{it} \qquad (3.9)$$

where:
  FD1 = First proxy of financial development, proxied by liquid liabilities to GDP (%)
  FD2 = Second proxy of financial development, proxied by deposit money bank assets to GDP (%)
  FD3 = Third proxy of financial development, proxied by bank deposits to GDP (%)
  YGR = Economic growth, proxied by GDP growth (annual %)
  GFCF = Investment, proxied by gross fixed capital formation (% of GDP)
  Δ = First difference operator
  ECT = Error-correction term
  ε = White noise error term
  i = Individual country
  t = Time period
  m = Lag length

3.2 Empirical Analysis and Discussion

3.2.1 The Panel Unit Root Test

In order to identify the order of integration of the variables used in the study, three panel unit root tests are employed: (1) Levin, Lin, and Chu "LLC" (2002); (2) Im, Pesaran, and Shin "IPS" (2003); and (3) augmented Dickey–Fuller (ADF). The results are reported in Table 3.2 for both country groupings − 16 French-speaking African countries and 12 English-speaking African countries.

The results of the panel unit root tests reported in Table 3.2 show that the data is conclusively and consistently stationary in first difference.

3.2.2 The Panel Cointegration Test

Given the nature of the data used in this study, unbalanced panel data analysis was employed. For the analysis of a long-run relationship among variables in this study, three panel cointegration tests are employed to ensure the veracity of the findings. These are (1) the Pedroni (2004) residual cointegration test, and (2) the Kao (1999) residual cointegration. The cointegration results are reported in Table 3.3.

Table 3.2 The Results of Panel Unit Root Tests.

	LLC t-Statistics		IPS W-Statistics		ADF − Fisher Chi-Square	
	Level	First Difference	Level	First Difference	Level	First Difference
French-Speaking African Countries						
FD1	2.27016	−6.19123***	2.52862	−6.2409***	22.6366	100.183***
FD2	0.09951	−4.04262***	−0.00217	−3.75338***	48.7377**	66.6868***
FD3	4.71505	−5.82357***	5.54618	−4.54959***	9.71317	77.6094***
GFCF	1.06559	−7.84338***	−0.13648	−8.75352***	31.2167	135.383***
YGR	−4.62***	−6.15334***	−6.06407***	−15.7457***	95.3279***	252.518***
English-Speaking African Countries						
FD1	−1.8079**	−5.85024***	−0.7872	−6.15241***	27.17	82.5998***
FD2	−2.1144**	−6.01379***	0.11709	−6.16217***	30.3551	85.6126***
FD3	−1.6536**	−6.09483***	0.41082	−5.8745***	18.2048	79.3059***
GFCF	−0.40303	−9.97350***	−0.50262	−10.0352***	25.0604	136.558***
YGR	−6.443***	−12.2536***	−6.4426***	−14.6264***	87.7275***	136.558***

Note: ** and *** indicate rejection of the respective null hypothesis at the 5% and 1% significance levels, respectively.

Table 3.3 Panel Cointegration Results.

	Panel a: French-Speaking Countries						Panel B: English-Speaking Countries					
	Model 1		Model 2		Model 3		Model 1		Model 2		Model 3	
	Statistic	Probability	Statistic	Probability	Statistic	Probability	Statistic	Probability	Statistic	Probability	Statistic	Probability

PANEL 1: Pedroni Residual Cointegration Test

Pedroni Panel Cointegration Test — Within-Dimension

	Statistic	Probability	Statistic	Probability	Statistic	Probability	Statistic	Probability	Statistic	Probability	Statistic	Probability
Panel v-Statistic	0.161099	0.4360	0.641100	0.2607	0.125918	0.4499	−2.375261	0.9912	−1.697851	0.9552	−2.689157	0.9964
Panel rho-Statistic	−5.095585	0.0000	−5.634313	0.0000	−5.234914	0.0000	−5.055616	0.0000	−5.281191	0.0000	−5.122991	0.0000
Panel PP-Statistic	−13.18666	0.0000	−14.90870	0.0000	−14.14191	0.0000	−12.46468	0.0000	−13.12684	0.0000	−13.05823	0.0000
Panel ADF-Statistic	−12.89729	0.0000	−14.91994	0.0000	−13.62259	0.0000	−12.72710	0.0000	−13.38754	0.0000	−13.20083	0.0000

Pedroni Panel Cointegration Test — Between-Dimension

	Statistic	Probability	Statistic	Probability	Statistic	Probability	Statistic	Probability	Statistic	Probability	Statistic	Probability
Group rho-Statistic	−3.675971	0.0001	−3.908196	0.0000	−3.565528	0.0002	−2.347321	0.0095	−2.488631	0.0064	−2.510448	0.0060
Group PP-Statistic	−18.07530	0.0000	−19.76674	0.0000	−21.00310	0.0000	−14.17722	0.0000	−12.94651	0.0000	−14.10805	0.0000
Group ADF-Statistic	−14.18417	0.0000	−15.64846	0.0000	−14.74892	0.0000	−11.13453	0.0000	−11.66405	0.0000	−11.29755	0.0000

PANEL 2: Kao Residual Cointegration Test

	t-Statistic	Probability	t-Statistic	Probability	t-Statistic	Probability	t-Statistic	Probability	t-Statistic	Probability	t-Statistic	Probability
ADF	−10.38541	0.0000	−11.10768	0.0000	−11.06569	0.0000	−11.21431	0.0000	−9.222109	0.0000	−10.95290	0.0000

Overall, the results of the two panel cointegration tests reported in Table 3.3 reveal that the variables in all three models (1–3) in both the French-speaking and English-speaking countries (i.e. Panel A and Panel B) are cointegrated; hence, the Granger-causality test could be performed.

3.2.3 Trivariate Granger-Causality Results

The Granger-causality test was performed to examine the causal relationship between YGR and the different proxies for financial development. The test is conducted after a VECM estimation with the assumption of cointegration between variables. This allows testing for Granger-causality in both the short and the long run. Short-run causality is given by the chi-squared statistic, while long-run causality relies on the significance of the ECT. Table 3.4 presents Granger-causality results for all models (Models 1–3) for both French-speaking and English-speaking African country groups.

The results reported in Table 3.4, Panel A, reveal that in French-speaking African countries, there is unidirectional Granger-causality from economic growth to financial development but only in the short run when financial development is proxied by FD1 and FD3. However, when FD2 is used to measure financial development, there is short- and long-run unidirectional Granger-causality from financial development to economic growth.

The results reported in Table 3.4, Panel B, show that English-speaking African countries exhibit a distinct unidirectional causal flow from economic development to financial development only in the short run when FD1 and FD3 are used to proxy financial development (Panel B, Models 1 and 3). However, the study failed to find a causal relationship between economic growth and financial development when FD2 is used as a proxy. Although contrary to expectations, these results are not unusual (see, among others, Shan et al., 2001; Nyasha & Odhiambo, 2015).

Other results show that in French-speaking African countries, there is (1) unidirectional causality from investment (GFCF) to FD1, FD2 and FD3 only in the short run; and (2) bidirectional causality between investment and FD2 in the short run. The other results of this study further reveal that English-speaking African countries exhibit (1) unidirectional causality from investment to economic growth in the short and long run in all the three models, and (2) unidirectional causality from FD2 to investment in the short run.

Table 3.4 Granger-Causality Results for All Models.

| | Independent Variable | | | | | | | | | | | |
| | Model 1 — FD1 | | | | Model 2 — FD2 | | | | Model 3 — FD3 | | | |
Dependent Variable	D(YGR)	D(FD1)	D(GFCF)	ECT	D(YGR)	D(FD2)	D(GFCF)	ECT	D(YGR)	D(FD3)	D(GFCF)	ECT
Panel A: French-Speaking African Countries												
D(YGR)	–	0.1182	1.4874	–0.8155***	–	11.8961**	2.7082	–0.7835***	–	2.8361	1.7242	–0.7997***
		(0.9983)	(0.8289)	(–7.2757)		(0.0181)	(0.6078)	(–7.0415)		(0.5856)	(0.7863)	(–7.1465)
D(FD1/2/3)	8.9602*	–	29.4725***	0.1387**	0.4653	–	25.6808***	0.0765	10.4689**	–	44.4041***	0.1016*
	(0.0621)		(0.0000)	(2.3191)	(0.9768)		(0.0000)	(1.3235)	(0.0332)		(0.0000)	(2.2194)
D(GFCF)	6.8956	3.7667	–	0.2697**	7.0173	13.8894***	–	0.2852***	7.5363	4.3040	–	0.2946***
	(0.1415)	(0.4385)		(2.5074)	(0.1350)	(0.0077)		(2.6593)	(0.1101)	(0.3664)		(2.7387)
Panel B: English-Speaking African Countries												
D(YGR)	–	0.9950	5.8696*	–0.7582***	–	4.4974	6.3502**	–0.7400***	–	1.2482	5.4292*	–0.7606***
		(0.6081)	(0.0531)	(–8.4903)		(0.1055)	(0.0418)	(–8.3063)		(0.5357)	(0.0662)	(–8.4292)
D(FD1/2/3)	7.1335**	–	1.4826	0.1320	1.3319	–	3.4029	0.1757*	5.6415*	–	2.0671	0.1277*
	(0.0282)		(0.4765)	(1.6304)	(0.5138)		(0.1824)	(2.1963)	(0.0596)		(0.3557)	(1.8050)
D(GFCF)	1.5108	0.2360	–	0.1565	2.0953	5.5972*	–	0.1507	1.7127	0.8103	–	0.1626
	(0.4698)	(0.8887)		(1.6141)	(0.3508)	(0.0609)		(1.5598)	(0.4247)	(0.6669)		(1.6589)

Note: Null hypothesis of 'no Granger causality' between dependent and independent variable. Chi-squared statistics and *P*-values in parentheses for short-run. ECT coefficients and t-stats in parentheses for long-run relation. *; **; and *** denote significance at 10%, 5% and 1% respectively. In brackets are standard errors.

4. Conclusion

This chapter has examined the causal relationship between financial development and economic growth in African countries using panel data for the period from 1990 to 2014. The study divided African countries into two groups, namely French-speaking and English-speaking countries. The study was motivated by conflicting findings that have been reported by previous studies and by the methodological weaknesses of some previous studies. In order to address the weaknesses of some previous studies, the study used a trivariate panel Granger-causality model, which incorporates investment as an intermittent variable between financial development and economic growth. The study also used three proxies to measure the level of financial development in French-speaking and English-speaking countries. These include (1) liquid liabilities (FD1); (2) deposit money bank assets (FD2); and (3) bank deposits (FD3). These proxies are in tandem with the financial systems currently prevailing in many African countries, which are largely bank-based in nature. The results of the panel Granger-causality show that the causality between financial development and economic growth differs significantly between French-speaking and English-speaking countries. The results also depend on the proxy used to measure the level of financial development as well as the time frame. When FD1 and FD3 were used as proxies for financial development, a demand-following response was found to predominate in both French- and English-speaking countries. However, when FD2 was used as a proxy, the study found a distinct unidirectional causal flow from financial development to economic growth (supply-leading) to prevail in French-speaking African countries but failed to find any causal relationship between financial development and economics growth in English-speaking countries in either direction.

Going forward, research will soon grapple with the causal relationship between financial inclusion (whose measures are different from those of financial development) and economic growth. Since indicators of financial inclusion are associated with inclusive growth, such research will increasingly gain prominence in developing African countries.

References

Abu-Bader, S., & Abu-Qarn, A. S. (2008). Financial development and economic growth: The Egyptian experience. *Journal of Policy Modelling, 30,* 887–898.

Adjasi, C. K. D., & Biekpe, N. B. (2006). Stock market development and economic growth: The case of selected African countries. *African Development Review, 18*(1), 144–161.

Agbetsiafa, D. (2004). The finance growth nexus: Evidence from sub-Saharan Africa. *Savings and Development, 28*(3), 271–288.

Ahmed, S. M., & Ansari, M. I. (1998). Financial sector development and economic growth: The South-Asian experience. *Journal of Asian Economics, 9*(3), 503–517.

Ahmed, A. D., & Wahid, A. N. M. (2011). Financial Structure and economic growth link in African countries: A panel cointegration analysis. *Journal of Economics Studies, 38*(3), 331–357.

Akinboade, O. A. (1998). Financial development and economic growth in Botswana, a test for causality. *Savings and Development, 3*(22), 331–348.

Akinlo, A. E., & Akinlo, O. O. (2009). Stock market development and economic growth: Evidence from seven sub-Sahara African countries. *Journal of the Economics of Business, 61*(2), 162–171.

Akinlo, A. E., & Egbetunde, T. (2010). Financial development and economic growth: The experience of 10 sub-Saharan African countries revisited. *The Review of Finance and Banking, 2*(1), 17–28.

Ang, J. B., & McKibbin, W. J. (2007). Financial liberalization, financial sector development and growth: Evidence from Malaysia. *Journal of Development Economics, 84*(1), 215–233.

Arestis, P., & Demetriades, P. (1997). Financial development and economic growth: Assessing the evidence. *The Economic Journal, 107,* 783–799.

Arestis, P., Luintel, A. D., & Luintel, K. B. (2005). *Financial structure and economic growth.* University of Cambridge, Centre for Economic and Public Policy. CEPP working paper No. 06/05.

Athanasios, V., & Antonios, A. (2012). Stock market development and economic growth: An empirical analysis. *American Journal of Economics and Business Administration, 4*(2), 135–143.

Bayar, Y., Kaya, A., & Yildirim, M. (2014). Effects of stock market development on economic growth: Evidence from Turkey. *International Journal of Financial Research, 5*(1), 93–100.

Beck, T., Levine, R., & Loayza, N. (2000). Finance and the sources of growth. *Journal of Financial Economics, 58,* 261–300.

Beck, T., & Levine, R. (2004). Stock markets, banks, and growth: Panel evidence. *Journal of Banking & Finance, 28*(3), 423–442.

Calderon, C., & Liu, L. (2003). The direction of causality between financial development and economic growth. *Journal of Development Economics, 72*(1), 321–334.

Caporale, G. M., Howells, P. G. A., & Soliman, A. M. (2004). Stock market development and economic growth: The causal linkage. *Journal of Economic Development, 29*(1), 33–50.

Caporale, G. M., & Pittis, N. (1997). Causality and forecasting in incomplete systems. *Journal of Forecasting, 16*(6), 425–437.

Carp, L. (2012). Can stock market development boost economic growth? Empirical evidence from emerging markets in Central and Eastern Europe. *Procedia Economics and Finance, 3,* 438–444.

Cheng, S. (2012). Substitution or complementary effects between banking and stock markets: Evidence from financial openness in Taiwan. *Journal of International Financial Markets, Institutions and Money, 22*, 508–520.

Choong, C., Yusop, Z., Law, S., & Liew, V. K. (2005). Financial development and economic growth in Malaysia: The perspective of stock market. *Investment Management and Financial Innovations, 4*, 105–115.

Christopoulos, D. K., & Tsionas, E. G. (2004). Financial development and economic growth: Evidence from panel root and cointegration tests. *Journal of Development Economics, 73*, 55–74.

Deb, S. G., & Mukherjee, J. (2008). Does stock market development cause economic growth? A time-series analysis for the Indian economy. *International Research Journal of Finance and Economics, 21*, 142–149.

Fase, M. M. G., & Abma, R. C. N. (2003). Financial environment and economic growth in selected Asian countries. *Journal of Asian Economics, 14*(1), 11–21.

Ghali, K. H. (1999). Financial development and economic growth: The Tunisian experience. *Review of Development Economics, 3*(3), 310–322.

Ghirmay, T. (2004). Financial development and economic growth in Sub-Saharan African countries: Evidence from time-series analysis. *African Development Review, 16*, 415–432.

Gokmenoglu, K. K., Amin, M. Y., & Taspinar, N. (2015). The relationship among international trade, financial development and economic growth: The case of Pakistan. *Procedia Economics and Finance, 25*, 489–496.

Graff, M. (1999). *Financial development and economic growth: A new empirical analysis.* Dresden discussion paper series in Economics, Nr. 5/99.

Graff, M. (2002). Causal links between financial activity and economic growth: Empirical evidence from a cross-country analysis, 1970–1990. *Bulletin of Economic Research, 54*(2), 119–133.

Guryay, E., Safakli, O. V., & Tuzel, B. (2007). Financial development and economic growth: Evidence from Northern Cyprus. *International Research Journal of Finance and Economics, 8*, 57–62.

Hondroyiannis, G., Lolos, S., & Papapetrou, E. (2005). Financial markets and economic growth in Greece, 1986–1999. *Journal of International Financial Markets, Institutions and Money, 15*(2), 173–188.

Ho, S. Y., & Odhiambo, N. M. (2013). Banking sector development and economic growth in Hong Kong: An empirical investigation. *International Business & Economics Research Journal, 12*(5), 519–532.

Hsiao, C., Appelbe, T. W., & Dineen, C. R. (1993). A general framework for panel data analysis – n with an application to Canadian customer dialed long distance service. *Journal of Economics, 59*(1–2), 63–86.

Hsiao, C., Luke, C. M. W., Mountain, D. C., & Tsui, K. Y. (1989). Modeling Ontario regional electricity system demand using a mixed fixed and random coefficients approach. *Regional Science and Urban Economics, 19*(4), 567–587.

Hsiao, C., Mountain, D. C., & Ho-Illman, K. (1995). Bayesian integration of end-use metering and conditional demand analysis. *Journal of Business & Economic Statistics, 13*, 315–326.

Hussain, F., & Chakraborty, D. K. (2012). Causality between financial development and economic growth: Evidence from an Indian state. *The Romanian Economic Journal, 15*(45), 27–48.

IM, K. S., Pesaran, M. H., & Shin, Y. (2003). Testing for unit roots in heterogeneous panels. *Journal of Econometrics, 115*(1), 53–74.

Jalilian, H., & Kirkpatrick, C. (2002). Financial development and poverty reduction in developing countries. *International Journal of Finance & Economics, 7*(2), 97–108.

Jedidia, K. B., Boujelbène, T., & Helali, K. (2014). Financial development and economic growth: New evidence from Tunisia. *Journal of Policy Modeling, 36*(5), 883–898.

Jung, W. S. (1986). Financial development and economic growth: International evidence. *Economic Development and Cultural Change, 34*, 333–346.

Kao, C. (1999). Spurious regression and residual-based tests for cointegration in panel data. *Journal of Econometrics, 90*(1), 1–44.

Kar, M., Nazlioqlu, S., & Aqir, H. (2011). Financial development and economic growth nexus in the MENA countries: Bootstrap panel granger-causality analysis. *Economic Modelling, 28*, 685–693.

King, R. G., & Levine, R. (1993). Finance and growth: Schumpeter might be right. *Quarterly Journal of Economics, 108*(3), 713–737.

Levin, A., Lin, C. F., & Chu, C. S. J. (2002). Unit root test in panel data: Asymptotic and fine-sample properties. *Journal of Econometrics, 108*(1), 1–24.

Lewis, W. A. (1955). *The theory of economic growth.* London: Allen and Unwin.

Lucas, R. (1988). On the mechanism of economic development. *Journal of Monetary Economics, 22*(1), 3–42.

Luintel, K. B., & Khan, M. (1999). A quantitative reassessment of the finance growth nexus: Evidence from a multivariate VAR. *Journal of Development Economics, 60*(2), 381–405.

Majid, M. S. A. (2008). Does financial development matter for economic growth in Malaysia? An ARDL bound testing approach. *Journal of Economic Cooperation, 29*(1), 61–82.

Marques, L. M., Fuinhas, J. A., & Marques, A. C. (2013). Does the stock market cause economic growth? Portuguese evidence of economic regime change. *Economic Modelling, 32*, 316–324.

Masoud, N., & Hardaker, G. (2012). The impact of financial development on economic growth: Empirical analysis of emerging market countries. *Studies in Economics and Finance, 29*(3), 148–173.

McKinnon, R. I. (1973). *Money and capital in economic development.* Washington: The Brookings Institution.

Nwosa, P. I., Agbeluyi, A. M., & Saibu, O. M. (2011). Causal relationships between financial development, foreign direct investment and economic growth. The case of Nigeria. *International Journal of Business Administration, 2*(4), 93–97.

Nyasha, S., & Odhiambo, N. M. (2015). Banks, stock market development and economic growth in South Africa: A multivariate causal linkage. *Applied Economics Letters, 22*(18), 1480–1485.

Odhiambo, N. M. (2004). Is financial development still a spur to economic growth? A causal evidence from South Africa. *Savings and Development, 28*(1), 47–62.

Odhiambo, N. M. (2008a). Financial depth, savings and economic growth in Kenya: A dynamic causal linkage. *Economic Modelling, 25*, 704–713.

Odhiambo, N. M. (2008b). Financial development in Kenya: A dynamic test of the finance-led growth hypothesis. *Economic Issues, 13*(2), 21–36.

Odhiambo, N. M. (2009a). Interest rate liberalization and economic growth in Zambia: A dynamic linkage. *African Development Review, 21*(3), 541–557.

Odhiambo, N. M. (2009b). Finance-growth nexus and inflation dynamics in Kenya: An empirical investigation. *Savings and Development, 33*(1), 7–25.

Odhiambo, N. M. (2009c). Finance-growth-poverty nexus in South Africa: A dynamic causality linkage. *The Journal of Socio-Economics, 38*, 320–325.

Omri, A., Daly, S., Rault, C., & Chaibi, A. (2015). Financial development, environmental quality, trade and economic growth: What causes what in MENA countries? *Energy Economics, 48*, 242–252.

Osuala, A. E., Okereke, J. E., & Nwansi, G. U. (2013). Does stock market development promote economic growth in emerging markets? A causality evidence from Nigeria. *World Review of Business Research, 3*(4), 1–13.

Patrick, H. T. (1966). Financial development and economic growth in underdeveloped countries. *Economic Development and Cultural Change, 14,* 174–189.

Pedroni, P. (2004). Panel cointegration; asymptotic and finite sample properties of polled time series tests, with an application to the PPP hypothesis: New results. *Econometric Theory, 20*(3), 597–625.

Quah, D. (1993). Empirical cross-section dynamics in economic growth. *European Economic Review, 37*(2–3), 426–434.

Rachdi, H., & Mbarek, H. B. (2011). The causality between financial development and economic growth: Panel data cointegration and GMM system Approaches. *International Journal of Economics and Finance, 3*(1), 143–151.

Robinson, J. (1952). *The rate of interest and other essays*. London: MacMillan.

Rousseau, L., & Wachtel, P. (1998). Financial intermediation and economic performance: Historical evidence from five industrialised countries. *Journal of Money, Credit, and Banking, 30,* 657–678.

Shan, J., & Jianhong, Q. (2006). Does financial development 'lead' economic growth? The case of China. *Annals of Economics and Finance, 1,* 231–250.

Shan, J. Z., & Morris, A. G. (2002). Does financial development 'Lead' economic growth. *International Review of Applied Economics, 16*(2), 153–168.

Shan, J. Z., Morris, A. G., & Sun, F. (2001). Financial development and economic growth: An egg and chicken problem? *Review of International Economics, 9*(3), 443–454.

Shaw, E. S. (1973). *Financial deepening in economic development*. New York: Oxford University Press.

Wood, A. (1993). Financial development and economic growth in Barbados: Causal evidence. *Savings and Development, 17*(4), 379–390.

World Bank. (2017a). *World development indicators* [Online] Available from: http://databank.worldbank.org/data/.

World Bank. (2017b). *Financial development and structure Dataset* [Online] Available from: http://www.worldbank.org/en/publication/gfdr/data/financial-structure-database.

Zang, H., & Kim, Y. C. (2007). Does financial development precede growth? Robinson and Lucas might be right. *Applied Economics Letters, 14,* 15–19.

Further Reading

Anagnostou, A., Kallioras, D., & Petrakos, G. (2016). Integrating the neighbours: A dynamic panel analysis of the EU-ENP countries'' trade relations. *Comparative Economic Studies, 58*(1), 17–42.

Chaiboonsri, C., Sriboonchitta, S., & Calkins, P. (2010). A panel cointegration analysis: An application to international tourism demand of Thailand. *The Thailand Econometric Society, 2*(2), 85–100.

Das, A., Chowdhury, M., & Akhtaruzzam, M. (2012). Panel cointegration and pooled mean group estimations of energy-output dynamics in South Asia. *Journal of Economics and Behavioural Studies, 5*(4), 277–286.

Holtz-Eakin, D., Newey, W., & Rosen, H. (1988). Estimating vector autoregressions with panel data. *Econometrica, 56*(6), 1371–1395.

Maddala, G. S., & Shaowen, W. (1999). *A comparative study of unit root tests with panel data and new simple test"* (pp. 631–652). Oxford Bulletin of Economics and Statistics, Special issue.

Narayan, P. K., Nielsen, I., & Smyth, R. (2008). Panel data, cointegration, causality and Wagner''s law: Empirical evidence from Chinese provinces. *China Economic Review, 19,* 297–307.

Örsal, D. D. K. (2007). *Comparison of panel cointegration tests.* SFB 649 Discussion Paper 2007-029. Berlin, Germany: Humboldt-UniversitÄatzu Berlin, School of Business and Economics Spanduerstr.1, 10099 [Online] Available from: http://sfb649.wiwi.hu-berlin.de.ISSN 1860-5664.

Pedroni, P., & Vogelsang, T. (2005). *Robust unit root and cointegartion rank test for panels and large systems.* Mimeo, Williams College.

THE ROLE OF FINANCIAL MARKETS AND INSTITUTIONS IN PRIVATE SECTOR DEVELOPMENT IN AFRICA[1]

Joshua Yindenaba Abor,[1]
Elikplimi Komla Agbloyor,[1] **Haruna Issahaku**[2]
[1]*Department of Finance, University of Ghana Business School, Accra, Ghana;*
[2]*Department of Economics and Entrepreneurship Development, University of Development Students, Ghana*

[1]This paper is part of the research project 'Delivering Inclusive Financial
Development & Growth', with funding from DFID and ESRC under the DFID-ESRC
Growth Research Programme Call 3.

1. Introduction

The private sector is deemed critical for job creation, provision of goods and services, honing skills and providing opportunities for entrepreneurs to create wealth and value. It is also fundamental in addressing global challenges bordering on inclusive growth, climate change, food security, poverty reduction, gender equity, and regional and global integration (IFC, 2011). In fulfilling these roles, the private sector faces both internal and external challenges. The internal challenges border on profitability, paying market rates and management capabilities, whereas the external challenges centre on the policy setting and access to markets and facilities (Aryeetey, 1998). No doubt, financial markets and institutions are key to addressing some of the challenges of the private sector.

Financial systems in Africa are generally costly, small, lacking in depth, and limited in outreach (Beck & Cull, 2014a), thus restricting the private sector's access to formal finance. This is borne out by the low performance of African countries in financial development indicators at the aggregate, firm and household levels (Beck & Cull, 2014b). This notwithstanding, Africa's financial system has evolved over the years in terms of structure, diversity, and stability. For financial markets and institutions in Africa to meet the demands of the private sector, it will require significant investments in financial infrastructure, corporate governance and legislative reform, which will allow for new financial service providers, new products and services, new lending techniques and better application of cutting edge technology and adoption of modern management practices to provide finance for all.

This chapter examines the roles played by various segments of Africa's financial system in fostering private sector development on the continent. This is important because the private sector is being widely recognized as the engine of growth in Africa. Therefore, any study that seeks to explore ways of contributing to the effectiveness of the private sector is of critical importance. Another reason why this study is imperative, is that finance is widely acclaimed as the most dominant constraint to private sector development in Africa and other parts of the developing world. Therefore, this study's quest to explore the avenues through which the private sector can deal with its most significant constraint is in the right direction.

While there is a reasonable amount of literature on private sector development and financial systems in Africa, significant gaps remain. Notably, the literature mostly concentrates on either private sector development (see Abid, 2016; AfDB 2011; Stampini, Leung, Diarra, & Pla, 2013) or financial markets and institutions (see Applegarth, 2004; IMF, 2016; Mu, Phelps, & Stotsky, 2013) without paying much attention to the links between the two. The limited studies that link the two often concentrate on small and medium enterprise (SME) financing (see Abor & Biekpe, 2007; Aryeetey, 1998; Beck & Cull, 2014a,b) and not the private sector as a whole. This study fills these gaps by reviewing private sector development in Africa and discussing how financial markets and institutions could boost private sector development.

The rest of the chapter is organized as follows: overview of Africa's private sector is presented in the ensuing section, followed by a discussion of the role of finance in promoting private sector development in Africa. It then discusses the constraints to extending financial inclusion in Africa and finally concludes by advising on the way forward.

2. Overview of Private Sector Development in Africa

This section discusses the features of Africa's private sector, its contributions to development and the challenges it confronts.

2.1 Characteristics of Africa's Private Sector

Many African economies were under state control during 5 decades of post-colonial rule. During this period, the state created agricultural marketing boards to control prices, embarked on import substitution industrialization, established large state-owned enterprises, instituted trade barriers, and established a massive public administration. These polices stifled and weakened the private sector. With state-led planning not yielding much in the way of results, most African countries liberalized their economies through the adoption of structural adjustment programs from the 1970s to 1990s. The reforms adopted created some space for the private sector to thrive. It is now being widely recognized that the private sector is the engine of growth and development in Africa.

Africa's private sector is relatively large. It accounts for four-fifths of production and two-thirds of investment as well as employing about 90% of the workforce (AfDB 2011). The large size of the private sector implies that its neglect will greatly slow growth and development on the continent, thus compromising the achievement of sustainable development goals (SDGs). Therefore, more attention should be paid to the private sector in terms of infrastructure upgrading and reforms to create a conducive business environment in order to bolster sustainable development. In terms of subregional analysis, most of Africa's relatively large private sector economies are found in 'Western Africa (Cote d'Ivoire, Guinea, Niger, Senegal and Togo), Central Africa (Cameroun, Republic of Congo) and Eastern Africa (Kenya, Sudan, Uganda and Tanzania)' (Stampini et al., 2013, p. abr.). The economies with relatively small private sectors are mostly oil exporting countries (Algeria, Angola, Equatorial Guinea, Libya and Nigeria), some very poor countries (Burundi, Burkina Faso, Guinea Bissau, Mali and Sao Tome and Principe) and Zambia and Botswana (Stampini et al. 2013).

Africa has one of the largest informal sectors in the world, only exceeded by those of Latin America and the Caribbean (LAC). Based on calculations for 41 African countries for the period 2007–2013, Abid (2016) estimates sub-Saharan Africa's (SSA's) informal sector's share of economic activity to average 42.9%. The subregional breakdown indicates 39.9% in North Africa, 40.0% in Southern Africa, 43.2% in East Africa, 45.2% in West Africa, and 45.5% in Central Africa. In a more recent study, Medina, Jonelis, and Cangul (2017) estimate the share of the informal economy of Africa in GDP to be about 38% over the period 2010–14. This is only outperformed by LAC with an informal economy of 40% of GDP. Other regions such as South Asia (34% of GDP) and Europe (24% of GDP) have relatively lower shares. In OECD countries, the informal economy is about 17% of GDP. It is worth noting that as is the case globally, the informal economy in Africa continues to decline over time.

The work of Medina et al. (2017) reveals significant heterogeneity in the distribution of the informal sector across SSA countries and along income classification. It is as low as 20%–25% of GDP in Mauritius, South Africa and Namibia and as high as 50% to 65% of GDP in Benin, Tanzania and Nigeria. The informality is estimated to average 40% in low-income economies and 35% in middle-income economies in SSA, implying that informality declines with increasing income. This is in line with global trends. Africa's relatively large informal economy has negative implications for productivity, job creation, and revenue mobilization since the sector is characterized by low productivity and employs a large share of the labour force but is largely outside the tax net.

Africa's formal sector is dominated by a large number of micro, small enterprises (MSEs) with few large firms. The few large firms are often foreign owned. This dualistic structure arises because capital-constrained indigenous entrepreneurs start small, with little or no expansion to enable them to reach medium and large enterprise status, while their foreign counterparts come with huge foreign direct investments and capital-intensive technologies and set up large enterprises. This leads to the missing middle phenomenon (a large number of MSEs, a small number of large-sized firms, but very few medium-sized firms) – a typical characteristic of initial stages of industrialization. Though MSEs contribute less to total production, they constitute the majority of businesses and employ a large share of the population, especially the poor. Medium and large firms constitute a third of all businesses, which is small compared with what pertains in other parts of the world. The underrepresentation of medium scale enterprises in Africa is attributable to entry barriers and high transaction costs, which make it difficult for small firms to transition into medium enterprises (AfDB 2011).

2.2 Contributions of Private Sector to Africa's Development

The private sector has an integral role to play in the socioeconomic development of Africa. The private sector is the main employer of active labour in Africa absorbing about 90% of the workforce. These jobs provide the majority of households with income to meet their expenditures on health, education, food, housing, security, communications and other welfare-enhancing items. The public sector is limited in terms of the degree to which it can expand to employ while remaining efficient. The private sector is more elastic in terms of creating new job avenues. Fig. 4.1 shows the share of public sector in total

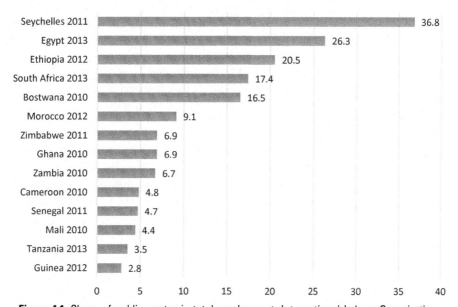

Figure 4.1 Share of public sector in total employment. International Labour Organization.

employment for a cross section of African countries. The size of the public sector varies markedly across the continent from as low as 2.8% in Guinea to as high as 36.8% in Seychelles. African countries with relatively large public sectors include Seychelles (36.8%), Egypt (26.3%), Ethiopia (20.5), South Africa (17.4%) and Botswana (16.5%). Those with relatively small public sectors include Guinea (2.8%), Tanzania (3.5%), Mali (4.4%), Senegal (4.7%) and Cameroun (4.8%). One implication of Africa's small public sector is that the private sector holds the key to resolving the rising unemployment on the continent.

One of the private sector's contributions to economic development is the creation of jobs. Firms in the private sector have different capacities for creating jobs. Fig. 4.2 shows the size distribution of firms across African countries based on employment shares. On the average, for most African economies, large enterprises are the leading employers followed by medium-sized enterprises and small enterprises respectively. Specifically, based on our calculations from various enterprise surveys, large enterprises' share in private sector employment is 39.6%, medium-sized enterprises' share in private sector employment is 33.9%, while small enterprises' share is 26.6%. These averages, however, mask country level peculiarities. For instance, in Guinea-Bissau, Liberia and South Sudan, small enterprises account for over 60% of private sector employment. Again, in Burundi and Gambia, medium enterprises constitute over 50% of private sector employment. In contrast, large enterprises contribute over 60% to private sector employment in Benin, Kenya, Lesotho, Madagascar, Malawi, Mauritius, Senegal and Togo. In the case of Ghana, large enterprises have the largest share in employment (47.9%), followed by medium enterprises (33.0%) and small enterprises (19.1%) respectively.

Another critical role played by the private sector is in the area of investment. The private sector in Africa leads the way in investment spending in various sectors of the economy, accounting for two-thirds of all investments in Africa. Gross fixed capital formation attributable to the private sector[2] is nearly 14% of GDP across various regions in SSA over the period 2013−15 (see Table 4.1). These investments have contributed immensely to the robust growth the continent has witnessed over the past 2 decades. More investments are required to provide road and transport

---

[2]Private investment covers gross outlays by the private sector (including private nonprofit agencies) in additions to its fixed domestic assets.

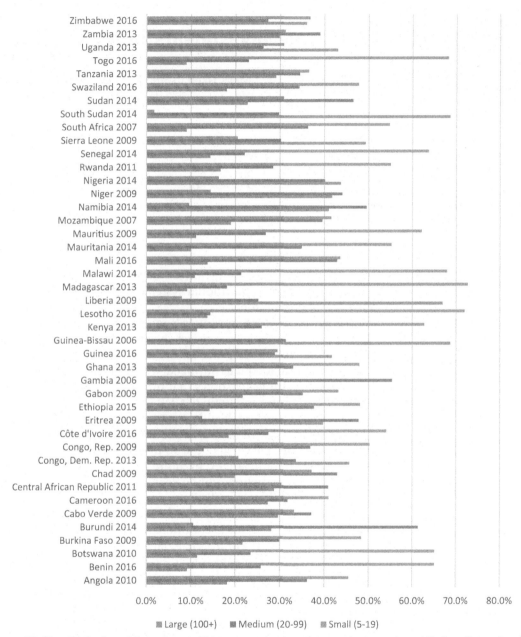

Figure 4.2 Size distribution of firms across African countries based on employment shares. Various Enterprise Surveys, www.enterprisesurveys.org.

Table 4.1 Private Investments in Africa.

	Gross Fixed Capital Formation, Private Sector (% of GDP)			
	2013	2014	2015	Period Average
Sub-Saharan Africa	14.0	14.0	13.7	13.9
Sub-Saharan Africa (excluding high income)	13.9	14.0	13.7	13.9
Sub-Saharan Africa (IDA & IBRD countries)	14.0	14.0	13.7	13.9

World Bank. (2016c). World development indicators. *Washington, DC: World Bank Databank, World Bank.*

infrastructure, establish factories, develop the power sector, improve health and educational systems if Africa must accelerate the pace of development.

The private sector contributes significantly to the health sector through investments in critical health infrastructure. These investments complement the efforts of the public sector to provide the often inadequate but needed health facilities, especially in rural areas. Table 4.2 shows that on the average, SSA's private health expenditure[3] as a ratio of GDP (3.1%) is higher than public sector expenditure[4] on health (2.4%) over the period 2012−14. This is contrasted with the Euro Area (public sector health expenditure is 8.0% of GDP versus 2.5% for private sector) and the global level (public sector health expenditure is 5.9% of GDP versus 3.9% for private sector) where public sector health expenditure outstrips private health expenditure.

In addition, the private sector contributes immensely to GDP and export revenues in the continent. According to AfDB (2011), Africa's private sector controls over 80% of total production in the continent. What this means is that the health of Africa's economy depends on how well the private sector performs.

[3]Private health expenditure includes direct household (out-of-pocket) spending, private insurance, charitable donations, and direct service payments by private corporations.
[4]Public health expenditure consists of recurrent and capital spending from government (central and local) budgets, external borrowings and grants (including donations from international agencies and nongovernmental organizations), and social (or compulsory) health insurance funds.

Table 4.2 Health Expenditure Shares Across the Globe.

Region	Sector	Health Expenditure (% GDP)			
		2012	2013	2014	Period Average
World	Public	5.9	5.9	6.0	5.9
World	Private	3.9	3.9	3.9	3.9
East Asia & Pacific	Public	4.9	4.6	4.6	4.7
East Asia & Pacific	Private	2.2	2.3	2.3	2.3
Europe & central Asia	Public	7.1	7.1	7.2	7.1
Europe & central Asia	Private	2.3	2.4	2.3	2.3
Euro area	Public	7.9	8.0	8.0	8.0
Euro area	Private	2.5	2.4	2.4	2.5
Latin America & Caribbean	Public	3.5	3.6	3.8	3.7
Latin America & Caribbean	Private	3.5	3.5	3.5	3.5
Middle East & North Africa	Public	2.9	3.1	3.2	3.1
Middle East & North Africa	Private	2.1	2.1	2.1	2.1
South Asia	Public	1.2	1.3	1.4	1.3
South Asia	Private	3.0	3.0	3.0	3.0
Sub-Saharan Africa	Public	2.5	2.5	2.3	2.4
Sub-Saharan Africa	Private	3.1	3.2	3.2	3.1

World Bank. (2016c). World development indicators. *Washington, DC: World Bank Databank, World Bank.*

2.3 Constraints to Private Sector Development in Africa

Africa's private sector is encumbered by a myriad of challenges, which prevent it from becoming an effective engine of growth. Top among these challenges are access to finance, weak and sometimes non-existent infrastructure, skills gap, unfavourable business environment and limited access to international markets. The most common constraints cited by African firms are access to finance and electricity (see Fig. 4.3). Lack of finance is preventing firms in the continent from expanding. It has been estimated that micro, small and medium-sized enterprises in Africa's formal sector face a financing gap of about USD 136 billion (AfDB/OECD/UNDP, 2016). The financing challenge is dire in the informal sector, where the majority of the enterprises do not even have bankable collateral. Long-term capital, which is critical

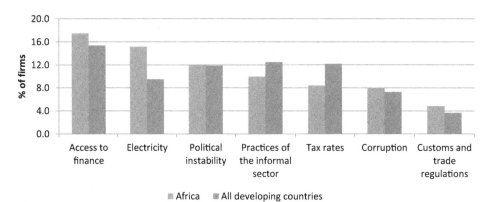

Figure 4.3 Most common operating challenges faced by African firms, 2015 or most recent year. Adapted from Enterprise Surveys, www.enterprisesurveys.org.

for business growth is hard to come by even for the formal sector. Beck, Maimbo, Faye and Triki (2011) estimate that 60% of loans in Africa have a tenure of less than 1 year; less than 2% of loans have a duration beyond 10 years. It is clear that both conventional and innovative financing strategies are required to fill the financing gap faced by Africa's private sector.

Poor transport and energy infrastructure characterize the business environment in most of Africa. What is sad about the situation is that there seems to be little progress and in some cases retrogression in the infrastructure base. Based on World Economic Forum, African Development Bank and World Bank (2017) estimates, the quality of energy supply in Africa has dropped by close to 3% over the past decade; the performance in quality of transport also fell by 6% in Africa, while on the average, ASEAN has improved by 7%. It is only the quality of roads that has seen improvements over the past decade. Without a strong infrastructure base, the quest for industrialization will remain a mirage for most African economies. Other constraints that have held the private sector down include political instability in some African countries, unfavourable tax regimes, corruption and burdensome custom and trade regulations.

The World Bank's *Doing Business* Report (2017) reveals significant difficulties in starting and operating a business in Africa. Significant gaps exist in a number of doing-business indicators between Africa and the best performing countries (frontier countries). Among the indicators, SSA performs reasonably well in starting a business (75.33 out of 100.00) (see Fig. 4.4). In four other indicators (dealing with construction permits, registering property, paying taxes and trading across borders), it is about

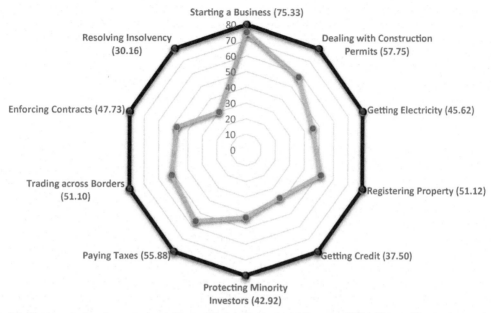

Figure 4.4 Distance to frontier scores on Ease of Doing Business Indicators -SSA. 'The rankings are benchmarked to June 2015 and based on the average of each economy's distance to frontier (DTF) scores for the 10 topics included in this year's aggregate ranking. The distance to frontier score benchmarks economies with respect to regulatory practice, showing the absolute distance to the best performance in each Doing Business indicator. An economy's distance to frontier score is indicated on a scale from 0 to 100, where 0 represents the worst performance and 100 the frontier'. Adapted from World Bank. (2017a). *Doing business 2017: Equal opportunity for all.* Washington, DC: World Bank.

halfway close to the frontier. The areas that need serious improvements include resolving insolvency, getting credit, getting electricity, protecting minority investors and enforcing contracts.

3. Driving Private Sector Development: The Role of Financial Markets and Institutions

Financial markets and institutions are imperative for the emergence of a vibrant private sector. Financial markets entail money, bond and stock markets that enable the trading of financial instruments (Abor, 2018). These markets can be physical or remote/electronic in nature. Financial institutions embody banks, savings and loans companies, insurance companies, investment companies, pension funds, credit unions and microfinance companies, amongst others, which carry out various financial intermediation functions. They could be deposit-taking establishments or non-deposit taking institutions. This section discusses the role financial markets and institutions play and can play in promoting private sector development in Africa.

3.1 Role of Financial Markets

Though substantial measures have been put in place to develop financial markets in Africa, progress has been quite slow. Financial markets in Africa lack depth and are inefficient but are accessible and stable (see Table 4.3). Depth of financial markets, measured as outstanding domestic debt securities as a percentage of GDP in SSA, is lower than the average scores for the developing world, high-income and developing countries in East Asia and the Pacific. In terms of access to financial markets (measured as the percent of market capitalization outside the top 10 largest companies), SSA ranks higher than high-income average and developing-world averages. This means that capital markets in Africa are relatively open to the private sector. It is second to financial markets in developing South Asia, which are the most accessible. Concerning stability of financial markets, stock markets in Africa are the most stable when compared with the averages of the developing world and high-income countries. What this means is that private sector companies can participate

Table 4.3 Financial Market Development Indicators in Developing Countries — Average 2005–14.

Financial Markets	Developing World	High Income	East Asia & Pacific	Europe & Central Asia	Latin America & Caribbean	Middle East & North Africa	South Asia	Sub-Saharan Africa
Depth	22	30	30	1	13	11	3	18
Access	48	45	56	50	37	51	62	56
Efficiency	20	44	32	24	7	13	24	5
Stability	20	20	23	24	18	20	20	15

Financial Markets—Depth: Outstanding Domestic Private Debt Securities/GDP; Access: Percent Market Capitalization Out of the Top 10 Largest Companies (%); Efficiency: Stock Market Turnover Ratio (%); Stability: Asset Price Volatility.
World Bank. (2017a). Doing business 2017: Equal opportunity for all. *Washington, DC: World Bank.*

in African capital markets with the comfort of stability afforded by those markets. However, financial markets in SSA are the least efficient in the developing world. African financial markets are characterized by low levels of stock market turnover ratios, poor capitalization, low liquidity, low number of bond issues and stock market listings, and weak financial infrastructure. Not all countries in Africa have stock markets. Currently, the African Securities Exchanges Association has 27 members serving 32 countries.

Bond markets (both government and corporate securities) in Africa are still at a nascent stage compared with other parts of the world. The capitalization of government bonds as a percentage of GDP in 2010 was 14.8% in SSA, which was lower than what pertained in Asian and Central European Countries (Mu et al., 2013). Mu et al. (2013) further estimate that the capitalization of corporate bonds in SSA is even lower with an average capitalization of 1.8% of GDP, compared with 26.5% for Canada and 98.6% for the United States. Thus, bond markets in Africa have much potential that can be harnessed for private sector development. The domestic bond markets in Africa are dominated by government securities, constituting nearly 90% of total market capitalization.

The key role financial markets play in private sector development is in the provision of long-term capital, which is scarce for businesses in Africa and generally all over the world. Businesses can raise long-term funds either by issuing bonds or stock through private placements, initial public offering or seasoned equity issues. The lack of long-term capital has been a binding constraint to the expansion of enterprises in Africa. With access to long-term funds, enterprises can borrow or issue equity and grow to their full potential. SMEs and start-ups do not often meet the stringent requirements of stock exchanges and are often deprived of opportunities available in the capital market. The solution to this is to create an alternative market (Alternative Market for SMEs) with low listing requirements which allows as many businesses as possible to go public and tap into more funds for investments. Alternative exchanges for SMEs can provide a lot of support to SMEs beyond the trading of securities. Additional support exchanges can offer to SMEs include linking SMEs to private equity, venture capital and angel investors, and facilitating SMEs access to additional professional services such as accounting, legal advice, underwriting, and stakeholder coordination and management (OECD, 2015).

A typical example is the Ghana Alternative Market (GAX), where SMEs and start-ups are offered an opportunity to raise long-term capital in the form of equity and bonds at relatively reduced costs. Incentives provided for firms of various stages of development to list on the GAX include pre-financing of IPOs, deferment of upfront fees, underwriting services, and access to a revolving fund to facilitate listing. In all, there are 14 stock exchanges for SMEs in Africa with more than 200 firms listed (Minney, 2016). These exchanges are BSE Venture Capital Market (Bostwana), Nile Stock Exchange (NILEX) (Egypt), GAX (Ghana), Growth Enterprise Market Segment (GEMS) (Kenya), MSE AltX (Malawi), Development & Enterprise Market (SEMDEM) (Mauritius), Casablanca Stock Exchange (BVC) (Morocco), Alternative Securities Market (ASeM) (Nigeria), Rwanda Stock Exchange (RSE) (Rwanda), AltX (South Africa), Enterprise Growth Market (EGM) (Tanzania), Tunis Stock Exchange Alternative Market (Tunisia) and Lusaka Stock Exchange (LuSE) (Zambia).

3.2 Role of Financial Institutions

Though financial institutions in Africa appear to have been making progress over the years, there is still a long way to go. Financial institutions in Africa are lacking in depth and breadth. The financial depth indicators in SSA shown in Table 4.4 fall below global averages. The average private credit provided by banks and other financial institutions over the period 2011–14 was 16.5% of GDP for SSA compared with a global average of 42.3% of GDP. This lack of financial depth implies that the private sector is not getting the credit it requires to take advantage of promising business opportunities. The lack of breadth in financial institutions is clearly seen in the fact that the number of bank accounts per 1000 adults is an average of only 150.3 in SSA compared with the world average of 511.7. The statistical representations are similar for bank branches per 100,000 adults. This means that fewer firms in SSA have access to formal financial services. In terms of stability and efficiency, African financial institutions are not too far behind the global averages. Bank net interest margin is 5.7% for SSA and 3.7% for the world implying that African banks are on the average less efficient relative to the world average. In terms of stability, bank Z-score is 8.0 for SSA compared with 9.9 for the world, indicating that African banks are quite stable but lag behind the global average.

Fig. 4.5 shows the percentage of the working capital of small, medium and large enterprises in Africa provided by banks. It shows that banks finance between 7.1% and 15.7% of the working capital of private enterprises in Africa. Clearly, the ability to obtain funds from banks increases with firm size in Africa, one of the notable exceptions being South Africa, where small enterprises

Table 4.4 Selected Indicators of Banking Sector Development in SSA.

Banking Sector Development Indicator		Year				Period Average
		2011	2012	2013	2014	
Depth						
Private credit by deposit money banks to GDP (%)	World	37.6	38.4	40.2	43.7	40.0
	SSA	16.4	16.4	16.5	15.7	16.3
Private credit by deposit money banks and other financial institutions to GDP (%)	World	39.3	41.2	42.8	45.7	42.3
	SSA	16.4	16.4	16.6	16.6	16.5
Deposit money banks' assets to GDP (%)	World	45.1	48.9	49.8	52.7	49.1
	SSA	21.0	20.8	22.8	23.8	22.1
Breadth						
Bank accounts per 1000 adults	World	433.1	461.0	499.1	653.5	511.7
	SSA	132.2	157.9	153.4	157.7	150.3
Bank branches per 100,000 adults	World	14.1	13.2	13.9	15.5	14.2
	SSA	3.7	3.8	4.2	4.1	3.9
Efficiency						
Bank net interest margin (%)	World	4.2	4.1	3.8	2.7	3.7
	SSA	6.6	6.1	6.4	3.7	5.7
Cost to income ratio (%)	World	55.8	55.0	56.2	51.5	54.6
	SSA	60.0	60.9	61.2	49.5	57.9
Stability						
Bank Z-score	World	10.0	9.9	9.9	9.9	9.9
	SSA	8.0	8.4	7.7	7.7	8.0
Bank nonperforming loans to gross loans (%)	World	4.1	4.1	4.4	4.4	4.2
	SSA	5.6	4.6	5.1	5.2	5.1

Financial Institutions—Depth: Private Credit/GDP (%); Access: Number of Accounts Per 1000 Adults, Commercial Banks; Efficiency: Net Interest Margin; Stability: Z-score.
World Bank. (2017a). Doing business 2017: Equal opportunity for all. *Washington, DC: World Bank.*

have a higher chance of obtaining funds than do medium enterprises. This has been backed by the work of Beck and Cull (2014a), who found that on the whole, African businesses are 19% less likely to obtain loans; small enterprises are 30% less likely to obtain bank loans than large firms; and medium enterprises are 13% less probable to obtain bank loans.

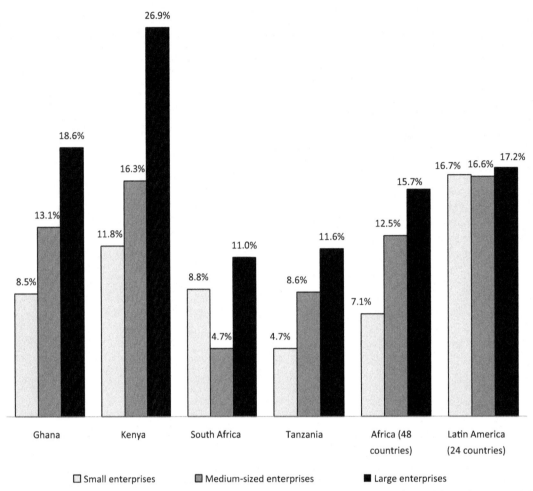

Figure 4.5 Proportion of working capital financed by banks in selected African countries and Latin America, 2015 or most recent year. Various enterprise surveys, www.enterprisesurveys.org.

3.3 Other Innovative Sources of Financing

Beyond traditional finance from banks and other financial institutions, there are other innovative avenues for sourcing funds and business support services for private sector development. These innovative sources help diversify the sources of funding to the private sector and reduce funding risk. Some of these innovative sources of support include remittances, private equity and venture capital funds, crowdfunding, structured trade finance, green bonds, and leasing and factoring, mobile money systems, and alternative capital markets for small and medium enterprises. Some of these new sources are explained in turn.

Remittances: In recent times, remittances have become an important source of development finance for developing countries and are playing roles relating to promotion of financial development, fostering growth, ensuring monetary stability and providing funding for migrant households (see Issahaku, Abor, & Harvey, 2017; Issahaku, Harvey, & Abor, 2016). Based on World Bank (2017) estimates, remittances to the SSA region in 2016 was 33 billion. In dollar terms, Nigeria was the largest remittance recipient, receiving $19 billion in 2016. Ghana, which was the second largest recipient in the region, received only $2 billion. In a number of developing countries, remittances exceed donor inflows, foreign reserves, private equity and portfolio inflows. A number of countries in SSA are highly dependent on remittances (see Fig. 4.6). Liberia is the most remittance dependent country in SSA, followed by the Comoros, the Gambia and Lesotho.

The usefulness of remittances rests on the fact that they are more stable than other capital flows, do not constitute debt to the host economy and are mostly countercyclical to economic business cycles. Thus, policies that stimulate the inflows of remittances can help provide relatively cheap capital for private sector development. An important barrier to remittance inflows is the cost of remitting. SSA is noted to be the costliest destination to send remittances and this significantly discourages migrants from remitting, especially through formal channels. Other bureaucracies such as cumbersome paper work and delays in claims processing further constrain inflows.

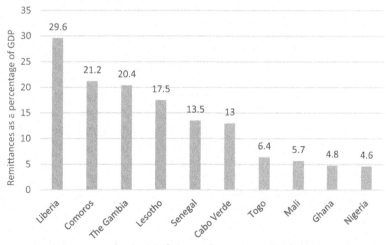

Figure 4.6 Remittance dependent countries in sub-Saharan Africa, 2016. World Bank. (2017b). *Migration and remittances: Recent developments and outlook, migration and development brief 27.* Washington, DC: World Bank.

Beyond remittances, return migrants have a crucial role to play in business development in Africa. They can apply the experience, exposure to technology, new knowledge and capital obtained abroad to promote entrepreneurship on their return to their country of origin. Black and Castaldo (2009) in a study based on Ghana and Côte d'Ivoire showed that return migration enhances entrepreneurship in those two countries. They further observed that returning migrants in Ghana were more likely to establish businesses in Ghana because of the friendlier business conditions in that country compared with Côte d'Ivoire at the time. This means that home country business environment is a key factor in determining business decisions of return migrants.

Private Equity: Private equity is a source of investment capital from high net worth individuals and institutions for the purpose of investing and acquiring equity stake in firms. Private equity firms focus on raising funds and managing these funds in order to yield favourable returns for their investors. Though private equity firms are currently playing a limited role in financing firms in Africa, they are growing with time. Private equity includes buyout, venture capital, growth, turnaround, private equity secondaries, mezzanine finance, private equity fund of funds, angel investments and other private equity. The 2016 *Preqin Global Private Equity & VC Report* shows that the aggregate capital raised by Africa-focused private equity funds from 2007 to 2015 was $20.4 billion. About 44% of this amount accrued from growth deals, 29% from buyout deals, 11% from venture capital deals, and 16% from all other equity deals. Out of a total of $4.5 billion raised by Africa-focused equity Funds in 2015, growth funds accounted for more than half ($2.5 billion). A total of $1.3 billion was raised through buyout, and venture capital accounted for $0.2 billion, while all other fund types raised half a billion dollars.

Crowdfunding: Crowdfunding is an innovative financing solution that allows firms to seek financing solutions from a large number of people through the internet. It allows firms to effectively utilize their networks wherever they are in the world to source funds for business development. Uptake of crowdfunding is low in Africa due in part to poor internet connectivity and the high cost of internet services. These have led to poor internet and social media patronage on the continent compared with other regions of the world. Other factors that have hindered crowdfunding activities in Africa include weak regulatory frameworks and standards relating to new payment systems, cross-country electronic funds transfers and transfer of equity (Berndt, 2016). The World Bank (2015) estimates the value of African crowdfunding market in 2015 to be only 0.5% of global crowdfunding activity. Thus, more needs to be done to improve the use of crowdfunding on the continent. This is especially the case because Estrin and Khavul (2016) have found that crowd-funding does not generate herding behavior; has low transactional costs; resolves the persistent market failures in funding entrepreneurial ventures; and reduces the biases in traditional forms of early stage entrepreneurial finance (sector, location and gender of the entrepreneur were found not to influence the success of a pitch).

Structured Trade Finance (STF): STF is an innovative approach to financing international trade, which focuses on transaction based lending. The advantage of STF is that funding decision is not based on balance sheet analysis, government guarantee or tangible assets as collateral but rather on the potential sale of the commodity for payment. Thus, in STF the emphasis shifts from the strength of the borrower to the underlying cash flow and structures that enhance safe financing. STF is particularly important in the case of Africa where it is difficult to obtain commercial finance. The African Export-Import Bank (AFREXIM) provided US$ 15.4 billion through STF deals during the period 2012−16. Banks and other lending institutions in Africa need to be encouraged to consider STF as opposed to the conventional method of balance sheet financing, which excludes most enterprises with viable trade transactions.

Alternative Markets for SMEs: An alternative market is a sub-market of a main stock exchange created to allow smaller companies with high growth potential to raise capital from the public market by floating shares with a more flexible regulatory system than is applicable to the main market. For instance, the JSE Limited created an Alternative Exchange (AltX) in 2003 and has since then has listed over 120 firms, raising over US$ 3.7 billion in secondary capital fund. About 63 companies remain listed on the AltX and many have progressed to the JSE's main board. In 2013, the Ghana Stock Exchange, the Nigeria Stock Exchange and the Nairobi Securities Exchange also launched the Ghana Alternative Market (GAX), Alternative Securities Market and the Growth Enterprise Market Segment respectively, targeting SMEs. The establishment of an alternative market offers a number of relative benefits for firms, including easier access to long term finance, reduced cost of access to long-term capital, potential improvement in the financial performance, attainment of some prestige status, opportunities for improving risk and liquidity management, better corporate governance structures, and business opportunities with foreign investors. In spite of the benefits of the Alternative Market, very few African firms have taken advantage to raise capital from the public equity market. Efforts at encouraging SMEs in Africa to take advantage of raising equity from such alternative markets need to be encouraged. There is the need to intensify public education in order to increase both the supply and demand side of share trading.

4. Challenges and Opportunities in Extending Financial Inclusion

Financial inclusion holds significant benefits to Africa's private sector. But these benefits are not being fully exploited due to some critical barriers. There are supply side barriers as well as demand side barriers. The supply side barriers originate from market failures and include distance, documentation, inefficiencies, regulatory and institutional weaknesses, and high transaction costs. Some individuals and business concerns are in locations far removed from the metropolitan centres where most financial institutions are located. The lack of motorable roads, unavailability of reliable electricity and internet connectivity make it a deterrent for financial institutions to establish branches and outlets in rural areas. The consequence of this is what we see in Table 4.4, where bank branches per 100,000 adults is an average of 14.2 for the world and only 3.9 for SSA over the period 2011–14. The advent of mobile banking and mobile money services has drastically reduced the nature of this challenge.

Most enterprises and individuals that are financially excluded are also those that do not have the elaborate documentations required in opening bank accounts, accessing credit and other financial services. The requirements of business and tax registration documents, titles to land and other collateral, the demand for national identity cards, evidence of electricity and water bill payments and other 'know your customer' (KYC) requirements, all combine to exclude some private entities from the formal financial system. The Financial Action Task Force (FATF) has cautioned that the overly cautious measures put in place to check money laundering and terrorism financing should not lead to the unintended consequence of financial exclusion for lawful firms and individuals (FATF, 2011).

Another supply side constraint is the perception by banks and other financial institutions of high transaction costs involved in extending financial services and products to the poor. These transactions costs often arise from poor identification and addressing systems, dispersed settlements and populations, weak infrastructure such as bad roads and inadequate and unstable power supply, unstable macroeconomic landscape, among others. Weak, uncompetitive and inefficient financial markets and institutions is another barrier to the delivery of financial services for all. Poor corporate governance systems, unwarranted governmental interference, lack of expertise in some cases, poor investment decision making among some banks and financial institutions in Africa are drawbacks to financial inclusion. These have led to high inefficiencies and have resulted in the collapse of some financial institutions in the continent.

The demand side constraints to financial inclusion include pervasive poverty, low levels of financial literacy, poor saving habits, trust issues, and cultural and psychological barriers. Demand side barriers are often described as self-imposed challenges which hinder firms and individuals from accessing and using financial products and services. Top on the list among the demand side barriers to financial inclusion is poverty. World Bank estimates show that poverty is pervasive in SSA with about 47% (501 million people) of the population living on $1.90 a day or less in 2012 (World Bank, 2016b). With low income levels, the poor segment of the population will prioritize food and survival needs ahead of financial inclusion by way of savings. An analysis based on the World Bank Global Findex database involving 37 African countries by Zins and Weill (2016) showed that 'lack of money' was the most frequent reason (70.8%) offered by respondents as to why they did not own formal accounts. This means that policies that seek to encourage financial inclusion must incorporate food security and basic survival needs of households.

Another self-reported barrier to financial inclusion is the cost of accessing financial services and products. The requirement of minimum balance to open and maintain an account, high interest rates by banks and microfinance institutions, high premiums by insurance companies, all exclude or diminish the participation of some category of individuals and businesses from the financial system. It is therefore not surprising that the next most important self-reported barrier in Africa based on the World Bank Global Findex database is the perception that it is 'too expensive' to open an account. There are also trust issues such as some individuals are afraid of losing their investments in the event of collapse of a bank or the financial institution they operate with. This problem is reinforced by lack of transparency in determining charges and fees, poor attitude of staff of financial service providers and examples of failed finance schemes and banks dotted around the continent.

Beck, Samuel, Issa, and Thouraya (2011) performed an analysis of demand side constraints cited by firms in Africa using the

World Bank Enterprise Surveys. They found that only 23% of Enterprises in Africa without a loan actually applied for one contrasted with 40% in other developing countries. The reasons given for the non-application for loans in order of importance include lack of demand, cumbersome application procedures, high interest rates, high collateral requirements, insufficient size and duration of loan, the need for bribe, and fear of rejection of loan application. High levels of illiteracy combined with low levels of financial literacy among individuals and enterprises is also a challenge to financial inclusion in Africa. Some individuals and firms lack awareness about the types of financial services and products that exist and how they can access and use them. Outreach programmes by banks, insurance companies and other financial institutions can help minimize these problems. Regulatory bodies such as Central Banks, Insurance Regulators, Pensions Authorities, and Securities and Exchange Commissions, among others, can also lend a helping hand in this direction.

In spite of the challenges impeding the promotion of financial inclusion, several opportunities for extending financial inclusion abound in the continent. The relatively stable macroeconomic and financial environment, infrastructure investments in roads, power, and technological support infrastructure across the continent, the increasing political stability, the large number of willing but unserved and underserved businesses and individuals, growth in adoption of mobile phone technology and increasing trends in internet and social media usage, and increasing population trends across the continent, all bode well for further extending financial inclusion. Furthermore, on-going legal reforms in the banking sector and other segments of the financial system, the revamping and resourcing of legal and legislative institutions, and moves to guarantee judicial independence in most countries, will help lower transaction cost and ensure protection for investors.

4.1 Conclusion and the Way Forward

Africa has a relatively large private sector, which contributes significantly to growth and sustainable development through job creation, provision of goods and services and opportunities for wealth creation. But, Africa's private sector needs better financing in order to be the engine of growth that it is supposed to be. Regrettably, finance is the most critical constraint stifling the growth of the private sector. These financial constraints weigh more heavily on micro, small and medium enterprises, which constitute the bulk of private enterprise in the continent.

In order to position the financial system in such a way as to benefit these enterprises, various stakeholders in the financial sector must play their roles well individually and collaboratively. Banks and other financial sector players must build capacity by training and equipping staff on the intricacies of reaching out to private businesses, especially, the underserved/unserved informal sector. Fostering good relationships with customers, and more transparency in fixing bank charges will also help resolve the trust issues between financial service providers and their clientele.

Innovative sources of finance, including remittances, private equity, crowdfunding, structured trade finance, green bonds, leasing and factoring, mobile money systems, and alternative capital markets for SMEs, are key to reaching the unreached segment of the private sector. The challenge is for financial regulators to ensure a regulatory and supervisory regime which is flexible enough to accommodate the unexpected nature of innovations but tight enough to detect and weed out financial fraud and fragility. The regulatory environment should also stimulate competition among financial sector players, as competition promotes innovation. Another responsibility that lies within the domain of regulators is consumer protection and financial education. Financial literacy and consumer protection will ensure that users of financial services are not exploited or unduly overburdened, but are knowledgeable enough and well empowered to make prudent financial choices.

For their part, governments can create an enabling environment for private sector financing by improving the efficiency and transparency of the judiciary and the courts, consolidating land and property rights, and investing in infrastructure such as roads, telecommunications, electricity and water, especially, in deprived areas. Such an enabling environment should lower transaction costs and enhance efficiency in the delivery of financial services to the private sector.

References

Abid, M. (2016). Size and implication of informal economy in African countries: Evidence from a structural model. *International Economic Journal, 30,* 571–598.

Abor, J. Y. (2018). *Financial markets and institutions: A frontier market perspective* (2nd ed.). Tema: Digibooks.

Abor, J., & Biekpe, N. (2007). Small business reliance on bank financing in Ghana. *Emerging Markets Finance and Trade, 43*(4), 93–102.

African Development Bank (AfDB). (2011). *Africa development report 2011: Private sector development as an engine of Africa's development.* Tunis: AfDB.

AfDB/OECD/UNDP. (2016). *African economic outlook 2017: Entrepreneurship and sustainable development*. Paris: OECD Publishing.

Applegarth, P. V. (2004). *Capital market and financial sector development in sub-Saharan Africa, a report of the Africa policy advisory panel*. Washington, DC: Center for strategic and international studies.

Aryeetey, E. (1998). *Informal finance for private sector development in Africa, economic research papers no. 41*. Abidjan: African Development Bank.

Beck, T., & Cull, R. (2014a). SME finance in Africa. *Journal of African Economies, 23*(5), 583–613.

Beck, T., & Cull, R. (2014b). Banking in Africa. In A. Berger, P. Molyneux, & J. O. S. Wilson (Eds.), *Oxford handbook of banking* (2nd ed.). New York: Oxford University Press.

Beck, T., Samuel, M. M., Issa, F., & Thouraya, T. (2011). *Financing Africa: Through the crisis and beyond*. Washington, DC.

Berndt, A. (2016). Crowdfunding in the African context: A new way to fund ventures. In L. Achtenhagen, & E. Brundin (Eds.), *Entrepreneurship and SME management across Africa, frontiers in African business research* (pp. 31–49). Singapore: Springer.

Black, R., & Castaldo, A. (2009). Return migration and entrepreneurship in Ghana and Côte d'Ivoire: The role of capital transfers. *Tijdschrift voor Economische en Sociale Geografie, 100*(1), 44–58. https://doi.org/10.1111/j.1467-9663.2009.00504.x.

Estrin, S., & Khavul, S. (2016). *Equity crowdfunding: a new model for financing entrepreneurship? (No. 462)*. Centre for Economic Performance, LSE.

Financial Action Task Force (FATF). (2011). *Anti-money laundering and terrorist financing measures and financial inclusion*. Paris: FATF/OECD.

IFC. (2011). *International finance institutions and development through the private sector*. Washington, DC: International Finance Corporation (IFC).

IMF. (2016). *Financial development in sub-Saharan Africa: Promoting inclusive and sustainable growth*. Washington, DC: International Monetary Fund.

Issahaku, H., Abor, J. Y., & Harvey, S. K. (2017). Remittances, banks and stock markets: Panel evidence from developing countries. *Research in International Business and Finance* (in press) https://doi.org/10.1016/j.ribaf.2017.07.080.

Issahaku, H., Harvey, S. K., & Abor, J. Y. (2016). Does development finance pose an additional risk to monetary policy? *Review of Development Finance, 6*, 91–104.

Medina, L., Jonelis, A., & Cangul, M. (2017). *The informal economy in sub-Saharan Africa: Size and determinants, IMF working papers, WP/17/156*. Washington, DC: International Monetary Fund.

Minney, T. (2016). Exchanges give SMEs a helping hand. *African Banker Magazine*, (May 5, 2016).

Mu, Y., Phelps, P., & Stotsky, J. G. (2013). Bond markets in Africa. *Review of Development Finance, 3*, 121–135.

OECD. (2015). *New approaches to SME and entrepreneurship financing: Broadening the range of Instruments*. Paris, France: OECD.

Stampini, M., Leung, R., Diarra, S. M., & Pla, L. (2013). How large is the private sector in Africa? *Evidence from national accounts and labour markets' South African Journal of Economics, 81*, 140–165. http://www.african-exchanges.org/en/about-asea#contentCarousel/learn-more-about-asea.

World Bank. (2015). *Crowdfunding in emerging markets: Lessons from East African startups*. Washington, DC: World Bank.

World Bank. (2016a). *Global financial development database*. Washington, DC: World Bank Databank, World Bank.

World Bank. (2016b). *Sub-saharan Africa poverty and equity data*.

World Bank. (2016c). *World development indicators*. Washington, DC: World Bank Databank, World Bank.

World Bank. (2017a). *Doing business 2017: Equal opportunity for all*. Washington, DC: World Bank.

World Bank. (2017b). *Migration and remittances: Recent developments and outlook, migration and development brief 27*. Washington, DC: World Bank.

World Economic Forum African Development Bank, & the World Bank. (2017). *The Africa competitiveness report 2017*. Geneva: World, Economic Forum.

Zins, A., & Weill, L. (2016). The determinants of financial inclusion in Africa. *Review of Development Finance, 6*, 46–57.

Further Reading

Abor, J. Y. (2017). *Entrepreneurial finance for MSMEs: A managerial approach for developing markets*. London: Palgrave Macmillan.

Allen, F., Demirguc-Kunt, A., Klapper, L., & Peria, M. S. M. (2016). The foundations of financial inclusion: Understanding ownership and use of formal accounts. *Journal of Financial Intermediation, 27*, 1–30.

Levine, R. (1996). Stock markets: A spur to economic growth. *Finance & Development, 33*(1), 8. http://www.imf.org/external/pubs/ft/fandd/1996/03/pdf/levine.pdf.

GEOGRAPHY OF FINANCIAL MARKETS AND INSTITUTIONS

5

FINANCIAL MARKETS AND INSTITUTIONS IN AFRICA: LANDSCAPE AND FINANCIAL INCLUSION

Sydney Chikalipah,[1] Daniel Makina[2]

[1]*Department of Finance and Tax, University of Cape Town, Cape Town, South Africa;* [2]*Department of Finance, Risk Management and Banking, University of South Africa, Pretoria, South Africa*

1. Introduction

Through their role as financial intermediaries of funds between surplus units (savers) and deficit units (borrowers), financial markets and institutions provide households and firms with the means for asset building. Funds intermediated through financial

Extending Financial Inclusion in Africa. https://doi.org/10.1016/B978-0-12-814164-9.00005-0

institutions can pave the way for savers and borrowers to gain access to other financial products and services. The ensuing financial relationship between parties enables account holders to establish credit histories that facilitate access to credit as well as enables them to take advantage of other financial services such as insurance, health and educational savings plans and other investments. Financial systems are considered well-functioning if they are offering appropriate services in an inclusive manner ensuring accessibility, availability and usage of formal financial services to the entire population including disadvantaged segments such as low-income households. They are viewed as healthy if they are well-regulated, stable and not prone to systemic risks. They are seen as competitive when many players offer a variety of financial services at arm's-length. These are the traits against which African financial systems should be evaluated to determine whether they are inclusive financial systems with a fair chance of leading inclusive growth.

With South Africa as an exception, a survey by Allen, Otchere, and Senbet (2011) found the financial sector in Africa to be largely underdeveloped and exhibiting dualism, whereby a mainstream market coexists with a parallel market that serves clients denied credit by the former. The underdevelopment is however not uniform as it varies within and across countries and regions. In fact, a bird's-eye view would observe a continuum of financial markets and institutions at different stages of development within and across countries. Furthermore, financial development exhibits differences arising from the colonial origin of countries; that is, whether such origin was Anglophone, Francophone or Lusophone.

Nevertheless, since the 1990s financial markets and institutions in Africa have benefited from strong economic growth that has averaged 5% annually, making the continent the second-fastest-growing region in the world after Asia. Furthermore, financial institutions have generally benefited from financial liberalization accompanied by the widespread emergence of stock markets. In addition, the improvement in governance and the business environment, growing middle class, increasing trade, implementation of sound macroprudential policies, and macroeconomic moderation have all contributed to the growth of the financial sector in Africa. Financial liberalization of financial institutions has led to the mushrooming of domestic banks in a sector previously dominated by foreign colonial banks, some which have become pan-African in the sense that they are established in more than one African country.

It is against this background that this chapter examines the landscape of financial institutions and markets, evaluating the extent to which they are extending financial inclusion. It is in its emphasis on financial inclusion that this work differs from the analysis of Allen et al. (2011), which also looked at financial systems in Africa. Additionally, this chapter uses most recent data covering the period 2010 to 2015. Despite the difference in emphasis, the two works complement each other.

2. An Overview of the Financial Sector

The growth of the financial sector in Africa since the late 1990s has been phenomenal. Moreover, the sector's prospects are getting brighter mainly due to the financial inclusion agenda, demographic changes, steady economic growth and ongoing financial sector reforms. Despite robust financial sector growth, over 500 million adults in Africa still lack access to formal banking services (Chikalipah, 2017; World Bank, 2015). Bank outreach on the continent remains well below global averages, similar to other components of the financial sector. For example, the insurance sector has a very low overall penetration of less than 3% across the African continent (PwC, 2016a).

Fig. 5.1 highlights the level of financial inclusion across the regions of Africa and selected countries. It can be observed that West Africa has the lowest rate of financial inclusion at 14%, with more than 90% of the adult population of countries such as Chad, Guinea and Niger lacking access to formal financial institutions. On the other hand, North Africa (excluding Morocco) has the highest financial inclusion level in the continent of 32%. Morocco has the highest financial inclusion rate in North Africa, with more than three-fifths of its adult population accessing formal financial services. In contrast, Egypt has the lowest financial inclusion rate at about 15%. Mauritius and South Africa are the most financially inclusive economies in Africa with 82% and 69% of their adult populations accessing formal financial institutions respectively.

The financial sector of Africa is largely shallow, and financial intermediation level is low compared with other regions of the world. According to the World Bank Global Findex report, the Middle East–North Africa region has the lowest financial inclusion rate at about 15%, followed by sub-Saharan Africa at 34% and South Asia at 46%, whilet the rest of the regions of the world have financial inclusion rates in excess of 50% (World Bank, 2014).

Fig. 5.2 reports the overall share of financial sector assets in Africa. Commercial banks make up the largest segment of the

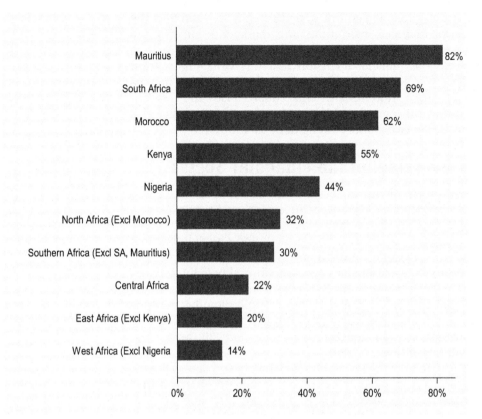

Figure 5.1 Financial inclusion in Africa (% of adults with a bank account). World Bank. (2015). *Economic indicators.* Washington DC, USA: World Bank Research - Databank.

financial sector and account for about 67% of total financial sector assets; the pension sector is second with 19%; and insurance and microfinance have a share of 11% and 1% respectively. The shares of financial assets across countries in Africa vary significantly. Countries like Benin, Congo Republic, Equatorial Guinea, Gabon, Liberia, Malawi, Mali, Nigeria, Nigeria, Senegal, Togo and Zambia have banking assets as a percent of the total financial sector in excess of 90%. In contrast, countries like Botswana, Lesotho Namibia, South Africa and Swaziland have bank assets as a percent of total financial sector assets of not more than 50%. Despite these variations, the banking industry, taken as a whole, still dominates the financial sector in Africa.

The stable and stellar growth of the nonbank financial sector, especially the insurance and pension industries, is reducing the dominance of commercial banks in the entire financial system of Africa, notwithstanding the low insurance penetration, which

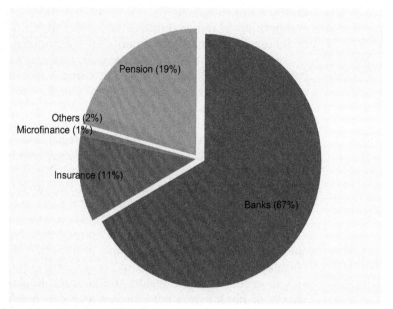

Figure 5.2 Total financial sector assets (%) in Africa 2015. The International Monetary Fund (IMF), African Development Bank (AfDB) and Central Banks financial stability Reports for financial year ending 2015.

shows less than 4% of Africans being insured — save for Mauritius, Namibia and South Africa. The insurance industry is the fastest growth component of the continent's financial sector, with an average growth rate exceeding 15% per year (AIB, 2016; EY, 2016; PwC, 2016a). The pension sector is also expanding steadily and currently provides a source of funding for major infrastructure development on the continent. Finally, the phenomenal growth of microfinance in Africa, averaging about 10% per annum, cannot be overlooked, albeit the industry has the smallest share of total financial sector assets at 1%. The stellar growth of the microfinance industry is largely witnessed in countries with low financial inclusion, such as Benin, Burkina Faso, Cameroon, Chad, Togo and Uganda.

3. The Banking Sector

As previously highlighted, commercial banks have been the main backbone of the financial sector in Africa. Financial liberalization and financial sector reforms, as well as the expansion of pan-African banks (PABs), has substantially changed the landscape of banking systems. The industry is now deeper, stable, and less susceptible to systemic banking crises. Notwithstanding these remarkable accomplishments, access to financial services in Africa has remained low. Furthermore, there is a lack of bank competition in many countries in Africa, which is partly caused by increased capital requirements for commercial banks.

At the end of the 2015 financial year, total bank assets in Africa exceeded $1.5 trillion (TAR, 2015). Africa's banking industry is relatively concentrated, with 15 of 850 banks controlling slightly more than half of total banks assets (see Fig. 5.3). Within this spectrum, about 30% of total bank assets in Africa come from South Africa—based banks, which are the most profitable on the continent (see Fig. 5.4). This is followed by Egypt with 22%; Algeria, Morocco and Nigeria with 8% each; and the remaining African countries accounting for about 24%. Regionally, North Africa has the largest share of total continental bank assets of 44%, followed by Southern Africa with 37%. West and East Africa have 12% and 5% respectively, while Central Africa has the smallest share at a mere 2%. It is important to note that there is a strong correlation between the level of financial inclusion and bank assets in each respective region and country. Regions with higher shares of bank assets have higher levels of financial inclusion, whereas those with low shares have equally low levels of financial inclusion.

The remarkable change in the African banking landscape in the recent decades has been the rapid growth of cross-border networks in the form of pan-African banking groups. By the

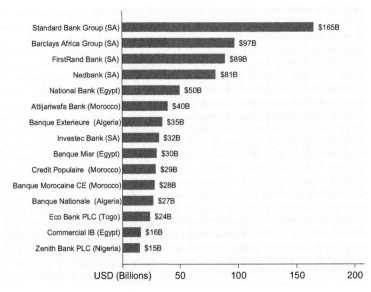

Figure 5.3 Top 15 African banks by assets in 2015. The International Monetary Fund (IMF) and Banks financial statements.

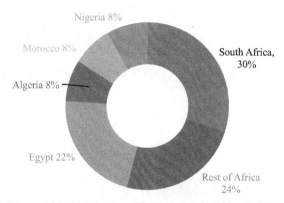

Figure 5.4 Geographical distribution of bank assets in Africa in 2015. The International Monetary Fund (IMF), Banks financial statements and Central Banks financial stability Reports for financial year ending 2015.

end of 2015, the top five PABs in terms of geographic footprint were: Ecobank (domiciled in Togo), with the largest presence in Africa, operating in 36 countries; Standard Bank (headquartered in South Africa), which has a presence in 20 countries; the United Bank for Africa (headquartered in Nigeria), which delivers bank services in 19 countries; Attijariwafa Bank (based in Morocco), which renders financial services in 13 countries; and Barclays Bank African Group (domiciled in South Africa), which operates in 11 countries.

Bank penetration in Africa, as earlier noted, remains low, compared with other regions of the world. Bank penetration is measured as the total number of adults accessing bank products and services in a country (Demirgüç-Kunt, Klapper, & van Oudheusden, 2015). North African countries are reasonably well penetrated compared with other regions in Africa, with 8 bank branches per 10,000 people as of 2015 (see Fig. 5.5). Egypt has the lowest financial inclusion in North Africa, with the number of bank branches per 10,000 people hovering around 3. Southern Africa overall stands at around 6 bank branches per 10,000 people, while West and Central Africa have about 2 bank branches per 10,000 people. East Africa has the lowest bank account penetration in the region at just 1.8 branches per 10,000 people. With regard to automated teller machines (ATMs), Southern Africa has over 50 ATMs per 100,000 people, followed by North Africa with 20, West Africa with 10, Central Africa with 6, and East Africa with 5 ATMs per 100,000 people. Table 5.1 presents the grouping of African countries in their colonial languages: English (Anglophone), French (Francophone) and Portuguese (Lusophone).

Figure 5.5 Bank penetration in Africa (branch network) in 2015. World Bank. (2015). *Economic indicators.* Washington DC, USA: World Bank Research - Databank.

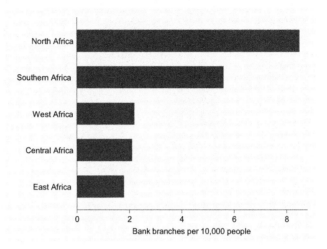

Table 5.1 Grouping of African Countries in Their Colonial Languages.

Francophone Countries				
Algeria	Benin	Burkina Faso	Burundi	Cameroon
CAR Φ	Chad	Côte d'Ivoire	Djibouti	Congo, DR⁺
Eq. Guinea	Gabon	Guinea	Madagascar	Mali
Mauritania	Morocco	Niger	Congo, rep	Rwanda
Senegal	Togo	Tunisia		

Anglophone Countries				
Botswana	Egypt	Gambia	Ghana	Kenya
Lesotho	Liberia	Malawi	Mauritius	Namibia
Nigeria	Sierra Leone	South Africa	South Sudan	Sudan
Swaziland	Tanzania	Uganda	Zambia	Zimbabwe

Lusophone Countries		
Angola	Guinea-Bissau	Mozambique

The symbols Φ and + denote Central Africa Republic and Democratic Republic, respectively.
Haspelmath, M. (2005). The world atlas of language structures *(Vol. 1). Oxford, United Kingdom: Oxford University Press.*

Francophone countries generally lag behind Anglophone countries in social and economic aspects. The economic divide is mainly attributed to lack of infrastructure, a poor corporate culture and bad governance in some French African-speaking countries. It is also the case for a handful of Portuguese-speaking countries in Africa, like Angola, Mozambique and Guinea-Bissau, which are lowest ranked on human development and also have poor environment for doing business. Equally important to note is that French- and Portuguese-speaking countries in Africa have experienced more civil wars in the last half-century than English-speaking countries have. To a large extent, the state of economic development explains the endemic low growth of the financial sector in these regions.

Based on the grouping of countries in Table 5.1, French-speaking countries have the lowest overall bank penetration of 23% of the adult population, followed by Portuguese-speaking countries with 27% and English-speaking countries with the highest penetration at 33%. The same is the case with the number of bank branches per 10,000 people — French-speaking countries with an average of 3.3, Portuguese-speaking countries with 3.4, and English-speaking countries with an average of 4.2. Significantly, English-speaking countries account for more than three-fifths of total bank assets in Africa. Lastly, it has been observed that, most if not all, the largest pan-African banks have significant footprints in countries with the same colonial languages, especially the Barclays African Group, FirstRand Group and Standard Bank. However, the pan-African Ecobank operates in all regions irrespective of language.

Crucially, the banking sector has been instrumental in extending financial inclusion in Africa. Financial inclusion has increased from about 24% of the adult population accessing formal financial services in 2010 to about 34% in 2015. Notwithstanding the substantial progress the banking sector has achieved in advancing financial inclusion, the industry is faced with vastly multifaceted bottlenecks. Some key bottlenecks include but are not limited to (1) high incidences of poverty levels among the population; (2) high financial and functional illiteracy; (3) underdeveloped infrastructure that hinders extending services in rural areas; (4) sparsely concentrated populations — particularly in rural areas, where three-fifths of the African population live; and (5) the high costs of maintaining a traditional bank account.

Since the early 2000s, the banking sector in Africa has seen gradual growth of about 2% per annum (Beck & Cull, 2014; Nyantakyi & Sy, 2015). Much of that growth is owed to financial sector reforms undertaken during the 1990s, which have significantly contributed to the development of the entire financial system. Furthermore, the capital bases for banks have been growing, risk management practices have considerably improved, and there has been steady expansion in consumer and commercial lending across the continent. Lending to the private sector as a percentage of GDP increased from 28% in 1980 to about 46% in 2015 (World Bank, 2015). The banking sector is yet to reach its full potential, as enormous market opportunities remain untapped. Some untapped opportunities include (1) a huge unbanked population, especially in rural areas; (2) the fastest growing middle class in the world; (3) small and medium enterprises (SMEs), which the traditional banking sector shuns in extending credit; and (4) infrastructure backlog, which when tackled would result in large-scale public and private spending that creates employment. However, for the banking sector to fully embrace these four market opportunities, a favorable business environment, stable macroeconomic fundamentals and quality institutions are necessary to support the growth of the banking industry.

4. The Pension Sector

Over the last 10 years, the pension industry on the continent has been growing at an average annual rate of 8%, with East Africa and Nigeria in particular witnessing growth in excess of 20% annually (PwC, 2015). Sector growth rates are projected to continue as coverage increases and pension regulations become simplified. The most noticeable development in the pension sector, according to the PwC (2015) report, is the creation of a three-pillar pension system in Ghana and Mauritius. The first pillar is a standardized state-run pension system, while the second pillar is a funded system in which both employees and employers make defined contributions. The third pillar is a voluntary scheme that caters for the rising category of middle-class employees. Fig. 5.6 lists the top 15 countries in Africa by total pension assets for the year ending 2015.

Based on available data of 34 countries, at the end of 2015, the total assets of the African pension sector was estimated at USD 430 billion, with South Africa accounting for about 72% of total pension assets. The 20 countries excluded from the analysis due to lack of data were Burundi, Cape Verde, Comoros, Djibouti, Democratic Republic of Congo, Equatorial Guinea, Eritrea, Ethiopia, Guinea, Guinea-Bissau, Liberia, Libya, Mauritania, São Tomé and Príncipe, Seychelles, Sierra Leone, Somalia, South

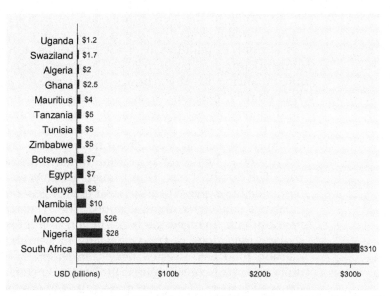

Figure 5.6 Total assets of pension funds in Africa at the end of 2015 (top 15 countries only). The African Development Bank (AfDB), Organisation for Economic Co-operation and development (OECD) and PricewaterhouseCoopers (PwC).

Sudan, Sudan and the Gambia. The pension sector in Africa is extremely concentrated, with 90% of assets located in four countries - Botswana, Namibia, Nigeria and South Africa. Southern Africa has the highest share of the total continental pension assets, representing 79%, North Africa has 9%, West Africa has 8%, and Central Africa and East Africa have 1% and 3% respectively.

Pension coverage is very low; overall under 10% of the active labor force in sub-Saharan Africa is covered, and these are usually civil servants and the small fraction of private sector workers who make contributions to pension funds. Only one in five old-aged persons receive an old-age pension. However, pension coverage varies significantly from country to country across the continent. The North African countries have the highest pension coverage, at over 60%. Southern African countries have pension coverage of about 13%, excluding Mauritius and South Africa with coverage of about 60%, the same as in North Africa. West African countries fall in third place with pension coverage of 9% across the active labor population, while Central and East African countries had only 6% of pension coverage in 2015. According to Help-Age International, only seven countries – Algeria, Botswana, Egypt, Lesotho, Mauritius, Namibia and South Africa – provide universal noncontributory pensions in Africa. In 2015, a few countries, namely Kenya, Uganda and Zambia, were piloting a universal old-age social pension scheme.

According to the New Partnership for Africa's Development agency, building infrastructure in Africa requires over $100 billion per annum. In addition, over $300 billion is needed to finance infrastructure projects until 2040. The huge shortfall in infrastructure financing in Africa brings in the role of pension funds. Traditionally, pension funds across the world invest largely in fixed-income assets and equity. By contrast, numerous pension funds in Africa have emerged as key investors in financing infrastructure projects as well. There have been a few examples of infrastructure financing by pension funds in Africa in the recent past. The South African Government Employees' Pension Fund has made huge investments in solar energy generation, hospitals, highways and telecommunication. The Tanzania's state-run pension fund financed the construction of a multimillion dollar six-lane toll bridge in Dar es Salaam. In Zambia, the state-run pension fund has invested heavily in shopping malls, housing units and road constructions. In Tunisia, a state pension fund financed construction of an airport. It is important to note that investments in infrastructure such in energy, telecommunications, roads and transport foster efforts in extending financial inclusion to rural areas where the majority of populations reside. Banks are only able to set up branches in rural areas when such basic infrastructure is in place.

Furthermore, similar to the banking industry, the general level of development of the pension sector, and coverage, varies based on colonial heritage (refer to Table 5.1). If we exclude North African countries, which have relatively high degree of pension coverage, the Anglophone countries have better developed pension sector and coverage compared with the Francophone countries. Lusophone countries have the worst developed pension sector in Africa. The common challenges faced by the pension sector in Africa include, among others, (1) large informal sectors which pay low wages; (2) weak legal and regulatory environments; (3) poor saving cultures resulting in low pension coverage among the self-employed; and (4) volatile macroeconomic environments.

5. The Insurance Sector

Insurance is the fastest growing segment of the finance sector in Africa, recording an average annual growth rate in excess of 15% since 2010, with Kenya, Morocco and Nigeria being the fastest-growing insurance markets (AIB, 2016; EY, 2016; PwC, 2016a). The insurance market is strongly related to economic growth.

The rise in household incomes translates into more insurable assets and directly increases insurance premium underwritings. Accordingly, the rapid growth of insurance industry has been propelled by the stellar economic growth in Africa since the early 2000s. Nevertheless, the insurance market is still underdeveloped and largely skewed toward non-life products, with a notable exception of Mauritius, Namibia and South Africa. Overall, the premiums for non-life insurance account for more than three-quarters of total insurance premiums in Africa. In marked contrast, life insurance dominates in South Africa owing to its well-established middle class and a more sophisticated financial system. Furthermore, South Africa has the second-highest life insurance penetration, about 11% in the world after South Korea.

Compared with other regions, insurance penetration in Africa is the lowest in the world, standing at 2.8% of the population overall in 2015. The low insurance penetration is mainly due to high levels of poverty, an underdeveloped financial sector, cultural and religious beliefs, rigid insurance regulations and lack of innovation and awareness. However, South Africa is an exception with insurance penetration of about 15%, followed by Namibia with 8%. The rest of the countries in Africa have penetrations of less than 2%, except seven countries that have a penetration rate of between 3% and 6% − these are Botswana (3.2), Kenya (3), Lesotho (3), Malawi (3), Mauritius (6), Morocco (3.2) and Swaziland (3). In terms of regions, East Africa, North Africa (excluding Morocco) and West Africa all have overall insurance penetrations of about 1%. Southern Africa (excluding Namibia and South Africa) has a penetration rate of 2.3%, while Central Africa has the least penetration at 0.5%. In addition to low penetration, access to the insurance sector in Africa is concentrated at the top 5% of the entire population. Even South Africa, with a well-developed insurance industry − insurance products are concentrated among the upper-middle class.

At the end of 2015, it was estimated total insurance assets in Africa amounted to $280 billion, and South Africa accounted for nearly three-quarters of all African insurance assets (AIB, 2016; EY, 2016; PwC, 2016a). Equally, of the 48 countries included in the analysis in this chapter, total insurance assets under management in 2015 amounted to $267 billion. Fig. 5.7 shows the geographical share of insurance premiums in 2015, excluding South Africa.

The trend is the same with the level of insurance penetration. Of total insurance assets across the regions, Southern Africa has $222 billion − South Africa alone contributing $210 billion, North Africa second with $32 billion, West Africa with $6.5 billion, East

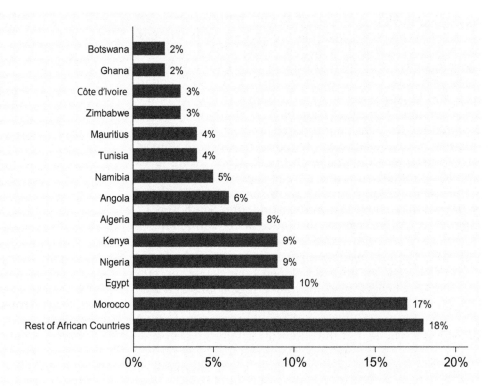

Figure 5.7 Share of African insurance premiums in 2015 (excl. South Africa). The African Insurance Barometer Market (2015).

Africa with $2 billion and Central Africa with $1.8 billion. A related point to note is that in 2015, total life and non-life premiums in Africa totaled $43.7 billion and $20.4 billion respectively. South Africa has superior dominance with an 86% share of Africa's entire insurance market. In terms of overall insurance growth, East Africa, North Africa and Southern Africa are the fastest growing regions on the continent, with annual growth exceeding 10%. What is heartening is that the insurance market is growing far much faster than the rate of economic growth. If this trend continues, the gap of access to insurance services will narrow significantly in the medium term.

6. Capital Markets

A well-developed and accessible capital market is an important component of a financial system. Unlike bank credit instruments, capital markets instruments are a source of long-term capital for large and small businesses. In the next subsections, stock markets, bond markets, mortgage markets and lease finance are discussed.

6.1 Stock Markets

Since the 1990s the World Bank has actively promoted stock market development among African countries through its affiliate, the International Finance Corporation (IFC), which provides technical expertise to advance this process. This has been justified on the basis that stock markets are part and parcel of the development of the financial sector as whole. Furthermore, emerging stock markets are seen as useful vehicles for attracting foreign portfolio investments and mobilizing savings for economic development.

In 1990 there were merely six stock markets in sub-Saharan Africa − Ghana, Kenya, Mauritius, Nigeria, South Africa and Zimbabwe − and three in North Africa − Egypt, Morocco and Tunisia. By the end of 2015, there were 28 stock exchanges representing 38 African capital markets. These 28 stock exchanges are located in the following countries: Algeria; Botswana; Bourse Régionale des Valeurs Mobilières (BRVM) is headquartered in Côte d'Ivoire (serving Benin, Burkina Faso, Côte d'Ivoire, Guinea Bissau, Mali, Senegal and Togo); Bourse Régionale des Valeurs Mobilières d'Afrique Centrale (BVMAC) is headquartered in Gabon (serves Central Africa Republic, Chad, Equatorial Guinea, Gabon and Republic of Congo); Cameroon, Cape Verde, Egypt, Ghana, Kenya, Libya, Malawi, Mauritius, Morocco, Mozambique, Namibia, Nigeria, Rwanda, Seychelles, Sierra Leone, Somalia, South Africa, Sudan, Swaziland, Tanzania, Tunisia, Uganda, Zambia and Zimbabwe.

Despite this rapid development, stock markets in Africa are still shallow, small in size and suffer from low liquidity with the exception of the Johannesburg Securities Exchange, which is the most active bourse on the continent. In 2015, it represented slightly over three-quarters of the combined US$ 1 trillion market capitalization of indices in Africa. When we measure the extent to which stock markets are serving the needs of African companies using initial public offering (IPO) data for the period 2013 to 2015, it can be observed that there were over 70 IPOs, and African companies raised capital in excess of US$ 4 billion (see Table 5.2).

Generally, the financial sector dominates the African IPO market with about 48% of the total value going to the sector, while the consumer goods and healthcare sectors account for 17% and 8% respectively. The industrials sector follows with 7%, and

Table 5.2 Initial Public Offerings (IPOs) by African Stock Exchanges.

Exchange Country	2013		2014		2015	
	Number of IPOs	Capital Raised (USD Million)	Number of IPOs	Capital Raised (USD Million)	Number of IPOs	Capital Raised (USD Million)
Botswana	0	0	0	0	1	9
BRVM	0	0	1	7	1	14
BVMAC	1	66	0	0	0	0
Egypt	0	0	1	109	4	752
Ghana	0	0	1	1	2	1
Kenya	0	0	1	7	1	35
Mauritius	0	0	1	9	0	0
Morocco	1	122	1	127	2	91
Mozambique	1	11	0	0	0	0
Nigeria	1	190	1	538	1	23
Rwanda	0	0	0	0	1	39
South Africa	4	261	9	742	12	658
Tanzania	1	2	2	6	1	15
Tunisia	12	191	6	125	2	43
Zambia	0	0	1	9	0	0
Totals	**21**	**843**	**25**	**1680**	**28**	**1680**

(i) **BRVM** serves Benin, Burkina Faso, Côte d'Ivoire Guinea-Bissau, Mali, Senegal and Togo; (ii) **BVMAC** serves Central Africa Republic, Chad, Equatorial Guinea, Gabon, and Republic of Congo.
PwC (2016b).

telecommunications accounts for 5% of the total IPO market. The other four sectors, viz basic materials, oil and gas, utilities and technology, share the remaining 15% of the total African IPO market.

Insofar as there has been sustained growth in the listings of companies on the African stock exchanges, the number of IPOs per year are still few compared with other regions of the developing world, with the exception of Latin America and the Caribbean. For example, in 2015 there were 1218 IPOs around the world which raised combined capital amounting to US$ 195.5 billion (EY, 2015). Of the 1218 IPOs, 12 were issued in central and south America, 28 in Africa, 58 in the Middle East and India, 188 in North America, 259 in Europe, and 673 in the Asia–Pacific (EY, 2015).

Generally, African stock markets do not provide a platform for start-ups and small businesses to raise capital. This leaves the SMEs and start-ups to rely on banks as a source of financing. On the other hand, banks in Africa shun the SME sector relative to other developing regions of the world. Bank lending often focuses on large corporate clients and on key sectors of the economy (manufacturing, trade, real estate and construction). According to the World Bank *Enterprise Survey* of 2014, over 90% of SMEs in Africa lack access to credit. This is attributed to high-risk characteristics of SMEs.

Stock markets in Africa are growing but at a slow pace. The many contributing factors to this slow growth include (1) low liquidity caused by few listed firms that trade infrequently; (2) weak legal and regulatory environments, (3) lack of robust electronic trading systems; and (4) few participating institutional investors. Overcoming these challenges would significantly contribute to the growth of stock markets in Africa.

Despite challenges, African stock markets have the potential to be a barometer of the economy and offer great investment opportunities. The future prospects of African stock markets look bright judging from recent developments. First, through increased participation of banks and pension funds as institutional investors, liquidity is on an upward trajectory. Second, the rising middle class in Africa is showing an appetite for stock market investment, thereby increasing the number of participants. Third, macroeconomic and political stabilization have been accompanied by improvements in the regulation and sophistication of stock trading systems.

6.2 Bond Markets

The African bond markets are also in embryonic stages of development. They are largely dominated by government securities, such as treasury bills, that are mostly of short duration. With the exception of South Africa, and to a limited extent the North African region, the corporate bond market is almost nonexistent in Africa. Nonetheless, the overall bond markets have grown steadily, from $3.2 billion in 2008 to about $19 billion in 2015 (PwC, 2016b). Of the $19 billion bond issuance, a total of $4.4 billion was corporate debt. Overall, between 2008 and 2015, sovereign bonds significantly contributed to the total bond market, accounting for as much as 87% of the total. In the recent past, a number of African countries have issued dollar-denominated sovereign bonds, viz Cameroon, Côte d'Ivoire, Ethiopia, Gabon, Kenya, Namibia, Nigeria, Rwanda, Senegal,

South Africa and Zambia. These sovereign bonds often finance the construction of new roads, railways and power generation. Table 5.3 lists the notable Eurobonds issued by African countries between 2011 and 2015.

Generally, the African corporate bond market is far from being the viable alternative for financing projects in the continent. The corporate bond market is concentrated in a few countries, namely Kenya, Mozambique, Namibia, Nigeria, South Africa, Tanzania, Uganda and Zambia. The few companies that issue corporate bonds are largely in financial services. The corporate bond market is predominantly active in South Africa, mainly due to the country's high level of industrial development, the

Table 5.3 Eurobond Issuance in Africa Between 2011 and 2015.

Country	Maturity Period (years)	Coupon Rate (%)	Amount (USD Million)	Year of Issue
Nigeria	10	6.75	500	28.01.2011
Senegal	10	8.75	500	13.05.2011
Namibia	10	5.50	500	03.11.2011
Zambia	10	5.38	750	20.09.2012
Morocco	10	4.25	1000	05.12.2012
Morocco	30	5.50	500	05.12.2012
Rwanda	10	6.63	400	02.05.2013
Nigeria	5	5.13	500	12.07.2013
Nigeria	10	6.38	500	12.07.2013
Ghana	10	7.88	1000	07.08.2013
Ghana	10	7.88	1000	07.08.2013
Zambia	10	8.50	1000	14.04.2014
Ghana	12	8.13	1000	11.09.2014
Kenya	10	6.88	1500	24.06.2014
Kenya	5	5.88	500	24.06.2014
Côte d'Ivoire	10	5.38	750	16.07.2014
Senegal	10	6.25	500	30.07.2014
Ethiopia	10	6.63	1000	04.12.2014
Tunisia	10	5.75	1000	26.01.2015
Côte d'Ivoire	12	6.38	1000	24.02.2015

European Investment Bank (EIB), Moodys and Institute of International Finance (IIF).

depth of the bond market and its attractiveness to international investors. Among the countries of the Maghreb region, Algeria, Morocco and Tunisia have growing corporate bond markets, albeit at a slow rate as their markets are still small.

6.3 Mortgage Markets

Over the next decade, it is projected that Africa will see new three megacities emerge, namely Dar es Salaam, Johannesburg and Luanda, joining the continent's three existing megacities – Cairo, Kinshasa and Lagos. The implication of the rising population and urbanization of African cities is that the bulk of the population is and will continue to rent homes, as buying is beyond reach for many. Save for South Africa, African mortgage markets are the smallest in the world, with less than 5% of adults having a home loan in 2015. Furthermore, mortgage finance overall in Africa is below 10% of GDP, similar to the region of South Asia. In the rest of the regions of the world, mortgage loans as a percentage of GDP vary from over 20% in East and Central Asia, the Middle East, Latin America and the Caribbean, to over 40% in Australia and New Zealand, Central Europe and North America. As depicted in Fig. 5.8, only seven countries in Africa, namely Cape Verde, Comoros, Mauritius, Morocco, Namibia, South Africa and Tunisia, have mortgage finance markets larger than 12% of GDP in 2015.

Among the countries with a ratio of mortgages to GDP less than 10% are Botswana at 7%, Kenya and Rwanda at 4% and Zimbabwe at 3%. The remaining African countries had 1% or less of mortgages as a percentage of their domestic GDP. One important observation is that there is a strong relationship between the level of financial inclusion and the level of mortgage market depth across Africa. Countries with high financial inclusion also have relatively higher levels of mortgages as a percentage of GDP. The main challenges facing the African mortgage market consist of unstable macroeconomic environments, underdeveloped financial systems, volatile and high lending interest rates and weak property rights – which are important in enforcing contracts. Notwithstanding these challenges, the mortgage market is gradually growing, especially in countries where the major pan-African banks (Attijariwafa Bank, Barclays African Group, Ecobank, FirstRand and Standard Bank) are operating. The industry is also being promoted through funding initiatives by the IFC, the International Monetary Fund, the World Bank and the Pan-African Housing Fund. In addition, an increasing number of countries in Africa are undertaking housing reforms to stimulate home ownership.

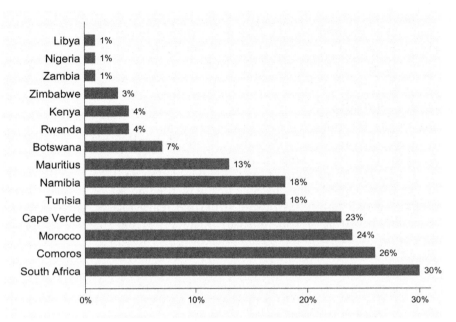

Figure 5.8 Mortgages as a percentage of GDP in selected African countries (2015). Centre for Affordable Housing Finance (CAHF, 2016), Housing Finance Information Network (HOFINET) and the World Bank.

6.4 Lease Finance

Lease finance is an important alternative to the long-established approach of financing equipment and capital goods. It enables a provider of finance, the lessor, to allow use of an asset by a borrower, the lessee, while paying for it in installments over an agreed period. This makes the facility more advantageous to small businesses that lack the required collateral to secure traditional bank credit. The leasing market in Africa is shallow and rudimentary, with a small presence in Egypt, Morocco, Tunisia and Nigeria, It is, however, substantial in South Africa. The lease finance penetration in Africa is below 5% as against a global average of over 20%. There is, however, lack of reliable data on Africa to derive a comprehensive analysis of the total continental lease finance portfolio.

Since 2008 the IFC has been providing lease financing to SMEs in 14 African countries: Burkina Faso, Cameroon, Cape Verde, Democratic Republic of Congo, Ethiopia, Ghana, Liberia, Madagascar, Mali, Mauritania, Rwanda, Senegal, Sierra Leone and Tanzania. The aim of the IFC facility is to increase access to finance and promote financial sector development on the continent.

Just like other segments of the financial sector in Africa, the main challenges faced by SMEs to access lease finance are numerous. Chief among them are few leasing firms, lack of financial documentation by SMEs, difficulties in enforcing contracts, and unstable macroeconomic environments. Notwithstanding challenges, the lease finance industry in Africa looks promising due to ongoing government supportive regulatory frameworks and financial support from the IFC and international investors such as Alios Finance.

7. Conclusion

The financial sector in Africa is rudimentary, with over two-thirds of the adult population lacking access to formal financial institutions, and over 80% of consumer transactions are conducted with cash. The commoditization of banking technology and the expansion of microfinance institutions and pan-African banks is giving an enormous boost to the 'universal financial access for Africa agenda' pioneered by the World Bank.

Going forward, the path of the development of the main components of the financial sector will vary from sector to sector. The banking sector will continue to dominate the financial system. The financial inclusion agenda as well as product innovation are likely to promote the growth of the banking industry. The cross-border network expansion undertaken by the pan-African banks will most likely exacerbate market concentration in Africa. The insurance and pension sectors are likely to reap the dividends in years to come, mainly from the rising middle-class and overall rapid growth of the African population. While the non-life insurance sector will continue to be the principal component of the insurance market in Africa, when income levels improve, life insurance is bound to register substantial growth. If economic growth is sustained at levels of at least 5%, stock markets, bond markets, mortgage markets and lease finance will continue to grow and provide alternative sources of finance for businesses in Africa.

References

AIB (African Insurance Barometer). (2016). *Africa insurance barometer market survey.* http://www.african-insurance.org/documents/Both%20Books.pdf.

Allen, F., Otchere, I., & Senbet, L. W. (2011). African financial systems: A review. *Review of Development Finance, 1*(2), 79–113.

Beck, T., & Cull, R. (2014). Banking in Africa. In *The oxford handbook of banking* (2nd ed.). Oxford, United Kingdom: Oxford University Press.

CAHF (Centre for Affordable Housing Finance). (2016). *Housing finance in Africa: A review of some of Africa's housing finance markets.* http://housingfinance africa.org/resources/yearbook/.

Chikalipah, S. (2017). What determines financial inclusion in Sub-Saharan Africa? *African Journal of Economic and Management Studies, 8*(1), 8–18.

Demirgüç-Kunt, A., Klapper, L., & van Oudheusden, P. (2015). Financial inclusion in Africa. In , *Policies and practices: Vol. 2. The oxford handbook of Africa and economics* (p. 388). Oxford, United Kingdom: Oxford University Press.

EY(Ernest & Young). (2015). *Ernest & young (EY) global IPO trends.* http://www. ey.com/Publication/vwLUAssets/EY-global-ipo-trends-2015-q1/$FILE/EY-Global-IPO-Trends-2015-Q1.pdf.

EY(Ernest & Young). (2016). *Sub-saharan Africa the evolution of insurance regulation.* http://www.ey.com/Publication/vwLUAssets/EY-sub-saharan-africa-the-evolution-of-insurance-regulation/$FILE/EY-sub-saharan-africa-the-evolution-of-insurance-regulation.pdf.

Haspelmath, M. (2005). *The world atlas of language structures* (Vol. 1). Oxford, United Kingdom: Oxford University Press.

Nyantakyi, E. B., & Sy, M. (2015). The banking system in Africa: Main facts and challenges. *Africa Economic Brief, 6*(5), 1–16.

PwC (PricewaterhouseCoopers). (2015). *Africa asset management 2020.* http:// www.pwc.lu/en/asset-management/docs/pwc-am-africa-2020.pdf.

PwC (PricewaterhouseCoopers). (2016a). *Insurance industry analysis.* http:// www.pwc.co.za/en/publications/insurance-industry-analysis.html.

PwC (PricewaterhouseCoopers). (2016b). *Africa capital market watch 2016.* https://www.pwc.co.za/en/assets/pdf/africa-capital-markets-watch-2016.pdf.

TAR (The Africa Report). (2015). *A record year for African Banks.* http://www. theafricareport.com/North-Africa/a-record-year-for-african-banks.html.

World Bank. (2014). *Global Findex: Measuring financial inclusion around the world.* http://www.worldbank.org/en/programs/globalfindex.

World Bank. (2015). *Economic indicators.* Washington DC, USA: World Bank Research - Databank.

Further Reading

Akinlo, T., & Apanisile, O. T. (2014). Relationship between insurance and economic growth in sub-Saharan African: A panel data analysis. *Modern Economy, 5*(2), 120–127.

Asabere, P. K., McGowan, C. B., Jr., & Lee, S. M. (2016). A study into the links between mortgage financing and economic development in Africa. *International Journal of Housing Markets and Analysis, 9*(1), 2–19.

Aterido, R., Beck, T., & Iacovone, L. (2013). Access to finance in sub-Saharan Africa: Is there a gender gap? *World Development, 47*, 102–120.

Beck, T. (2013). *SMEs finance in Africa: Challenges and opportunities. Banking in sub-Saharan Africa* (pp. 75–87). European Investment Report https://www. econstor.eu/bitstream/10419/88938/1/776005626.pdf#page=80.

Beck, T., & Hesse, H. (2009). Why are interest spreads so high in Uganda? *Journal of Development Economics, 88*(2), 192–204.

Beck, T., & Levine, R. (2004). Stock markets, banks, and growth: Panel evidence. *Journal of Banking & Finance, 28*(3), 423–442.

Brookings. (2017). *Leveraging African pension funds for financing infrastructure development*. https://www.brookings.edu/research/leveraging-african-pension-funds-for-financing-infrastructure-development/.

HAI (HelpAge Internation). (2016). *Old age income security in Africa annual report*. http://www.helpage.org/resources/publications/.

Lawry, S., Samii, C., Hall, R., Leopold, A., Hornby, D., & Mtero, F. (2017). The impact of land property rights interventions on investment and agricultural productivity in developing countries: A systematic review. *Journal of Development Effectiveness, 9*(1), 61—81.

Madestam, A. (2014). Informal finance: A theory of moneylenders. *Journal of Development Economics, 107*, 157—174.

Makina, D. (2012). Mortgage market, character and trends: Africa. In S. J. Smith, M. Elsinga, L. F. O'Mahony, S. E. Ong, S. Wachter, & K.-H. Kim (Eds.), *International encyclopaedia of housing and home* (Vol. 4, pp. 410—414). Oxford: Elsevier.

McAuslan, P. (2013). *Land law reform in eastern Africa: Traditional or transformative?: A critical review of 50 Years of land law reform in eastern Africa 1961—2011*. Abingdon, United Kingdom: Routledge.

Njue, M. N., & Mbogo, M. (2017). Factor hindering SMEs from accessing the financial products offered by Banks. *International Journal of Finance, 2*(3), 67—85.

Pilossof, R. (2016). Possibilities and constraints of market-led land reforms in southern Africa: An analysis of transfers of commercial farmland in postcolonial Zimbabwe, 1980—2000. *Journal of Agrarian Change, 16*(1), 32—49.

PSDA (Private Sector Development in Africa). (2014). *Pension funds and private equity*. https://www.fsdafrica.org/knowledge-hub/documents/pension-funds-and-private-equity-unlocking-africas-potential/.

Punnett, B. J. (2017). *Africa: Open for business LEAD: Leadership effectiveness in Africa and the African diaspora* (pp. 1—18). New York: Springer. Palgrave Macmillan.

Rofman, R., Apella, I., & Vezza, E. (2014). *Beyond contributory pensions: Fourteen experiences with coverage expansion in Latin America*. Washington DC, USA: World Bank Publications.

Rossouw, G. J. (2005). Business ethics and corporate governance in Africa. *Business & Society, 44*(1), 94—106.

UN (United Nations). (2013). *United Nations report - microfinance in Africa*. http://www.un.org/en/africa/osaa/pdf/pubs/2013microfinanceinafrica.pdf.

UN (United Nations). (2014). *United Nations report - world urbanisation prospects*. https://esa.un.org/unpd/wup/publications/files/wup2014-highlights.Pdf.

WEF (World Economic Forum). (2016). *What is the future of economic growth in Africa*. https://www.weforum.org/agenda/2016/05/what-s-the-future-of-economic-growth-in-africa/.

6

A SURVEY OF MICROFINANCE INSTITUTIONS AND INFORMAL FINANCE IN AFRICA

Sydney Chikalipah,[1] Daniel Makina[2]

[1]*Department of Finance and Tax, University of Cape Town, Cape Town, South Africa;* [2]*Department of Finance, Risk Management and Banking, University of South Africa, Pretoria, South Africa*

1.   Introduction

Microfinance is essentially the provision of financial services to poor people who for several reasons are shunned by the traditional banking sector. The concept dates back to the 18th century when Ireland experienced a famine. In response, an Irish nationalist, and the author of *Gulliver's Travels*, Jonathan Swift, started a £500 fund to lend money to poor tradesmen whereby they would pay in small weekly installments without interest. Over the years

Extending Financial Inclusion in Africa. https://doi.org/10.1016/B978-0-12-814164-9.00006-2

more schemes mushroomed throughout the developing world to cater to the rural and urban poor, leading to the establishment of microfinance institutions such as ACCION International in Venezuela and Grameen Bank in Bangladesh in the 1960s and 1970s respectively. Professor Muhammad Yunus, the founder of Grameen Bank, who popularized the concept of microfinance, was awarded the 2006 Nobel Peace Prize for his contribution.

In Africa microfinance has long existed in the form of informal finance provided by rotating savings and credit associations (ROSCAs) or traditional village savings and loan associations (VSLAs), whereby a group of villagers saves a small amount each month and lends the accumulated funds to a member. Understandably, due to low financial inclusion in Africa, the informal finance sector is huge, with millions of adults utilizing the service. However, microcredit from the informal sector is often characterized by short maturity, high interest rates, small monetary value and draconian payment terms.

Modern microfinance which has now become widespread in Africa was pioneered by donor organizations such as Care International UK that modernized the operations of the ROSCAs or VSLAs along the principles employed by Grameen Bank in Bangladesh. Other microfinance approaches employed included specialized lending to microenterprises by banks funded by international nongovernmental organizations (NGOs). Microfinancing has brought enormous benefits to the financially excluded segment of the society in Africa. These benefits included (1) facilitating microsavings, (2) provision of microcredit, (3) reduction of transaction costs for both lenders and borrowers via peer monitoring and group lending, and (4) some degree of empowerment, particularly for poor women.

In the last 2 decades, the microfinance industry in Africa has substantially evolved and so has its line of products offered to the poor. Besides microcredit and microsavings, microfinance institutions (MFIs) also offer innovative products and services like microconsignment, microfranchise, microinsurance, microleasing, microhousing, microenterprise short courses and mobile money transfers. The CGAP (2006) suggests that the large number of financially excluded people in the developing world can only gain access if financial services for the poor are integrated into the three levels of the financial system, namely the micro, meso and macro levels (CGAP, 2006).

Micro level interventions involve identifying microfinance clients and service providers. Poor people need a variety of services that include insurance, remittances and transfer, pensions, loans for emergency needs, microenterprise loans and safe places to save. Microfinance clients are often self-employed and typically home-based entrepreneurs. In rural areas they are small farmers and small-scale business operators engaging in peripheral income-generating activities. In urban areas, microfinance clients are more diverse and include street vendors, shopkeepers, service providers, artisans, etc. Research by CGAP (2006) has identified three broad features of microfinance clients:

- It is observed that most clients come from moderately poor and vulnerable nonpoor households, with some clients from extreme-poor households also participating;
- Programmes that explicitly target poorer segments of the population generally have a greater percentage of clients from extremely poor households; and
- Truly destitute households are outside the reach of microfinance programmes.

Indeed, in the literature it is observed that microcredit in particular may not be appropriate for the destitute and the hungry with no prospects of paying back such loans. Financial and nonfinancial services such as small grants, infrastructure improvements, employment and training programmes could be more appropriate for the destitute.

Meso level interventions involve building financial infrastructure such as payments and clearing systems that facilitate financial inclusion. Usually small financial institutions such as MFIs that serve the poor have no direct access to the payments system.

Macro level intervention pertains to the involvement of government in building inclusive financial systems. CGAP (2006, p. 76) identifies three ways in which governments can get involved in the financial system. First, governments deliver financial services directly and indirectly, usually by disbursing credit to preferred groups or channeling resources to financial institutions through wholesale arrangements. Usually, governments are not good at offering credit to poor people. However, government-owned banks, especially postal banks, do have a good track record of mobilizing savings or facilitating money transfers of poor clients in remote areas. Secondly, governments set policies, such policies ensuring macroeconomic stability, liberalizing interest rates, and establishing banking regulation and supervision which make viable microfinance possible. Thirdly, governments can proactively promote inclusion by offering fiscal incentives to financial institutions to serve the poor or low-income people.

Since MFIs alone cannot meet the huge demand for loans by small and informal sector businesses, it is essential that commercial banks also become involved in offering microfinance as well as the commercialization of MFIs. Indeed, the commercialization of MFIs in Africa has been on the rise, a forerunner being the K-REP Bank in Kenya. Other early examples of commercial banks that have been set up to offer only microfinance include Centenary Rural Development Bank in Uganda and the National Microfinance Bank in Tanzania. Today in almost every African country, commercial microfinance banks operate alongside other banks in the traditional banking sector.

Commercial banks that have moved into microfinance are mainly state banks – cases of preexisting, privately owned commercial banks that have started microfinance operations are still few. Baydas, Graham, and Valenzuela (1997) give some insights into why private commercial banks shy away from microfinance. Some are due to perceptions borne from the experience of failed programmes by governments in the provision of finance to the poor. Furthermore, private commercial banks are answerable to shareholders who are more concerned with the bottom line and maximization of shareholder returns which might not be obtained from microfinance activities. In addition, the standards and regulatory requirements that they need to comply with are not appropriate for microfinance. There are also cultural barriers whereby staff and managers of private banks often perceive the poor as unbankable. Furthermore, the organizational structures, procedures, products and delivery methodologies of private commercial banks are not designed for dispensing microfinance.

Notwithstanding the challenges, there are now a number of private commercial banks that are dispensing microfinance as one of their product. The two early pioneers are the Commercial Bank of Zimbabwe and the Co-operative Bank of Kenya that started microfinance operations during the 1990s with support from the British Department for International Development, and whose experiences had been positive.

2. Microfinance Paradigms

MFIs are distinguished by their legal charter. The legal charter defines the mission objectives. There are five different forms of MFIs, which can be categorized as cooperative and credit unions (CCUs), microbanks (MBs), nonbanking financial institutions (NBFIs), nongovernmental organizations (NGOs), and rural banks (RBs):

- **A Cooperative or Credit Union (CCU)** is a nonprofit member-based financial intermediary that offers a range of financial services for the benefit of its members, including lending and deposit mobilization. In many countries, CCUs are regulated either by central banks or by the societies' regulatory authority.

- A **Microbank (MB)** is a licensed financial intermediary regulated by a supervisory agency, usually the central bank. It may provide a number of financial services such as deposit taking, lending, payment services as well as money transfer services. Similar to MBs are **Rural Banks (RBs),** which are banking institutions that target clients who live and work in rural and peri-urban areas who predominantly engage in agricultural-related activities.
- A **Nonbanking Financial Institution (NBFI)** is a financial institution that provides similar services to those of a bank except with regard to deposit taking. The common types of NBFIs are life assurers, general assurers, asset management companies and pension funds. NBFIs are licensed under a separate category because of low capital requirements and limitations on the financial services they can offer. They are often supervised by a separate state agency.
- A **Nongovernmental Organization (NGO)** is an organization registered as nonprofit for tax purposes. The financial services of NGOs are restricted and do not often involve mobilizing microsavings from customers. NGOs are typically not regulated by banking supervisory authorities, but they offer microcredit as part of the development work to assist the poor in developing countries.

2.1 Microfinance Credit Lending Models

A wide range of microcredit lending methods are currently being used by MFIs in Africa. The lending methods are closely related, and MFIs typically employ two or more delivery methods when extending financial services to the poor.

- **Loan Solidarity Groups**: These are joint liability loan groups comprising at least five homogeneous individuals sharing virtually similar probabilities of loan repayments. This voluntary formation of small groups reduces the risks of default, and the collective responsibility of group members replaces the traditional banking practice of requiring collateral. Furthermore, the joint liability groups drastically eliminate the adverse selection problem, and moral hazard. Also, the MFI benefits from peer monitoring due to group members being jointly liable for the loan repayment.
- **Individual loans**: These are provided directly to borrowers as either household credit or a small business loan. The individual loan lending methodology forms the largest part of microcredit programmes, and commonly involves equipping microcredit borrowers with complementary services,

including cash flow management, saving techniques, record keeping, cost control and inventory management.

Generally, under both lending approaches there is a requirement for either compulsory or voluntary savings. The requirement of compulsory savings is based on the view that the poor must be taught financial discipline. In contrast, the voluntary savings are premised on the notion that the poor in society have also the ability to save and what they need are products and services tailored according to their needs. Compulsory savings are often a condition for receiving a loan, normally expressed as a percentage of the loan. In fact, compulsory savings could be considered part of a loan product rather than an actual saving product since they are so closely tied to receiving and repaying loans. On the other hand, voluntary savings do not form part of the condition for accessing credit services and microsavers can deposit and withdrawal funds without restrictions.

2.2 Microfinance Schools of Thought

The modern microfinance industry is predicated on two broad schools of thoughts, namely: the institutionalist approach, sometimes called the capitalist approach, and the welfarist approach (Brau & Woller, 2004). The institutionalist approach advocates for commercialization of the microfinance industry so that it becomes self-sustainable financial intermediation. Moreover, donor funding is viewed as uncertain and unsustainable. If MFIs are not financially self-sustainable, they may not remain in operation for the foreseeable future. Under this approach, profit oriented MFIs charge relatively higher lending interest rates compared with not-for-profit MFIs. It is expected that the higher lending rates reflect commensurate risks and guarantee profitability as well as insulate the institutions from constantly seeking financial support from donors.

On the other hand, the welfarist approach is premised on the poverty alleviation school of microfinance and emphasizes on serving a large number of poor customers. It views microfinance as a policy instrument for poverty reduction, which can be achieved via empowering the economically disadvantaged communities. According to this approach, MFIs must aim to expand client outreach, even when it is not economically viable to do so. The operational deficit should be subsidized with financial support from the international donors, government and social investors. It is for this reason a majority of nonprofit MFIs charge relatively lower lending rates compared to the profit-oriented MFIs. Noticeably, due to endemic poverty in Africa, the welfarist approach is the dominant school of thought in the continent.

3. The Evolution of Microfinance in Africa

Historically, the microfinance industry in Africa can be tracked as far back as the 1970s when the services were known as agricultural support programmes (ASPs) or farm input subsidies programmes (FISPs). The programmes were aimed at training and supporting rural subsistence farmers to engage in commercial farming through provision of inputs and agricultural extension services. The ASPs somewhat failed to strengthen and promote agricultural development in Africa because the programmes were not sustainable. Instead, they created a government dependency culture among farmers. The farmers perpetually expected farming input support each farming season. In most African countries such programmes ended in the late 1980s. However, in some countries like Zambia, the FISP is still in existence and still faces the challenges of the dependency syndrome. The modern microfinance movement in Africa reemerged in the early 1990s. Since then the industry has continued to register sustained growth year-on-year. Notably, the microfinance industry is increasingly becoming a core component of financial inclusion. There has been paradigm shift of not only viewing the microfinance sector as poverty alleviation initiative, but as a financial inclusion tool for fighting poverty.

In the last 2 decades, the microfinance industry in Africa has seen unprecedented growth, averaging at 15% per annum (UN, 2013). More recently, there are twice more microsavings accounts as there were microcredits accounts. The remarkable growth of microsavings accounts is a clear testimony that the poor treasures saving more than microcredit. According to the *2015 Microfinance Information eXchange* market report, there were a total of over 40 million microsavings accounts against 20 million microcredit accounts in Africa.

As at the end of 2015, there were 4134 MFIs in Africa (see Fig. 6.1). Geographically, 2333 were registered in West Africa, with Nigeria having the highest figure of about 950 MFIs; 733 were registered in Central Africa with Cameroon having the biggest share of about 500 MFIs; 562 were registered in Southern Africa with 562, with Mozambique having a dominant share of 300 MFIs; 331 were registered in North Africa, with Egypt having the biggest share of 281 MFIs; and about 175 were registered in

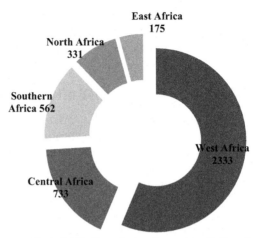

Figure 6.1 Geographical distribution of microfinance institutions in Africa at the end of 2015. Microfinance Information eXchange MIX (2015) reports, Central Banks financial stability Reports (2015).

East Africa. The lowest penetration of microfinance in East Africa is due to the significant penetration of mobile money service, an alternative microfinance facility (e.g. M-Pawa, M-Pesa, M-Shwari and MTN mobile money). Equally to note, the East African region has the highest usage of mobile money services in the world, with over 20 million subscribers in Kenya alone.

Microfinance is more active in countries with low financial inclusion, particularly in countries such as Cameroon, Chad, Egypt, Mozambique, Nigeria and Senegal. In 2015, the microfinance sector assets equaled USD 16.5 billion, representing about 14% of global microfinance assets. Fig. 6.2 highlights the geographical distribution of microfinance assets across the five regions of Africa in 2015.

The microfinance industry in Southern Africa, though having relatively fewer MFIs, has the dominant share of assets to the tune of USD 5.8 billion, with South Africa having the biggest share of about USD 1 billion. West Africa is second with about USD 3.7 billion in microfinance assets, with Nigerian MFIs leading with about USD 1.1 billion in assets. North African MFIs come in third with USD 3.4 billion in assets, with Egypt accounting for almost half of the entire portfolio. East African MFIs recorded about USD 1.9 billion in assets, while Central Africa reported the lowest microfinance assets of about USD 1.7 billion, with Cameroon having the lion's share of approximately 60%. Some notable MFIs that have emerged in the five regions of Africa are shown in Table 6.1.

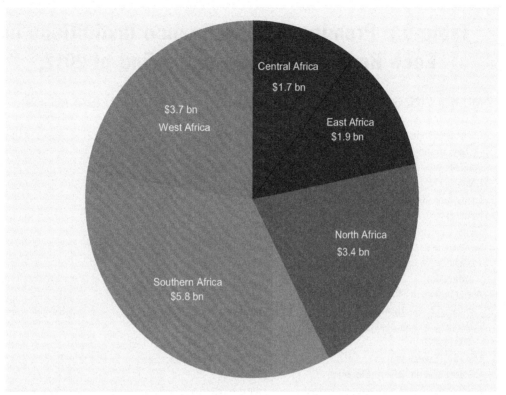

Figure 6.2 Total assets of microfinance institutions, per region, at the end of 2015. African Development Bank (AfDB) 2015 reports, Microfinance Information eXchange MIX (2015) reports, Central Banks financial stability Reports (2015).

4. Microfinance Interest Rate Ceilings

The microfinance industry in Africa is characterized by persistently higher lending interest rates compared with those of other regions of the developing world. Unsurprisingly, microcredit interest rates are often higher than commercial bank interest rates. Specifically, during the period 2003 to 2015, microcredit interest rates averaged 34% in Africa, 30% in Latin America and the Caribbean (LAC), 28% in the Middle East and North Africa (MENA), and 22% in Asia (MIX, 2015, 2016). In all four regions, inflation and commercial bank lending rates averaged 8% and 20%, respectively, during the period in question (Chikalipah, 2017c).

An increasingly common policy intervention by monetary authorities to curb higher microcredit interest rates is imposing interest rate ceilings. Interest rate ceilings (or caps) are justified

Table 6.1 Prominent Microfinance Institutions in Each Region of Africa at the End of 2012.

MFI Name (Country)	Region	Assets (USD Millions)
Cameroon cooperative credit union league (**Cameroon**)	Central Africa	293
ProCredit bank (**Congo, DR**)	Central Africa	168
Union des MECK (**Comoros**)	Central Africa	47
Equity bank (**Kenya**)	East Africa	2507
National microfinance bank (**Tanzania**)	East Africa	1378
Centenary bank (**Uganda**)	East Africa	381
Al Amana microfinance (**Morocco**)	North Africa	292
Foundation Banque populaire micro-credit (**Morocco**)	North Africa	206
Assiut Businessmen association (**Egypt**)	North Africa	125
Capitec bank (**South Africa**)	Southern Africa	3162
Opportunity international bank of Malawi (**Malawi**)	Southern Africa	73
FINCORP (**Swaziland**)	Southern Africa	71
Crédit mutuel du Senegal (**Senegal**)	West Africa	273
Réseau des caisses populaires du Burkina (**Burkina Faso**)	West Africa	236
FUCEC (**Togo**)	West Africa	167

Microfinance Information eXchange (MIX) for the year 2011 and 2012. In the absence of 2012 data, 2011 data was used instead in this table.

by authorities as a means to protect consumers from usury and exploitation. Cameroon and Zambia are notable cases where microcredit interest rates exceeded 100% before monetary authorities imposed interest rate ceilings. The two countries introduced interest rate ceilings in 2013, imposing maximum rates of 25% and 42%, respectively. Table 6.2 list the countries in Africa with interest rate ceilings at year-end 2015. It is evident that the majority of African countries impose interest rate ceilings on MFIs.

Some argue that interest rate ceilings do not necessarily protect the poor borrowers, but rather hurt them because they force MFIs to retreat from the market. The vulnerable poor clients would then revert to the unregulated informal credit markets, which are monopolized by individual moneylenders who charge

Table 6.2 Countries With Interest Rate Ceilings Based on 2015 Data.

Region	Countries	Total
Central Africa	Cameroon, Central African Republic (CAR), Chad, Congo Republic, Equatorial Guinea and Gabon	6
East Africa	Eritrea, Ethiopia, and Sudan	3
North Africa	Algeria, Egypt, Libya, Mauritania and Tunisia	5
Southern Africa	Namibia, South Africa, Zambia, and Zimbabwe	4
West Africa	Benin, Burkina Faso, code d'Ivoire (Ivory coast), Ghana, Guinea, Guinea-Bissau, Mali, Niger, Nigeria, Senegal and Togo	11
Total number of countries with interest rate ceilings		**29**

CGAP and African Development Bank report (AfDB).

higher interest rates. For instance, in the early 2000s, the central bank of West Africa, the Banque Centrale des Etats de l'Afrique de l'Ouest, imposed an interest rate ceiling of about 27% for all nonbank lenders. The result was that many MFIs scaled back the provision of credit to the poor, and a number of MFIs closed down their rural branch networks. Similar scaling down by MFIs were reported in Morocco and Tunisia following the introduction of interest rate ceilings.

5. Regulation of Microfinance Institutions

The 2007–09 global financial crisis has raised issues of the adequacy and appropriateness of regulatory regimes of financial institutions. The orthodox approach has been a preference for large banks deemed easier to regulate and supervise and which are assumed to exercise due diligence more strongly than smaller institutions. However, the lessons from the crisis include the fact that big financial institutions can also engage in excessive risk taking and in regulatory arbitrage, practices that have been contributory factors to the crisis resulting in large institutions. One consequence of the crisis, may be that the 'big bank' model could be replaced by one characterized by a larger number of smaller operators. If it materializes this could possibly advance the financial inclusiveness agenda since smaller banks might be more willing to tap the previously excluded potential customers.

One of the debates on financial inclusion via microfinance provision has been how best to deal with microfinance regulation and supervision. It is generally accepted that as microfinance matures it is likely to migrate towards institutions that are licensed and supervised by the central bank or other financial authorities. In this respect, governments should only apply the more burdensome prudential regulation when the financial system and depositors' money are potentially at risk. In other words, they should apply nonprudential regulations to MFIs. Prudential regulations would ordinarily include capital adequacy to ensure that a financial institution has enough equity in case of a crisis, and reserve and liquidity requirements to ensure there is enough cash to pay off depositors in the event of a run on a bank. In contrast, nonprudential regulations include measures such as registration with some authority for transparency purposes, keeping adequate accounts, prevention of fraud and financial crimes, and adherence to consumer protection requirements. The CGAP (2006) suggests adjustments to standard banking regulations to accommodate the special characteristics of microfinance as shown in Table 6.3.

A growing number of countries have introduced industry-specific microprudential regulations for the microfinance sector in Africa (see Box 6.1). The enactment of microfinance specialized laws has enabled the following: (1) the education and protection of customers, (2) establishment of centralized industry database, (3) easy supervision of industry participants, (4) increased engagement with credit reference bureaus, and (5) protection of country's financial system by preventing the contagion effect in an event of a bankruptcy of one institution. With regards to the overall regulatory environment of the financial sector, it is imperative to design the regulatory structures in tiers to recognize the differences in the structure of ownership, governance, capital, funding and risks faced by different financial institutions so as to keep regulations appropriate, simple and straightforward.

Most African countries have specific microprudential regulations for the microfinance industry. In this regard, MFIs are regulated based on their established legal charter. As previously mentioned, the five different legal charters comprise CCUs, MBs, NGOs, NBFIs, and RBs. CCUs and NGOs operate mostly

Table 6.3 Possible Adjustments to Prudential Regulations for Microfinance.

Standard Banking Regulations	When Applied to Microfinance
Minimum capital requirements	Need to balance promotion of microfinance with the capacity to supervise
Capital-adequacy ratios	Many need more equity because of repayment volatility
Limits on unsecured lending	Impractical for character-based lending, i.e., lending on the basis of social characteristics of client rather than collateral
Registration of collateral	Too expensive for tiny loans
Requirements for branches: Security standards, working hours, daily clearing of accounts, limitations on location	May interfere with innovations that reduce costs and bring more convenient services to clients
Standard loan documentation requirements	May be too expensive and time-consuming for tiny loans

CGAP (Consultative Group to Assist the Poor). (2006). Access for all: Building inclusive financial systems. *Washington DC, USA.*

as not-for-profit organizations, whereas MBs and NBFIs are principally profit-oriented organizations, with the former often engaging in deposit-taking.

6. Technology-Aided Microfinance

Recent technological developments in the form of mobile money have their roots in East Africa, where in the early 2000s Kenya launched its flagship M-Pesa, which is a mobile phone-based service that now facilitates a number of financial services including remittance transfers, savings, credit and microinsurance. The mobile money service has since spread to other different parts of Africa under different names. The use of mobile money has been one by-product of large-scale mobile phone penetration in Africa. The ability to store value and transfer money, usually small amounts, has enabled low-income populations to have mobile money accounts without necessarily having a bank account. Such mobile money accounts do not require onerous documentation and large minimum balances as bank accounts. Mobile network operators (MNOs) remain

Box 6.1 Microfinance Regulatory Framework in Africa as of 2015.

A. Microfinance Tiered Regulation Approach

Since late 2000s, many countries in Africa have introduced specialized microfinance regulation and supervision. The African countries with specialized microfinance laws adopts a tiered approach, defining four categories of financial institutions that can offer microfinance services:

Tier 1: Commercial banks.

Tier 2: Credit (only) institutions

Tier 3: Microfinance-deposit-taking institutions (MDIs) allowed to take deposits from the public and supervised by the central banks.

Tier 4: Non-deposit-taking institutions (NDIs) and small member-based institutions.

B. Regulation and Supervision of MFIs in Africa at year-end 2015

(I) Countries in Africa with specialized microfinance law (40): Algeria; Benin; Burkina Faso; Burundi; Cameroon; Cape Verde; Central African Republic (CAR); Chad; Comoros; Congo Democratic Republic; Congo Republic; Cote d'Ivoire (Ivory Coast); Egypt; Equatorial Guinea; Eritrea; Ethiopia; Gabon; Ghana; Guinea; Guinea Bissau; Kenya; Lesotho; Liberia; Madagascar; Malawi; Mali; Mauritania; Morocco; Mozambique; Niger; Nigeria; Rwanda; Senegal; Sudan; Uganda; The Gambia; Togo; Tunisia; Zambia; Zimbabwe.

(II) Countries in Africa that were regulating MFIs under nonbank financial institutions (8): Angola; Botswana; Namibia; Tanzania; Somalia; South Africa; South Sudan and Swaziland.

(III) Countries with no specialized microfinance law and drafting legislation (6): Djibouti; Libya; Mauritius; São Tomé and Principe; Seychelles; and Sierra Leone.

This text box is based on data obtained from: (1) Central banks financial stability reports, (2) CGAP (2006) and (3) International Monetary Fund (IMF) individual country reports.

the significant players in delivering mobile money. Moreover, over two-third of money mobile services are operationally managed by MNOs.

According to the Groupe Spéciale Mobile Association report, the sub-Saharan African region alone accounted for slightly over 52% of the active mobile money service across the world in 2015. The scale of mobile money growth in Africa has been phenomenal, rising from less than three countries offering mobile money service in 2006 to 48 countries by 2015. This shows how fast the mobile money industry is growing in Africa. By end of 2015 there were over 100 million active mobile money users

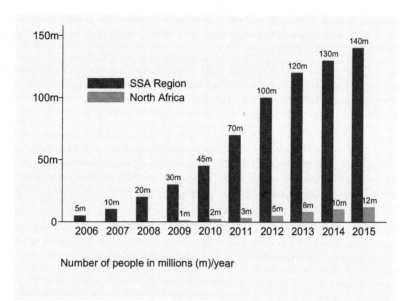

Figure 6.3 Growth of mobile money customers in Africa from 2006 to 2015. Groupe Spéciale Mobile Association GSMA (2015) report.

(see Fig. 6.3). Equally, there were over 140 mobile money operators in the entire Africa region in 2015. Furthermore, over 30 million unregistered customers in Africa performed an over-the-counter (OTC) mobile money transaction in 2015. The OTC mobile money transactions are executed via an agent's account on behalf of the customer. In countries such as Burundi, Cameroon, Chad, Democratic Republic of the Congo, Gabon, Ghana, Guinea, Kenya, Lesotho, Liberia, Madagascar, Rwanda, Swaziland, Tanzania, Uganda, Zambia and Zimbabwe, there are already more mobile money accounts than traditional bank accounts (GSMA, 2015).

Until recently, mobile money has solely facilitated the transfer of money between individuals and settling household bills. Over time mobile money services have now evolved to include: cross-border remittance transfer, mobile credit, mobile savings and mobile insurance. According to GSMA (2015), the mobile money industry in Africa processed more than 8 billion transactions, which translate into total ecosystem payments (inflows) worth USD 6 billion. This represents an increase of twofold since 2011. Of the total transactions recorded in 2015, purchase of airtime top-ups dominated the industry's transactions with 66% followed by person-to-person (P2P) transfers representing

23%, household bill payments with 6.8%, merchant payment with 2% and the rest 2.2% represents other miscellaneous transactions.

Considering that mobile service operators and microfinance institutions target the same clientele, it is for this fact that some microfinance institutions and mobile money providers are collaborating to overcome operational challenges. These are high transaction costs of providing financial services to the poor, low population density especially in rural areas, underdeveloped infrastructure and high incidences of extreme poverty. The level of trust amongst mobile money users has significantly increased in the past decade. This is demonstrated by the fact that the median mobile money balance has increased from USD 2 in 2010 to about USD 10 in 2015. The increasing trust in the service has been a contributing factor to stellar growth of the mobile money industry in Africa.

7. Microinsurance

One important microfinance product offered to the poor communities in Africa, is microinsurance. According to a 2015 Microfinance Insurance Centre (MIC) report, there are over 200 microinsurance providers in Africa with a combined portfolio of about USD 800 million. In terms of penetration, over 60 million people are covered, representing slightly over 5% of overall regional outreach coverage. Similar to the banking industry, Africa has lowest microinsurance penetration in the world which is largely attributed to endemic poverty. Based on the World Bank data, the wealth composition in Africa is as follows: (1) only 1% of the African population are considered rich and earn above USD 20 per day; (2) about 6% are middle class, which translates into daily earnings of between USD 10 and 20; (3) while 39% are classified as lower class and earn between USD 2 and 10 per day; and lastly (4) 54% of the population are categorized as poor and earn less than USD 2 a day.

South Africa dominates the microinsurance market, accounting for over 80% of premiums and assets. A large number of African countries are witnessing spectacular growth in the microinsurance market (MIC, 2015). These include Namibia, Tanzania and Zambia that have experienced growth in excess of 400% between 2011 and 2014. The common types of products covered by microinsurance providers include: accidents, agriculture, credit life, health, life and property. In terms of the growth of premium underwriting, agriculture microinsurance is the

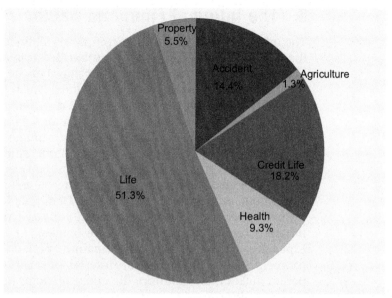

Figure 6.4 Microinsurance product coverage in Africa at the end of 2015. Micro Insurance Centre (MIC). (2015).

fastest growing product, followed by accidents and health (Churchill & Merry, 2017). Fig. 6.4 below illustrates the coverage of microinsurance products in 2015.

The claims ratio for microinsurance across products in Africa is relatively low when compared to that of developing regions such as Asia and Latin America. According to MIC (2015) report, the aggregate median of claim ratio between 2011 and 2015 averaged about 25% in the whole of Africa. The low claim ratio has been attributed to a number of reasons that include (1) lack of awareness and understanding of the claim process by microinsured clients; (2) difficulty securing supporting documentation given that most end users are poor; (3) a complex claim process; and (4) small claim pay-outs, which in some cases are less than the costs plowed into the claim process.

Despite the growth of the microinsurance market, microinsurance providers are yet to exploit fully the low-income market of Africa. Some of the challenges the hinder the stellar growth of the microinsurance industry include, among others, the high illiteracy, which results in high financial illiteracy as well; the lack of technical expertise on some market frontiers; and the lack of infrastructure necessary to distribute microinsurance products.

8. The Informal Financial Sector

The informal financial sector encompasses all financial activities that take place outside regulatory authorities. It is a sector that is highly dependent on personal relationships between the provider and the user. There are many institutions, which fall under the informal financial sector such as: nongovernmental organizations, savings and credit associations, farmers' associations, self-help groups, unregulated microfinance institutions, moneylenders, and deposit collectors. Prior empirical studies have established a negative association between the overall degree of financial inclusion and access to the informal financial sector in an economy (for a review, see Demirgüç-Kunt, Klapper, & van Oudheusden, 2015). As previously indicated, the credit from informal sector, mainly from moneylenders, in most cases is expensive, come with a very short maturity period and draconian payment terms. The extortionate interest rates and short maturity period makes the credit from the informal sector unattractive for business purposes.

The informal credit market is very active in rural areas where the formal financial institutions have no operational reach. Rural subsistence farmers occasionally access informal financing to purchase farming inputs and also for consumption smoothing between the planting and harvest time. Through surveys, FinMark Trust has documented the size of the informal financial sector in terms of adults utilizing the sector in a number of African countries. Fig. 6.5 below reports the percentage of adults accessing the informal financial sector in 20 African countries.

Uganda is seen to have the highest share of its adult population, 42%, using the informal finance market which is almost twice the percentage of those accessing the formal financial sector (refer to Fig. 6.5). On the other extreme end, Mauritius has the lowest percentage of the adult population using the informal financial sector. In a nutshell, there is an inverse relationship between the overall level of financial inclusion in a country and access to informal financial sector of the economy. Based on the Global Findex, 2014 data, there are over 100 million adults in Africa using the informal methods of finance. This evidently shows how vast the informal financial sector is utilized in Africa and the potential opportunity for the formal financial institutions to exploit.

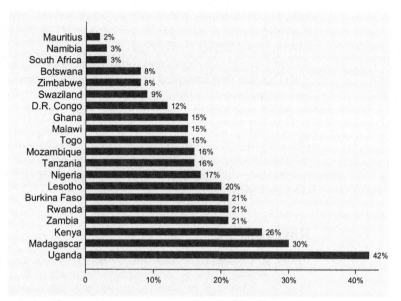

Figure 6.5 Percentage of the adult population accessing the informal financial sector in selected African countries. FinScope. (2015). *FinMark Trust — annual reports.* (http://www.finmark.org.za/).

9. Looking Ahead

Going forward, the provision of microfinance will be technology-aided. It will not be the preserve of financial institutions. Non-financial firms such as financial technology (FinTech) firms are already entering the microfinance market and are either competing with traditional MFIs or collaborating with them. On the other hand, MFIs appear uniquely positioned to benefit from emerging FinTech. Mobile technology has already resulted in mobile money that has significantly changed and will continue the financial inclusion landscape in Africa. In addition, FinTech will revolutionize the operations of MFIs. New business-to-business (B2B) FinTech solutions will aid MFIs to improve internal operational efficiencies and lower the cost of doing business. This in turn will lower prices of financial services enabling the extension of financial inclusion to previously excluded populations.

The future MFI will utilize B2B FinTech applications such as artificial intelligence (AI), blockchain technology, and data analytics, among others. AI will facilitate cognitive analysis and assist credit officers to evaluate the creditworthiness of financially excluded segments of the population. Blockchain (distributed ledger) technology will facilitate digitization and enable the consideration of new forms of collateral, while data analytics will facilitate better prediction of risks.

Increasingly, policymakers and regulators will come to terms with the fact that financial innovation is the hallmark of the modern economy. Accordingly, they will respond by providing an enabling regulatory environment that promotes innovation rather that stifles it. As many players enter the microfinance market, national payment systems, which currently are the preserve of large banks, will become accessible to MFIs. All such developments that will be spurred by FinTech will deepen financial inclusion in Africa.

References

Baydas, M., Graham, D., & Valenzuela, L. (1997). *Commercial banks in microfinance: New actors in the microfinance world.* USAID.

Brau, J. C., & Woller, G. M. (2004). Microfinance: A comprehensive review of the existing literature. *Journal of Entrepreneurial Finance, 9*(1), 1–27.

CGAP (Consultative Group to Assist the Poor). (2006). *Access for all: Building inclusive financial systems.* Washington DC, USA.

Chikalipah, S. (2017c). The nexus between microcredit nominal interest rates and inflation in sub-Saharan Africa: Evidence from panel vector autoregression analysis. *Enterprise Development & Microfinance, 28*(4), 355–370.

Churchill, C., & Merry, A. (2017). Transforming Africa through risk management: Insurance matters. In *Developing Africa's financial services: The importance of high-impact entrepreneurship* (pp. 61–78). Emerald Publishing Limited.

Demirgüç-Kunt, A., Klapper, L., & van Oudheusden, P. (2015). Financial inclusion in Africa. In , *Policies and practices: Vol. 2. The oxford handbook of Africa and economics* (p. 388). Oxford, UK: Oxford University Press.

FinScope. (2015). *FinMark Trust — annual reports.* http://www.finmark.org.za/.

Global Findex. (2014). *Measuring financial inclusion around the world.* http://www.worldbank.org/en/programs/globalfindex.

GSMA (Groupe Spéciale Mobile Association). (2015). *State of the industry report, mobile money.* www.gsma.com//mobilefordevelopment/wp-content/uploads/2016/04/SOTIR_2015.pdf.

MIC (Micro Insurance Centre). (2015). *The landscape of microinsurance Africa 2015. The world map of microinsurance.* Micro Insurance Network (NIC). www.microinsurancecentre.org/resources/documents/business-case-for-microinsurance/the-landscape-of-microinsurance-in-africa-2015-preliminary-briefing-note.html.

MIX (Microfinance Information eXchange). (2015). *Financial year 2015 sub-Saharan Africa regional Snapshort. Microfinance information exchange (MIX) reports.* Washington DC, USA.

MIX (Microfinance Information eXchange). (2016). *Financial year 2011 sub-Saharan Africa regional Snapshort. Microfinance information exchange (MIX), Reports number 36.* Washington DC, USA.

UN (United Nations). (2013). *United Nations report on microfinance in Africa.* http://www.un.org/en/africa/osaa/pdf/pubs/2013microfinanceinafrica. pdf.

Further Reading

Acemoglu, D., Gallego, F. A., & Robinson, J. A. (2014). Institutions, human capital, and development. *Annual Review of Economics, 6*(1), 875–912.

AfDB (African Development Bank). (2011). *Africa in 50 years' time report.* https://www.afdb.org/fileadmin/uploads/afdb/Documents/Publications/Africa%20in%2050%20Years%20Time.pdf.

Agier, I., & Szafarz, A. (2013). Microfinance and gender: Is there a glass ceiling on loan size? *World Development, 42*(0), 165–181.

Aker, J. C., & Mbiti, I. M. (2010). Mobile phones and economic development in Africa. *The Journal of Economic Perspectives, 24*(3), 58.

Akudugu, M. A. (2013). The determinants of financial inclusion in western Africa: Insights from Ghana. *Research Journal of Finance and Accounting, 4*(8), 1–9.

Allen, F., Carletti, E., Cull, R., Qian, J., Senbet, L. W., & Valenzuela, P. (2014). *Improving access to banking: Evidence from Kenya.* World bank Research - Databank.

Ananya, R. (2010). *Poverty capital: Microfinance and the making of development.* New York, NY: Routledge.

Asabere, P. K., McGowan, C. B., Jr., & Lee, S. M. (2016). A study into the links between mortgage financing and economic development in Africa. *International Journal of Housing Markets and Analysis, 9*(1), 2–19.

Assefa, E., Hermes, N., & Meesters, A. (2013). Competition and the performance of microfinance institutions. *Applied Financial Economics, 23*(9), 767–782.

Aterido, R., Beck, T., & Iacovone, L. (2013). Access to finance in sub-Saharan Africa: Is there a gender gap? *World Development, 47*, 102–120.

Banerjee, A., & Duflo, E. (2011). *Poor economics: A radical rethinking of the way to fight global poverty.* New York, USA: Public Affairs.

Bateman, M., & Chang, H. (2012). Microfinance and the illusion of development: From hubris to nemesis in thirty years. *World Economic Review, 1*, 13–36.

Batuo, M. E. (2015). The role of telecommunications infrastructure in the regional economic growth of Africa. *The Journal of Developing Areas, 49*(1), 313–330.

Beck, T., & Maimbo, S. M. (2012). *Financial sector development in Africa (directions in development - finance).* Washington, DC, USA.

Bell, R., Harper, A., & Mandivenga, D. (2002). Can commercial banks do microfinance? Lessons from the commercial bank of Zimbabwe and the Co-operative Bank of Kenya. *Small Enterprise Development, 13*(4), 35–46.

Bond, J. (2016). Infrastructure in Africa. *Global Journal of Emerging Market Economies, 8*(3), 309–333.

Calderón, C., & Servén, L. (2004). *The effects of infrastructure development on growth and income distribution.* Washington DC, USA: World Bank Publications.

Caudill, S. B., Gropper, D. M., & Hartarska, V. (2009). Which microfinance institutions are becoming more cost effective with time? Evidence from a mixture model. *Journal of Money, Credit, and Banking, 41*(4), 651–672.

Chikalipah, S. (2017a). What determines financial inclusion in Sub-Saharan Africa? *African Journal of Economic and Management Studies, 8*(1), 8–18.

Chikalipah, S. (2017b). Institutional environment and microfinance performance in sub-Saharan Africa. *African Development Review, 29*(1), 16–27.

Citi. (2013). *Microfinance barometer* (4th ed.). Paris, France: Convergence - Citi Bank.

Collier, P., & Dollar, D. (2002). Aid allocation and poverty reduction. *European Economic Review, 46*(8), 1475–1500.

Cotler, P., & Almazan, D. (2013). The lending interest rates in the microfinance sector: Searching for its determinants. *Journal of Centrum Cathedra, 6*(1), 69–81.

Cull, R., Demirgüç-Kunt, A., & Morduch, J. (2009). *Banks and microbanks.* Washington DC, USA: The World bank Policy Research Working Paper.

Demurger, S. (2001). Infrastructure development and economic growth: An explanation for regional disparities in China? *Journal of Comparative Economics, 29*(1), 95–117.

Duffy-Deno, K. T., & Eberts, R. W. (1991). Public infrastructure and regional economic development: A simultaneous equations approach. *Journal of Urban Economics, 30*(3), 329–343.

Dupas, P., & Robinson, J. (2013). Why don't the poor save more? Evidence from health savings experiments in Kenya. *American Economic Journal, 103*(4), 1138–1171.

Fosu, S. (2013). Banking competition in Africa: Subregional comparative studies. *Emerging Markets Review, 15*, 233–254.

Ghosh, S., & Van Tassel, E. (2013). Funding microfinance under asymmetric information. *Journal of Development Economics, 101*, 8–15.

Hanushek, E. A. (2013). Economic growth in developing countries: The role of human capital. *Economics of Education Review, 37*, 204–212.

Hartarska, V., Parmeter, C. F., & Nadolnyak, D. (2010). Economies of Scope of lending and mobilising deposits in microfinance institutions: A semiparametric analysis. *American Journal of Agricultural Economics, 93*(2), 389–398.

Helms, B., & Reille, X. (2004). *Interest rates ceiling and microfinance: The story so far.* Washington DC, USA: Consultive Group to Assist the Poor (CGAP).

Hendricks, L., & Chidiac, S. (2011). Village savings and loans: A pathway to financial inclusion for Africa's poorest households. *Enterprise Development & Microfinance, 22*(2), 134–146.

Hudon, M., & Ashta, A. (2013). Fairness and microcredit interest rates: From Rawlsian principles of justice to the distribution of the bargaining range. *Business Ethics: A European Review, 22*(3), 277–291.

Hulme, D. (2000). Impact assessment methodologies for microfinance: Theory, experience and better practice. *World Development, 28*(1), 79–98.

Janda, K., & Svárovská, B. (2013). Performance of microfinance investment vehicles. *Journal of Economics, 1*(61), 47–66.

Kessides, I. N. (2012). Regionalising infrastructure for deepening market integration: The case of East Africa. *Journal of Infrastructure Development, 4*(2), 115–138.

Madestam, A. (2014). Informal finance: A theory of moneylenders. *Journal of Development Economics, 107*, 157–174.

Makina, D. (2009). *Recovery of the financial sector and building financial inclusiveness* (Working Paper 5). United Nations Development Programme; Comprehensive Economic Recovery in Zimbabwe 2009.

Mbengue, D. M. (2013). *The worrying trend of interest rate caps in Africa.* Washington DC, USA: Consultive Group to Assist the Poor (CGAP).

Mbiti, I., & Weil, D. (2011). Mobile banking: The impact of M-pesa in Kenya. *NBER, 17129*(1).

Mersland, R., & Strøm, R. (2009). Performance and governance in microfinance institutions. *Journal of Banking & Finance, 33*, 662–669.

Milford, B. (2010). *Why microfinance doesn't work? The destructive rise of local neoliberalism* (1st ed.). London, United Kingdom: Zed Books.

Mitra, S. K. (2009). Exploitative microfinance interest rates. *Asian Social Science, 5*(5), 87–93.

MMU (Mobile money for the Unbanked). (2013). *State of the industry.* https://www.gsma.com/mobilefordevelopment/wp-content/uploads/2015/03/SOTIR_2014.pdf.

Morduch, J., & Armendariz, B. (2010). *The economics of microfinance.* Cambridge. Massachusetts, USA: MIT Press.

Munnell, A. H. (1992). Policy watch: Infrastructure investment and economic growth. *The Journal of Economic Perspectives, 6*(4), 189–198.

Norton, B. (2014). Introduction: The millennium development goals and multilingual literacy in African communities. *Journal of Multilingual and Multicultural Development, 35*(7), 633–645.

Perkins, P., Fedderke, J., & Luiz, J. (2005). An analysis of economic infrastructure investment in South Africa. *South African Journal of Economics, 73*(2), 211–228.

Quayes, S. (2015). Outreach and performance of microfinance institutions: A panel analysis. *Applied Economics, 47*(18), 1909–1925.

Richardson, D. (2003). Going to barricades with microsavings mobilization: A view of the real costs from the trenches. *The MicroBanking Bulletin, 9*, 9–13.

Robinson, C. (2014). *Literacy encyclopedia of quality of life and well-being research* (pp. 3631–3636). Springer.

Sachs, J. (2006). *The end of poverty: Economic possibilities for our time.* New York, USA: Penguin Books.

Sapundzhieva, R. (2011). *Funding microfinance-A focus on debt financing.* Washington DC, USA: Microfinance Bulletin.

Tchouassi, G. (2012). Can mobile phones really work to extend banking services to the unbanked? Empirical lessons from selected sub-Saharan Africa countries. *International Journal of Developing Societies, 1*(2), 70–81.

UNESCO (United Nations Educational, Scientific and Cultural Organisation). (2014). *International literacy data.* Paris, France: UNESCO Institute for Statistics.

WEF (World Economic Forum). (2016). *What is the future of economic growth in Africa.* https://www.weforum.org/agenda/2016/05/what-s-the-future-of-economic-growth-in-africa/.

Wilson, A., Ugwunta, D., Okwo, M., & Eneje, B. (2014). How telecommunication development aids economic growth: Evidence from itu ict development index (IDI) top five countries for African region. *International Journal of Business, Economics and Management, 1*(2), 16–28.

Woller, G. (2002). The promise and peril of microfinance commercialization. *Small Enterprise Development, 13*(4), 12–21.

Woller, G., Dunford, C., & Woodworth, W. (1999). Where to microfinance. *International Journal of Economic Development, 1*(1), 29–64.

Yunus, M., & Bank, G. (1994). *Grameen Bank: Experiences and reflections.* Dhaka, Bangladesh: Grameen Bank.

7

FINANCIAL SECTOR REGULATION AND GOVERNANCE IN AFRICA

Jacob Oduor, Jammeh Kebba

Research Department, African Development Bank, Abidjan, Côte d'Ivoire

CHAPTER OUTLINE

Extending Financial Inclusion in Africa. https://doi.org/10.1016/B978-0-12-814164-9.00007-4

1. Background

The importance of governance in supporting efficient intermediation of financial resources for development cannot be overemphasized. Governance in a broad sense refers to the institutions and practices put in place in a sector to guide the conduct of players in that sector. In the financial sector, it involves the set of rules, institutions and practices that ensure that the interests of corporate agents (managers) are closely aligned with their principals (shareholders) and other stakeholders, including the government. These include market conduct rules, disclosure obligations, protection of the rights of minority shareholders, fiduciary requirements among others. There are at least three reasons why the enabling of regulations and good governance are important cornerstones for the development of Africa's financial sector: (1) their role in deepening the financial sector, (2) improving stability and (3) accelerating financial inclusion.

This chapter explores the governance landscape in Africa, assessing the successes and failures of prudential reforms implemented over the years and discussing the role of governance in supporting financial inclusion. The exploration shows that while sound financial sector regulation is hampered by several challenges, it has helped improve financial sector stability and financial inclusion in Africa.

The rest of the chapter is organized as follows: the remainder of Section 1 relates the importance of strong regulations and good governance on financial sector depth, stability, and financial inclusion. Section 2 explores the regulatory and governance institutions in Africa. Section 3 examines the efficacy of the past prudential reforms citing successes and failures, while Section 3 discusses the role of regulations and governance in supporting financial inclusion. Section 4 concludes, highlighting lessons learnt and best practices that may be adopted by other countries to foster stability and financial inclusion.

1.1 Strong Regulations and Good Governance as a Means of Financial Sector Deepening

A well-functioning financial sector plays a catalytic role in economic development through efficient allocation of productive resources, and governance stands at the core of efficient resource allocation. As shown in Fig. 7.1, countries having more efficient and advanced financial sectors, measured by the ratio of private credit to GDP, tend to have higher real per capita income. Improvements in governance are therefore important for financial sector deepening.

1.2 Regulations, Governance and Financial Sector Stability

Governance is also an important anchor to financial sector stability. Poor governance can have serious economic and social ramifications on the economy in general because the sector is the custodian of the wealth of households, private firms and governments. The 2008–10 global financial crisis was mainly a result of poor governance structures in the global financial landscape and exposed weaknesses in global financial regulations and governance. Honohan Cheltenham and Thorsten Beck (2007) argue that banking crises in Africa were mainly caused by governance-related problems in the sector, either at the bank or regulatory level, as well as by bad banking practices

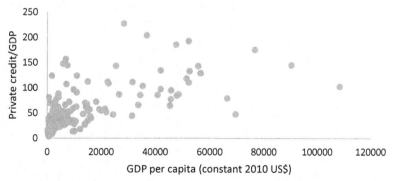

Figure 7.1 Financial development and GDP per capita, 2016. World Development Indicators Database, World Bank. Note: Sample size: 162 countries.

for countries whose banking sectors were dominated by both state-owned banks and those with mainly private banking systems. A number of studies have found that strong regulations help improve financial stability. Bolt and Tieman (2004), for instance, argue that more stringent capital regulation led banks to set stricter acceptance criteria for granting new loans, thereby reducing their exposure to default risk.

Historical trends indicate that financial sector crises are more prevalent in Africa than in the rest of the world. In the past 2 decades, many African countries have implemented financial sector reforms meant to improve governance. These reforms have to a great extent focussed on enhancing financial sector regulations and governance. These reforms have resulted in notable successes in stabilizing Africa's financial sector. The implementation of financial sector reforms in most African countries, consolidated with prudential and market conduct supervision and regulation, has improved financial stability in Africa over the past 2 decades. Laeven and Valencia (2008) record that Africa experienced 43 systemic banking crises between 1975 and 1995, compared with 56 episodes for the rest of the world. Since then, Africa has recorded only one systemic crisis — Nigeria in 2009 — compared with 47 episodes in the rest of the world, underscoring the increased stability of Africa's financial sector. The wave of privatization of government-owned banks during and after the structural adjustment programmes of the 1980s and 1990s also helped to improve institutional governance.

1.3 Regulatory and Governance Impacts on Financial Inclusion

Good governance is also important in improving financial inclusion through increased efficiency, reduced transaction costs and increased confidence in the financial system. Efficiency is also associated with increased competition and a deeper financial system, which helps to increase the reach of financial services to the underserved. Improving financial sector governance is therefore important for accelerating financial inclusion. This is notably important for Africa, where financial inclusion remains a challenge. Data from the Global Financial Development database show that domestic credit to the private sector as a percentage of GDP, a commonly used measure of financial inclusion, stands at 24.4% compared with 45.5% and 134.3% for Latin America and the Caribbean, and the high-income OECD countries, respectively.

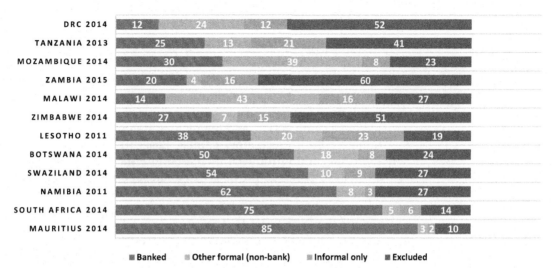

Figure 7.2 Financial inclusion in selected African countries. FinScope (database), FinMark Trust, Johannesburg.

Fig. 7.2 uses data from the FinScope and FinAccess surveys to show that financial inclusion is as low as 12% in some countries in Africa, and the percentage of those without access to formal banking services is large in a majority of the countries. The figure also evidences the widespread use of semiformal (microfinance providers, etc.) and informal financial services in Africa.

2. Landscape of Financial Regulations and Governance of Financial Institutions in Africa

The role of financial sector regulators are mainly two: ensuring financial stability to prevent financial chaos and consumer protection by ensuring that financial institutions offering financial services do so in a responsible manner. The landscape of financial regulation and governance in Africa is changing fast, particularly as a result of technological innovations and the wave of financial sector liberalization that swept across the continent beginning in the early 1990s. In this section, we review some regulatory and governance milestones in the African financial sector, highlighting successes, failures and trajectories for the future.

2.1 Micro Prudential Regulations

2.1.1 Supervisory Standards and Implementation of the Basel II and III Accords

The Basel Core Principles for Effective Banking Supervision (BCPs) are the de facto minimum standards for sound prudential regulations and effective banking supervision. Basel I was adopted in December 1992 and mainly required banks to keep a minimum of 8% of regulatory capital. Basel III replaced Basel I in June 2004 and introduced increased internal risk monitoring. In 2010, in response to the 2008–10 financial crisis, the Basel Committee introduced Basel III, which increased the capital requirement ratio from 8% to 10.5% by 2019 to strength the capital requirements of Basel II. According to a survey of the status of Basel II implementation conducted by Fuchs, Losse-Muller and Witte (2010), BCP 1.2 (the independence, accountability, and transparency of bank supervisors), BCP 7 (the risk management process in bank supervision), BCP 18 (the abuse of financial services), and BCP 23 (the corrective and remedial powers of supervisors) are the principles that pose compliance challenges for many African countries. Compliance challenges mainly emanate from a lack of regulatory independence, the weak supervisory capacity of most regulatory authorities, a lack of qualified staff and unavailability of analytical tools and skills.

While there is no obligation on non-members of the Basel Committee to implement the Basel regulatory requirements, many African countries, including those that are not members of the Basel committee, have an incentive to implement the regulations because implementation signals increased stability of the country's financial system. Implementation of Basel III is already ongoing in a number of countries worldwide, especially in Europe. However, most African countries are still operating under the Basel I regulatory regime. In 2008, South Africa became one of the first African countries to introduce the full-fledged version of Basel II, pillar 1. While Basel III comes with increased stability assurance, African countries may not be immediately exposed to some of the risks that Basel III attempts to mitigate, including major on- and off-balance sheet risks and derivative-related exposures, because most African banks do not actively participate in derivatives, repurchase agreements, and securities financing. South Africa and Tunisia have opted to adopt Basel III in its entirety. Some African countries, however, have committed to adopt provisions of the Accord that they feel are suited to their jurisdictions and level of financial sector development. South Africa started implementing Basel III on schedule in

Table 7.1 Status of Implementation of Basel Regulatory Accords (Status as at 2015).

Basel II Implementation Ongoing	Basel IIII Implementation Started
Algeria	Angola
Madagascar	Botswana
Namibia	DRC
Nigeria	Egypt
Seychelles	Gambia
Tanzania	Ghana
	Kenya
	Lesotho
	Liberia
	Malawi
	Mauritius
	Morocco
	Mozambique
	Swaziland
	Tunisia
	Uganda
	Zambia
	Zimbabwe

Financial Stability Institute Survey on Basel II, 2.5, and III implementation, July 2015.

January 2013. Egypt, Kenya and Nigeria, on the other hand, have decided to implement Basel II and III concurrently, exercising discretion as to which aspects of the two accords they will implement in line with the realities of their respective economies (Table 7.1).

2.1.2 Regulation of New Financial Innovations

Recent innovations in the financial sector have also posed regulatory challenges. Mobile phone payment systems are becoming more popular across the continent. The providers of these services in many cases are non-bank institutions that fall outside the regulatory umbrella of regulators and may pose risks to the system as well as customers. For example, one of China's biggest online peer-to-peer lending schemes, Ezubao, turned out to be a Ponzi scheme that had collected over USD 9 billion from more than 900,000 investors by the time it closed down in February 2016. These risks present a dilemma for African financial regulators in light of their traditional objectives (efficiency, financial stability, consumer protection and the integrity of the sector). Understanding the innovations and putting in place appropriate regulatory frameworks has been considerably slow in some African countries. Increased financial inclusion has been recorded in countries where authorities have allowed innovations to grow followed by regulations, rather than developing regulations before innovations can be adopted. For instance, there were no regulations on mobile-banking when M-Pesa was introduced in Kenya. Similarly, Islamic banking worked well in South Africa before any regulations were introduced, as regulators applied the same regulatory laws to Islamic and conventional banks. However, the tight regulation of M-Pesa in South Africa partly led to its failure. Countries where mobile payment systems have not taken off due to regulatory bottlenecks, Europe's approach, in creating a separate regulatory category of payment institutions and separating the regulation of payment services from the regulation of credit institutions, (Box 7.1).

Box 7.1 Regulatory Sandboxes for FinTechs

These digital disruptions pose new challenges to regulators and supervisors, who are often steps behind financial innovations. Too much regulation chokes innovation and financial inclusion, and too little regulation exposes consumers (and the financial system in general) to great risk. Additionally, the challenge that regulators face is not only how much to regulate but what to regulate. One sees this playing out to some extent in Africa, where countries do not have an all-encompassing FinTech-specific legal framework. Considering Kenya and South Africa as the FinTech leaders in Africa, `*FinTech businesses are regulated by a variety of statutes and rules governing various financial products, services and market participants, as well as other provisions of more general application*' (Didenko, 2017). Rather than formulating a single set of FinTech regulations, regulators in these countries generally respond to the more pressing issues individually as and when the need arises. This is clearly demonstrated by the responses of the South African Reserve Bank and the Central Bank of Kenya (CBK) to the risks associated with virtual currencies. However, there have been notable developments in FinTech regulation in both Kenya and South Africa with the development of `regulatory sandbox'-type frameworks to encourage innovation within a controlled environment.

2.1.3 Cross-Border Micro-Prudential Regulation

Cross-border regulation is becoming an important issue among regulators in Africa due to increasing volume of cross-border financial operations. Banking services dominate the range of financial services offered across the borders. As of May 2018, Ecobank had the largest cross-border network with operations in 36 countries across Africa (see Fig. 7.3). One of the main challenges facing both regulators and financial institutions is lack of harmonization of regulations across borders. As a starting point, effective supervision of cross-border financial institutions requires harmonized supervision between supervisory authorities in home and host countries.

Cross-border regulatory landscape is dotted with different frameworks, mainly bilateral agreements between the host and home country regulatory authorities. A number of countries including Nigeria require memorandum of understanding with the home country before allowing a foreign bank to set a subsidiary in Nigeria. However, more efforts need to be made to harmonize the regulations at the continental or sub-continental level. Bilateral agreements may not be sufficient to deal with systemic crisis that may affect more than one country. Further, differences in regulatory capacity (human and financial) in different countries make it difficult to implement the regulations in a harmonized way. Lack of centralized information centers makes it difficult for supervisors to have the same set of information to make similar conclusions.

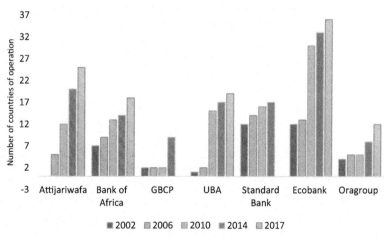

Figure 7.3 Cross-border banking operations in Africa. Respective Bank Annual reports and websites.

Information asymmetry is caused by confidentiality of information that restricts regulatory authorities from sharing with external third parties. Changes must necessarily be effected through legislative changes that anchor the policies.

2.2 Macro-Prudential Regulations and Standards

Prudential regulations seek to promote sound practices and limit risk-taking by financial institutions. Whereas micro-prudential regulations seek to enhance the safety and soundness of individual financial institutions, macro-prudential standards focus on safeguarding the soundness of the financial system as a whole. Macroeconomic shocks that hit the whole economy due to high exposure to a few sectors such as natural resources may have adverse and widespread implications for the financial sector as a whole. However, most regulatory authorities in Africa lack full-fledged surveillance units and capacity for macro-prudential surveillance. Macroeconomic modelling and analysis capacity to develop early warning instrument to identify system-wide risks, for instance, is lacking in most African countries. However, Beck et al., (2011) notes that apart from institution-specific factors, most regulators in African central banks do not have the legal authority to intervene based on macro-prudential risks. Thus, regulators and governments in Africa need to work together in designing and clearly determining the conditions and extent to which macro-prudential regulators can intervene when they detect systematic risks.

2.2.1 Macro-Prudential Regulatory Instruments

A number of macro-prudential instruments exist that can be used to address system-wide risks. Among these instruments include cap on loan-to-value ratio, cap on debt-to-income ratio, cap on leverage (to limit asset growth by tying banks' assets to their equity), countercyclical capital requirements (to avoid excessive balance-sheet shrinkage during stress), time-varying reserve requirements (to control capital flows with prudential purposes), and liquidity coverage ratio (to prevent the accumulation of excessive short-term debt).

Minimum capital and reserve requirements are the most widely used prudential instruments in Africa. In 2004, the Central Bank of Nigeria raised the minimum required capital of commercial banks from $15 million to $190 million. This resulted in mergers and acquisitions within the industry, reducing the number of banks from 89 in 2004 to 24 in 2006. In 2007, the minimum capital requirement for commercial banks in Zambia was increased from $358,240 to $2.2 million. In Algeria, amendments introduced in 2008 boosted minimum capital for banks from USD 39 million to USD 155 million. In Kenya, commercial banks had a deadline of December 2012 to build up their capital base from $3.3 million in 2008 to $12.5 million by the end of 2012; while in Uganda, a new statutory instrument was issued on 5 November 2010 which required commercial banks to build up their minimum paid-up share capital to $3.9 million by 1 March 2011 and $9.9 million by 1 March 2012.[1] Oduor, Odongo, and Ngoka (2017) note that increased regulatory capital requirements meant to mitigate macro-prudential risks have instead increased the instability of Africa's financial sector. They argue that capital regulations based on risk-weighted assets encourage innovation that allows banks to circumvent regulatory requirements and hold more risky assets by understating their risks through the use of complex in-house risk-assessment models.

2.3 Market Conduct Regulations

Whereas the primary objective of prudential regulatory authorities is to safeguard the soundness and stability of the financial sector, market conduct regulators seek to regulate, supervise and improve the 'conduct' of financial institutions in order to enhance the integrity of the financial system. Generally, market conduct regulations are a set of principles aimed at protecting consumer welfare while enforcing minimal ethical codes of conduct. However, conduct regulations have also developed to include areas such as organizational systems, corporate governance and incentives, competition and anti-trust, and professionalism. Conduct regulators look not only at the conduct of individual financial institutions and their organization, but also at the individuals in the institutions and how the conduct of individuals and financial institutions affect customer outcomes.

Market conduct legislative frameworks in most African countries are fragmented, inconsistent, and incomplete across the financial system, which compromises effective market conduct supervision. As a result, persistent and widespread poor customer outcomes as well as unfair treatment of customers have highlighted the need for stronger regulatory supervision of the conduct of financial institutions in Africa. Weaknesses

---

[1]See Financial stability reports and Bank supervision reports of respective countries.

identified in most African countries include weak corporate culture, mind-set and behaviour; lack of transparency and disclosure; poor governance and control structures; inappropriate incentives; high, opaque and complex fee structures; and the design and sale of inappropriate products.

2.3.1 Consumer Protection Laws and Regulations in Africa

Consumer protection laws and regulations are government interventions to ensure fair interactions between consumers and service providers. In the financial sector, as in many other sectors, service providers usually have more market power and information about the service than consumers do. This information asymmetry may lead to consumer exploitation if not well regulated. Market conduct regulations can be under the mandate of government's regulatory authorities or in the hands of independent bodies established by the financial services providers. Market conduct regulations may include elimination of unfair practices, fraud prevention, introduction of greater transparency, promotion of marketplace competition, and education of customers to increase their awareness of financial services.

Although consumer protection legislations are in place in most African countries, enforcement mechanisms and monitoring capacity are weak in many of these countries, thwarting the effective application of existing regulations. Moreover, the regulations oftentimes lag behind innovations in the financial sector and therefore tend to be outdated. Consumer protection mechanisms in the areas of non-bank FinTech services, for instance, are limited. Besides, apart from local dispute settlement mechanisms, formal independent third-party dispute resolution mechanisms are almost non-existent. South Africa is the leader in Africa in terms of consumer protection laws and regulations. The 2002 Western Cape Consumer Affairs (Unfair Business Practices) Act empowers regulators to investigate consumer complaints and effectively implement consumer protection services. The 2008 Consumer Protection Act consolidates these achievements to further safeguard consumer rights and consumer education.

2.4 Corporate Governance of Financial Institutions in Africa

The boundaries of corporate governance for banks and other financial institutions stretch beyond equity governance to include debt governance as opposed to the general corporate governance that focusses only on equity governance. Whereas equity governance only considers shareholders, debt governance takes into consideration debt holders, insurance policyholders and other creditors. Failures in corporate governance of financial institutions has been widely cited as one of the contributing factors that led to the 2008 financial crisis. The Basel Committee on Banking Supervision is one of the first institutions to outline minimum requirements for bank governance under the title 'corporate governance' in1999.[2] In 2006, a revised version was published to set up eight principles of good corporate governance, seven of which focussed on the board, while one concerned the bank (governance in a transparent manner).[3] However, after the 2008 financial crisis, the 2010 Basel Committee report introduced 14 principles: 4 for board practices, 1 for senior management, 4 for risk management and internal control, 2 for bank structure, 2 concerning compensation, and 1 for disclosure and transparency.[4] A two-tier board with clear separation of the management and control functions is among the prominent suggestions put forward for good corporate governance of financial institutions.

2.4.1 Appointment of Directors of Financial Institutions

The appointment of the board of directors is of utmost importance in safeguarding the health of financial systems. The board is the key organ responsible for the overall corporate governance of financial institutions. In most African countries, a director of a financial institution can only serve after written approval of the concerned regulatory authorities. Section 29(4) of Botswana's banking act stated that before appointing or replacing a director in Botswana, a bank must provide to the Bank of Botswana all information required and sufficient for deciding whether to approve the proposed appointment. The Bank of Botswana will render a decision and notify the bank of its decision in writing within 30 days from the date that all the needed information is received. Similarly, banking acts of Ghana and Kenya also dictate that no person can be appointed as a director or removed from office without written approval of the Bank of Ghana and the CBK,

---

[2]Basel Committee on Banking Supervision, Enhancing Corporate Governance for Banking Organizations, September 1999.

[3]Basel Committee on Banking Supervision, Enhancing governance for banking organizations, revised version, February 2006.

[4]Basel Committee on Banking Supervision, Principles for enhancing corporate governance, October 2010.

respectively. In addition, if a financial institution becomes insolvent, the CBK will take over the responsibility of appointing directors to be liquidators of the institution; and the appointment shall have the same effect as the appointment of a liquidator by the court under the provisions of the Companies Act. Pursuant to the recommendations on good corporate governance by the Basel Committee, supervisory agencies in Africa often screen directors under a 'fit and proper test'. For example, CAP 488 of Kenya's banking act ensures that no person is appointed or elected as a director unless the CBK certifies the person as fit and proper to manage or control the institution.

2.4.2 Regulations Regarding Significant Owners

The main objective of good corporate governance is to overcome the inherent conflicts of interest in the corporate governance of financial institutions. In compliance with the BCPs, many African countries have introduced codes of corporate governance best practices to regulate significant owners. Although these codes differ across African countries in their scopes and objectives, some are common among many African countries. These include the use of supervisory 'fit and proper tests' for significant shareholders, the combination of executive and non-executive directors on the board, the separation of duties between CEO and chairperson, and the creation of board committees responsible for specific tasks, such as the nomination, audit, risk management and remuneration committees (Courteau, Pietra, Giudici, & Melis, 2017). There also exist ownership threshold limits and regulations in many African countries that necessitate the requirement to obtain approval. For instance, the maximum single shareholding cap for any investor, including related parties, is 5% and 10% of total equity in Ethiopia and Ghana respectively. In Nigeria, the codes of corporate governance for development financial institutions, for mortgage refinance companies and for primary mortgage banks all specify that an equity holding of 5% and above by any investor requires the approval of the Central Bank of Nigeria. Where such shares are purchased through the capital markets, such institutions are required to apply for a letter of 'no-objection' from the Central Bank of Nigeria immediately after the transactions are executed. Further, the Code of Corporate Governance for Microfinance Banks pegs government shareholding at 10% of total equity in order to discourage government from being a significant shareholder in such institutions.

2.4.3 Regulations Regarding Insider Loans

Regulations regarding insider loans have been of importance in Africa since the 1995 Nigerian banking crisis which adversely affected investors' confidence. During this crisis, several bank CEOs and board directors were arrested for non-performing loans that were given to themselves, friends and relations. This led to the proliferation of regulations regarding insider loans in Nigeria and the rest of the African continent. For example, Nigeria's Banks and Other Financial Institutions Act (BOFIA) prohibits banks from advancing, without prior written approval of the Central Bank of Nigeria, unsecured loans or credit facilities of an aggregate amount more than ₦50,000 to any of their directors or to any firm, partnership, public or private company in which they may have an interest. The Act also prohibits banks from advancing unsecured loans or credit facilities to their officers and employees, which in the aggregate for any one officer or employee, is an amount which exceeds 1 year's emolument to such officer or employee. For insider loans secured by acceptable collateral, BOFIA prohibits banks from advancing such loans to any director, officer or employee, or to any firm, partnership, public or private company in which they may have an interest, an amount exceeding 1% of the paid-up capital of the bank at any time. The banking acts of South Africa, Kenya, Botswana and Ghana have similar regulations regarding insider loans. For instance, Ghana's banking act prohibits banks from advancing loans or credit facilities against the security of its own shares, the shares of its holding company, the shares of its subsidiaries, or the shares of any of the subsidiaries of its holding company. The Act also restricts banks from advancing unsecured loans to any of its (1) directors or significant shareholders, (2) companies in which a director or a significant shareholder is interested, (3) holding or subsidiary companies of the company in which a director is interested, or (4) directors' or significant shareholders' relatives, unless the prior written approval of the Bank of Ghana is obtained in respect of that unsecured loan. Where the loan is given on a secured basis, the aggregate secured loan shall not exceed 10 percent of the bank's net own funds. Section 44 prohibits banks from granting any unsecured loan or advance to any of their officers and employees an aggregate amount exceeding the officer's or employee's 2 years' salary. In both cases, banks are prohibited from writing off or waiving fully or partially without the permission of the bank's board and the prior written approval of the Bank of Ghana.

These regulations have helped improve corporate governance in the financial system in Africa. However, bank directors and managers have colluded with regulatory supervisors in some instances to conceal insider loans advanced through proxy companies. This was the case with Chase Bank in Kenya, which was put under statutory management by the CBK after about USD 800 million of unreported insider loans were discovered. This emphasizes the fact that strong regulations are in themselves not sufficient to guarantee good corporate governance in the financial sector. It highlights the importance of having a strong supervision department at the regulatory authorities with enough capacity to scrutinize the financial reports of the financial institutions.

2.5 Licensing

Under the laws of all African countries, as in other parts of the world, institutions are not allowed to carry out any business of a financial nature or to carry in their names words like bank and insurance unless they hold a valid corresponding licence granted by authorized regulatory authorities. In Kenya for example, the Kenyan Banking Act (CAP 488) clearly states that no person should (1) *'transact any banking business or financial business or the business of a mortgage finance company unless it is an institution or a duly approved agency conducting banking business on behalf of an institution which holds a valid license,'* and (2) *'unless it is a financial institution or mortgage finance company and has obtained the consent of the Central Bank, use the word "finance", or any of its derivatives or any other word indicating the transaction of financial business or the business of a mortgage finance company, or the equivalent of the foregoing in any other language, in the name, description or title under which it transacts business in Kenya'.* The objective of regulation in providing licence for financial institutions is to facilitate the development of a strong, sound and viable financial system that stimulates economic growth and development. Apart from Ethiopia, all African countries grant licences to foreign entities to enter their financial sector as far as they satisfy the country's regulatory requirements. Ethiopia maintains a strict regulation that does not permit foreign entry in her banking system. Even though the strict licensing process in most countries is aimed at guaranteeing safety of the financial system, political influence sometimes play a big role in the granting or refusal to grant licences to financial institutions. This may introduce vulnerabilities, as some institutions may not have the requisite capacity to offer financial services (Box 7.2).

Box 7.2 Political barriers to entry: Opposition to M-Pesa licensing in Kenya

In 2007 and 2008, the then Kenyan Finance Minister, John Michuki, ordered a probe of the M-Pesa mobile money transfer system because it was alleged that it posed dangers to the financial system. At that time, the Kenyan commercial banks were fighting to prevent telecommunication companies from engaging in money transfer services, arguing that it was a violation of the Banking Act. The then governor of the CBK, Prof. Njuguna Ndungu, and then Permanent Secretary in the Ministry of Communications, and Dr Bitange Ndemo, however, stood up to the opposition by the commercial banks and the subsequent political pressure and made a strong case for the licensing of mobile payments. Kenya would have lost a big opportunity had the technocrats yielded to political pressure to block Safaricom, the technology company, from launching the M-Pesa money transfer service. Because of M-Pesa, Kenya is now considered a global example of how technology can help improve financial inclusion among the informal unbanked.

Ironically, when Equity Bank, one of Kenyas big banks, got a licence in September 2014 to roll-out a new money transfer service using an independent SIM card (not reliant on any telecommunication companys network), Safaricom tried to put a political barrier to the entry of Equity Bank into the money transfer business, claiming that the system was vulnerable to fraud. Safaricom also argued that the approval was granted before legislation was enacted to support it. In the same month, Kenyan Parliaments House committee on Energy and Communication formed an 11-member committee to supervise investigations into Equitys technology following fears expressed by Safaricom that the roll-out could expose customers private data to illegal access. The Communications Authority of Kenya and CBK, however, dismissed the claims made by Safaricom. The case went to court and was dismissed in May 2015, allowing Equity to roll out the service.

2.6 Regulatory Effectiveness Through Information Sharing and Reporting

Promoting regulatory effectiveness through information sharing and reporting is at the heart of efforts to enhance the integrity of financial systems. Effective information sharing makes it possible for financial institutions to provide supervisory authorities with the relevant information needed to safeguard the stability and soundness of the financial system as well as providing law enforcement authorities with intelligence needed to combat money laundering, terrorist financing and other financial crimes. Financial institutions also count on the public sector to share information on geographical vulnerabilities and the behaviour of targeted suspects in order to monitor their transaction flows and better manage their risk exposures. Importantly, the size of international capital flows and the increasing occurrence of multinational money laundering schemes make cross-border information sharing an important element for the effectiveness of domestic information-sharing arrangements.

2.6.1 Information-Sharing Arrangements Among Regulators

African countries and regional bodies have put in place a number of information-sharing arrangements in order to improve coordination and collaboration between stakeholders, especially among supervisors. Among the most prominent initiatives to enhance cross-border information sharing in Africa is the College of Supervisors of the West African Monetary Zone, which was established to enhance information among supervisors in the region and enhance their regulatory effectiveness. Similarly, member states of the Economic and Monetary Community of Central Africa (Cameroon, Central African Republic, Chad, Equatorial Guinea, Gabon and Republic of the Congo) also have an information-sharing framework through the Bank of Central African States and the Banking Commission for Central Africa. Other bilateral information-sharing arrangements exist between financial institutions within and between different countries in Africa.

2.6.2 Reporting Requirements to Financial Sector Regulators

There are several reporting requirements that financial institutions must comply with in all African countries. To enhance financial safety and soundness, most African central banks require licensed financial institutions to annually produce audited financial statements guided by the International Financial Reporting Standards accompanied by the auditor's management letter and a statement on the effectiveness of internal controls signed by the financial institution's board of directors. In Nigeria and South Africa, licensed financial institutions are required to observe the 'Financial Reporting Council Revised Guidelines/Regulations' and the 'Financial reporting framework' respectively as part of the comprehensive disclosure requirements of the Central Bank of Nigeria and South African Reserve Bank. In Ghana, Section 49 of the Banking Act (Act 673) mandates banks to '*report to the Bank of Ghana, the particulars of each large financial exposure, in the form and at the intervals, that the Bank of Ghana may require.*' Among the compliance requirements to be disclosed in the annual reports of licensed financial institutions include the qualifications and experience of each director, the details of the remuneration package of directors, the number of board meetings held in the year as well as the attendance of every board member. The Kenyan banking act's minimum disclosure requirements also mandates financial institutions to publish their annual audited accounts in a national newspaper within 3 months of the end of each financial year. These reporting requirements are aimed at promoting financial transparency in order to protect the integrity as well as enhance the soundness and stability of financial systems in the African continent. The effectiveness of the reporting depends however on the abilities of regulatory authorities to understand the financial reports and spot mistakes, errors and misreporting. If the capacity of the regulatory in this respect is weak, the financial institutions may be incentivized to misreport.

2.7 Regulatory Compliance, Offences and Penalties

Misconduct in the financial system has potential negative effects on both the stability of the financial sector and the real economy. As part of efforts to deter financial misconduct and to encourage regulatory compliance, fines and penalties are levied against financial institutions that violate financial sector requirements and regulations. African countries have widely used fines and other money penalty regimes as measures for addressing financial misconduct. However, there are great regulatory arbitrage regarding the design of bank enforcement architecture in the African continent. This regulatory arbitrage raises the need to develop common regulatory approaches across African countries and at the continental level. Experiences in the United States of America have shown that a holistic and coordinated approach to the activities of financial institutions is prerequisite for effective regulatory enforcement using money penalty regimes especially in criminal misconduct cases such as fraud. In other cases, regulatory authorities are mandated to put under statutory management, financial institutions that violate and put the health of the financial system in jeopardy. Such was the case with three banks (Dubai Bank, Imperial Bank and Chase Bank) put under statutory management by the CBK in 2015 and 2016 after they were found to have flouted regulatory requirements.

2.7.1 Enforcement of Regulations

Enforcing financial regulations requires various strategies. Enforcement options in Africa range from imposition of administrative penalties to criminal prosecution. Supervisory actions also include licence suspension or revocation as well as orders to undertake or prohibit certain actions. Despite making great improvements in strengthening financial sector regulations, Africa has not made great progress in effective enforcement of such regulations to ensure compliance within the financial industry. With some few exceptions, many regulators in Africa have limited enforcement power, low institutional capacity and resource constraints which further curtail their ability to enforce financial sector regulations. This challenge is exacerbated by the rapidly changing banking environment as well as increased globalization and cross-border banking.

However, stringent regulatory monitoring in some countries is done with the objective of raising fiscal revenues rather than instilling discipline on a routine basis. For example, after years of relatively lax enforcement, regulatory authorities in Nigeria shifted to stricter regulatory compliance involving waves of landmark fines against major financial institutions signaling a drive by government to increase revenues from alternative sources. In 2015 and 2016, the Central Bank of Nigeria levied fines against Skye Bank (N4bn/$20m), United Bank of Africa $14.57m and First Bank $9.54m for various regulatory infractions. The Financial Reporting Council also sanctioned fines against Stanbic IBTC to the tune of a $5m fine.

2.7.2 Penalties for Non-Compliance With Regulations

Penalties are widely used in Africa as a mechanism to deter noncompliance with financial sector regulations. In some African countries such as Ghana, financial institutions are given the opportunity to report themselves for failing to comply with regulatory requirements. Section 26 of Ghana's 2004 Banking Act mandates banks that fail to comply with the prescribed minimum capital adequacy ratio to promptly notify the Bank of Ghana of the particulars of that non-compliance. However, a bank that fails to maintain the prescribed minimum capital adequacy ratio and fails to notify the Bank of Ghana commits an offence and is *'liable to pay to the Bank of Ghana on each day that the deficiency continues as penalty one-half* per *mille of the difference between'* the required capital adequacy ratio that the bank should maintain and the actual level that the bank maintains. Similarly, if a bank fails to satisfy the prescribed minimum capital adequacy ratio and such deficiency is not rectified within 3 months such a bank may be prohibited from granting loans or accepting deposits. For failure to comply with the required liquidity ratio, central banks in Africa extensively use penalty regimes, such as (1) fee on the difference between the total amount of required liquid assets and the actual amount of liquid assets held by the financial institution, (2) directive to prohibit the payment or distribution of dividend to its shareholders, (3) directive advising banks to discontinue or limit granting of credit or the making of investments and capital expenditure. In addition, the institution is liable to pay a penalty in respect of each day during which the deficiency continues. In Ghana, this amount is calculated as one half per mille of the deficiency which exists on that day. Directors and/or the chief executive officer of non-compliant banks commit an offence and are also liable to penalty charges. Kenya's 1999 Banking (penalties) Regulations also states that any financial institution that fail to comply with financial sector regulations is liable to a penalty not exceeding one million shillings. The various penalty regimes help to instill discipline and ensure compliance with the regulations.

2.7.3 Rights of Appeal Against Sanctions

In almost all African countries, financial institutions have rights to appeal against sanction orders of regulatory authorities. Most of these appeals are directed either to the regulatory authorities, Ministries of Finance or to the Supreme Courts. In the Gambia, financial institutions have rights to appeal in writing against suspension or revocation of licence within 10 (ten) days from receiving the notice. The Central Bank of the Gambia may grant a hearing in considering the petition against the suspension or revocation, and within 30 (thirty) days from the date of the receipt of the petition shall communicate its decision on the appeal to the concerned institution. A financial institution aggrieved by the decision of the central bank after the petition has rights to appeal to the Supreme Court of the Gambia. In Ghana, such appeals against orders from the Bank of Ghana are directed to the Minister of Finance within 14 days from the date of receipt of the Bank's order. The Minister shall subsequently give a hearing to the financial company and the Bank of Ghana and take a decision on the appeal within 1 month from the date of receipt of the appeal. Best practice requires that appeals are directed to independent tribunals like is the case in South Africa and not politicians like Ministers of Finance who may have vested interests in the financial institutions. In addition to the Ombud Council, South Africa also has the Financial Services Tribunal as an independent tribunal with powers to reconsider decisions by financial sector regulators against financial institutions in the country.

2.8 Institutionalization of Financial Sector Regulation

Africa has made great improvements in strengthening financial sector regulations over the past 2 decades. However, progress in financial sector regulations has not always translated to progress in the institutionalization of such regulations. Limited enforcement power, low institutional capacity, and resource constraints are key limitations that have been identified to pose severe challenges in institutionalizing financial sector regulations in Africa. Several regulatory institutional models exist in Africa.

2.8.1 Twin Peaks Model—Case Study of South Africa

The Twin Peaks Model divides financial regulation into two broad parts: market conduct regulation (which includes consumer protection) and prudential regulation (Godwin, 2017). Each of these financial regulation functions are entrusted to a separate specialized regulator. The Twin Peak Model in South Africa has a 'prudential regulator', the Prudential Authority, and 'The Financial Sector Conduct Authority' responsible for market conduct regulation. The goal for shifting towards a twin peaks system for financial regulation was to separate and strengthen market conduct and customer protection from the other regulatory objective of ensuring a more resilient, stable and sound financial system. The Twin Peaks model of financial regulation has both advantages and disadvantages. On the merit side the model creates two peak regulators with dedicated objectives and clear mandates and allows each regulator to focus on its core mandate. In addition specialized regulators are more likely to be better prepared to keep pace with the continuing growth of financial conglomerates and the growing complexity of financial markets. If also reduces the risk that one aspect of regulation—such as prudential regulation—will dominate the regulatory landscape. On the downside, the model may create regulatory overlaps between the dual regulatory bodies and may increase the risk of information-sharing failures due to cooperation and coordination problems between the regulators.

2.9 Powers, Responsibilities and Independence of Regulatory Bodies

The responsibilities and powers of financial regulatory bodies in Africa vary across countries ranging from setting or approving regulatory laws for financial institutions, setting or approving prudential standards and requirements, monitoring and ensuring compliance with these regulations and prudential measures, ensuring that consumer protection measures are effective and enforced, cooperating with other domestic regulatory agencies as well as with the regulatory authorities of other countries in regard to cross-border issues. In addition, regulatory bodies in most African countries are conferred the responsibilities and powers to carry out onsite and offsite inspections, including unannounced inspections, as well as to issue penalties against financial institutions for noncompliance of regulations. In practice however, majority of African regulatory bodies are faced with limited enforcement power due to limited regulatory independence and resource constraints. The lack of political will of governments in many African to depoliticize the appointment of regulators and to transfer regulatory authority to an independent regulator has greatly hampered sound regulation in Africa. Although some African countries have now created 'independent' regulatory agencies, many of these institutions are not fully independent. Governments often put pressures on 'independent' regulatory agencies to amend or over-turn decisions even in cases where these agencies are established and empowered with legal mandates for regulatory decision-making. This clearly demonstrates the gap that exist between financial sector regulations and practices in Africa.

2.10 Human Resource Capacity of Regulatory Authorities

Low human resource capacity has emerged to be one of the acute challenges confronting regulatory authorities in Africa. The problem of inadequately trained, experienced and competent regulators has greatly compromised the quality, credibility, and impact of financial sector regulation in the continent. According to a survey conducted in Botswana, Ethiopia, Ghana, Kenya, Lesotho, Tanzania, Uganda, and Zambia by Gottschalk and Griffith-Jones (2010), the lack of skills, technical capacities, and staff constitutes the biggest challenge facing African regulators to deal with Basel II issues. As a result, most bank regulators in these sub-Saharan African countries have not yet implement Basel II in their respectively countries. Moreover, the appointment of regulators, as part of government responsibilities in most African countries, remains largely politicized leading to the appointment of commissioners without the requisite skills, competent and experience. African regulators also experience high turnover of management and

Board members, compared with regulators in other parts of the world, hampering institutional development and memory. Although the building and acculturation of sound governance, management, and organizational systems and practices take time, there is an urgent need to build the professional capacity of regulators in Africa since the need for trained, experienced, and competent regulator staff increases with increased independence of financial sector regulators.

2.11 Role of Regulations on Financial Inclusion

Regulation may have different impacts on financial inclusion depending on how they affect the cost of financial services. While a number of regulatory requirements, help increase transparency and efficiency hence reducing cost of financial services and increases financial inclusion, other financial sector regulations may stifle financial sector inclusion. We explore the two possible outcomes of regulation in this section.

2.11.1 Regulations With Adverse Effects on Financial Inclusion

As discussed in the introductory section of this chapter, strong regulation and good governance have two main objectives (other than deepening the financial sector). These are improved stability and increased financial inclusion. Regulations that are meant to improve financial sector stability do not always achieve the twin objective of increasing financial inclusion. Increased regulatory capital build-up, for instance, may lead to mergers creating monopolies and reducing competition in the financial sector. This results in increased cost of financial services and reduced financial inclusion.

We use annual bank level panel data from Bank Scope covering the period 2000–11 from 167 banks across 37 African countries to assess the impacts of increased regulatory capital on financial inclusion. We measure the size of the banking sector relative to the size of the economy by the ratio of domestic credit provided by the banking sector to GDP. Countries with this ratio above 100% are classified as large banking sector economies while countries with the ratio falling between 100% and 50% are classified as medium sized banking sector economies. Countries with the ratio less than 50 are classified as small-sized banking sector economies. The results reported in Table 7.2 below shows that increased regulatory capital, has no impact on financial inclusion in African countries that have small banking sector but increases financial inclusion in countries with large

Table 7.2 Impact of Increased Regulatory Capital on Financial Inclusion in Africa

Financial inclusion					
	Coefficients				
Model (Gross Loans)	Whole (44)	Small banking sector countries (45)	Big banking sector countries (46)	Foreign (47)	(48)
Regulatory Capital Ratio	-153.73 (0.79)	-199.52 (0.73)	45333.16** (0.02)	199.40 (0.74)	-1037.488* (0.423)
Startup procedures to register a business	-59286.59** (0.00)	-107286.10** (0.01)	-52588.79** (0.00)	-101135.50** (0.03)	-37927.24** (0.004)
Procedures to enforce a contract	51355.43* (0.06)	62178.34** (0.03)	-		
Money supply	2774.19* (0.06)	-	4673.63** (0.00)		
cap*contract	-	-	-1028.20** (0.01)		
cap*legalrights	-	-	-2495.04** (0.02)		
cap* startupprocedure	-	-	2006.35** (0.01)		
Constant	-1226927.00 (0.15)	-958118.40 (0.17)	73642.66 (0.51)	1302488.00** (0.01)	512711.3** (0.00)
sigma_u	454573.86	559220.66	257284.48	577080.83	191862.02
sigma_e	157708.43	181077.43	29260.17	215875.86	79707.439
Rho	0.89	0.91	0.99	0.88	0.8528118

Note: **means significant at 5% and * at 10%. The figures in parenthesis are the p-values

banking sectors. The results imply that regulatory requirements mean to consolidate to increase financial sector stability may have adverse impacts on financial inclusion in countries where the financial sector is small relative to the size of the economy.

2.12 Regulations That Support Financial Inclusion

Regulatory measures meant to increase efficiency, governance and market conduct on the other hand have the effect of increasing financial inclusion by reducing the cost of financial services. The explosion in FinTechs and the enabling regulatory environment accorded these innovations in most countries have led to an increase in financial inclusion. The 2017 Global Findex database shows that the share of adults who have an account with a financial institution or through a mobile money service rose globally from 54% in 2004 to 63% in 2017 in developing economies. The importance of enabling regulation cannot be as clear as is the case in Kenya. World Bank 2015 reports that in 2011, the number of Kenyans that had access to a financial account of any kind stood at 42% to about 82% in 2017, while those who use accounts in financial institutions only without mobile money accounts dropped from 20% in 2014 to about 16% in 2017. One of the main reasons for the rapid increase in financial inclusion in Kenya is an enabling regulation. The CBK allowed Safaricom, the mobile phone company that was piloting M-Pesa, to start piloting the innovation without too much regulatory bottlenecks. Countries that have insisted on regulation before piloting have seen a lesser penetration of these innovations.

3. Conclusion

Over the past 2 decades, Africa has made great improvements in strengthening financial sector regulations and governance. Many African countries have reviewed and subsequently reformed their financial sector legislations including market conduct, prudential, information sharing and reporting, and consumer protection laws as well as regulations concerning significant owners and insider loans. Nonetheless, a number of challenges still remain. Lack of regulatory independence and weak supervisory capacity, including lack of qualified staff and unavailability of analytical tools and skills, have constraint financial sector supervision in many African countries. In addition, politicization of the appointment of directors and operations of regulatory authorities hamper the effectiveness of the institutions. Lack of proper and independent institutional frameworks also compromises the achievement of the mandates of the regulatory bodies. New institutional frameworks like the 'Twin-Peak Model' adopted by South Africa can provide lessons for other African countries interested in separating and improving the effectiveness of the prudential and market conduct mandates of the regulatory bodies.

Increasing trend in cross-border financial services provide an opportunity for countries to collaborate and harmonize regulatory requirements to improve financial inclusion. Further, the rise of Fintechs poses new challenges to regulators as they are provided mainly by telecommunication institutions that are outside the regulatory armpit of the financial sector regulators. The adoption of technology in the financial sector is also outpacing the development of supporting regulations. Countries can may choose to follow the example of Kenya and let innovation precede legislation or choose to develop legislation first. Letting innovation to precede legislation will however require that the capacity of regulators is high to be able to monitor on a continuous basis the potential risks of the innovations as they are rolled out. Financial stability consequences of FinTech innovations can be very high if the attendant risks are not closely monitored and mitigated in time.

References

Beck, T., Maimbo, S., Faye, I., & Triki, T. (2011). *"Financing Africa: Through the Crisis and Beyond"*. The World Bank: World Bank Publications. No. 2355.

Bolt, W., & Tieman, A. (2004). *Banking competition, risk, and regulation*. IMF. IMF Working Paper 4/11.

Courteau, L., Pietra, R. Di, Giudici, P., & Melis, A. (September 2017). The role and effect of controlling shareholders in corporate governance. *Journal of Management & Governance, 21*(3), 561–572, 2017.

Didenko, A. (December 2017). *Regulatory challenges underlying FinTech in Kenya and South Africa*. Bingham Centre for the Rule of Law, British Institute of International and Comparative Law, 2017.

Fuchs, M., Losse-Müller, T., & Witte, M. (2010). *The reform agenda for financial regulation and supervision in Africa*. Unpublished working paper. Washington, DC: World Bank.

Godwin, A. (2017). Introduction to special issue – The twin peaks model of financial regulation and reform in South Africa. *Law and Financial Markets Review, 11*(4), 151–153.

Gottschalk, R., & Griffith-Jones, S. (2010). Basel II implementation in low-income countries: Challenges and effects on SME development. In Ricardo (Ed.), *The Basel capital accords in developing countries: Challenges for development finance.*

Honohan Cheltenham, P., & Thorsten Beck, T. (2007). *Making finance work for Africa*. Washington, DC: World Bank.

Laeven, L., & Valencia, F. (2008). *Systemic banking crises: A new database*. IMF Working Paper 08/224. Washington, DC: International Monetary Fund.

Oduor, J., Odongo, M., & Ngoka, K. (2017). "Capital requirement, bank competition and stability in Africa? (accepted for publication on 19th Jan 2017) *Review of Development Finance, 1*(Special Issue).

Further Reading

BCBS (Basel Committee on Banking Supervision). (October 2006). *Core principles for effective banking supervision*. Basel, Switzerland: Bank for International Settlements. http://www.bis.org/publ/bcbs129.pdf.

Mehran, H., & Mollineaux, L. (2012). *Corporate governance of financial institutions*. Federal Reserve Bank of New York Staff Reports. no. 539 January 2012; revised February 2012.

4

EMPIRICAL EVIDENCE FOCUSING ON AFRICA

8

MACROECONOMIC DETERMINANTS OF FINANCIAL INCLUSION: EVIDENCE USING DYNAMIC PANEL DATA ANALYSIS

Kidanemariam Gebregziabher Gebrehiwot,[1] Daniel Makina[2]

[1]*Department of Economics, Mekelle University, Ethiopia;* [2]*Department of Finance, Risk Management and Banking, University of South Africa, Pretoria, South Africa*

Extending Financial Inclusion in Africa. https://doi.org/10.1016/B978-0-12-814164-9.00008-6
Copyright © 2019 Elsevier Inc. All rights reserved.

1. Introduction

Empirical evidence has shown that well-functioning, healthy and competitive financial systems are an effective tool in spreading opportunity and fighting poverty through offering people services to meet a wide range of needs such as savings, credit, payment and risk management (see Honohan and Beck, 2007, among others). Indeed it has been demonstrated in the literature that financial development stimulates economic growth and the causal relationship operates through three linkages, viz. (1) financial deepening promotes economic growth; (2) economic growth stimulates financial development; and (3) financial development and economic growth influence each other. Hence, it is logical to say that inclusive development in an economy requires inclusive financial systems that ensure accessibility, availability and usage of formal financial services to the entire population. Thus, a pro-inclusive growth economy should have financial inclusion as one of its strategies of spreading opportunity and fighting poverty.

Notwithstanding the positive impacts of financial inclusion, a global survey by Dermiguc-Kunt and Klapper (2012a) shows that half the world is unbanked, as only 50% of adults reported having an account at a formal financial institution – a bank, credit union, cooperative, post office or microfinance institution. Formal account use is reported to differ sharply between high-income and developing economies. In high-income economies, 89% of adults reported having an account at a formal financial institution, whereas it was only 41% in developing economies.

Improving the economic wellbeing of low-income groups has always remained at the centre stage of development policies of governments and donor agencies alike (Wagle, 2012). Different policy paradigms have been theorized and put into the development policy framework of developing countries since the 1950s. A review by Ellis and Biggs (2001) focussing on rural development shows that policy strands dominating the past half-century in most developing countries include: community development, the main emphasis being on small-farm growth (1950s and 1960s); integrated rural development, still with the emphasis being on small-farm growth (1970s); state-led rural development (1970s) to market liberalization (1980s); sustainable livelihoods (where microcredit is one component) (1990s); and poverty reduction development strategies (2000s).

Tackling poverty by addressing the needs of the unbanked and thus focussing on financial inclusion as an instrument of poverty reduction in developing countries was initiated roughly 30 years ago following the group-credit model of Mohammed Yunus of the Grameen Bank (Chibba, 2009). Despite the substantial positive economic and social contribution of financial systems to overall economic growth, the attention given to financial inclusion has been marginal until recently (Chibba, 2009; Demirgüç-Kunt and Klapper, 2012a; Rousseau and Watchtel, 1998; Triki and Faye, 2013).

According to Triki and Faye (2013), Africa is home to 50 million micro, small and medium businesses, 69% of which operate in the informal sector but contribute 58% of total employment and 33% of the continent's GDP, making them critical for socio-economic growth. Using 1-year growth rates in employment as a measure of firm growth, the OECD (2009) reports that about 15% of small and medium enterprises in Africa are high-growth firms (i.e. with 1-year growth in employment greater than or equal to 20%). However, the source of financing for their growth is only 8% bank-financed compared with an average of 11% in other developing countries (Demirgüç-Kunt and Klapper, 2012b). In recognition of the role that can be played by financial sector reforms in promoting financial inclusion and development, the issue of financial inclusion has attracted the attention of the UN organs, governments, and international development institutions. Inclusive financial systems are now widely recognized in policy circles of not only developing countries, but also for developed countries. Several countries across the globe now look at financial inclusion as the means of a more inclusive growth, wherein each citizen of a country is able to have the minimum access and entitlement to the different financial service products, so as to improve their financial status, adding to the nation's progress.

At the national level, series of legislative measures have been initiated in different countries across the globe. For example, in the United States, the Community Reinvestment Act (1997) requires banks to offer credit throughout their entire area of operation and prohibits them from targeting only rich neighbourhoods. In France, the 1998 law on exclusion emphasizes an individual's right to have a bank account. The German Bankers' Association introduced a voluntary code in 1996 providing for an entitlement of an 'everyman' current banking account that facilitates basic banking transactions. In the United Kingdom, a 'Financial Inclusion Task Force' was constituted by the government in 2005 in order to monitor the development of financial inclusion (Sarma and Pais, 2011).

At the global level, the World Bank has sponsored 'Principles for Innovative Financial Inclusion' to serve as a guide for policy and regulatory approaches with the objective of fostering safe adoption of innovative, adequate, low-cost and competitive financial delivery models. New international bodies, such as the Alliance for Financial Inclusion (AFI), have been established with the main objective of advancing financial inclusion for the needy. The International Monetary Fund (IMF) has launched a new database on financial inclusion, and the International Finance Corporation together with the Consultative Group to Assist the Poor and AFI have spearheaded the G-20 discussion regarding the agenda of financial inclusion. The Bill and Melinda Gates Foundation pledged $2.5 billion for a 5-year period to support access to financial services (Ardic, Heimann, & Mylenko, 2011). To support the on-going efforts, the World Bank Group has initiated the Financial Access indicators and reports to partially satisfy the higher demand for financial inclusion–related information (Ardic et al., 2011).

Despite all of these initiatives and efforts at both international and national levels, the progress so far made, especially in Africa, is not promising. According to the available data, compared with an average of 33% for South Asia, 39% for Latin America and Caribbean, 45% for Europe and Central Asia and 55% for East Asia and Pacific, the share of adults with access to formal financial institutions in Africa falls below 23%, and many adults in Africa use informal methods to save (Demirgüç-Kunt and Klapper, 2012a).

As observed by Triki and Faye (2013), factors explaining the underdeveloped financial sector and its limited outreach in Africa include low and volatile income levels, inflationary environments, high illiteracy rates, inadequate infrastructure, governance challenges, limited competition within the banking industry, and the high cost of banking. Yet none of these factors have been empirically tested in a conclusive fashion. Despite the high levels of attention given to financial inclusion, most academic work has remained confined to finance and economic growth (Goldsmith, 1969; Gertler & Gilchrist, 1994; King & Levine, 1993a, 1993b; Nissanke and Aryeetey, 2005). However, to understand the role of financial development on development, it is necessary to understand the factors underpinning financial inclusion. Empirical work focussing on the factors influencing financial inclusion is scant save for the works of Sarma and Pais (2011) and Allen, Demirguc-Kunt, Klapper, Soledad, and Peria (2012), among the few. However, we observe that the results of Sarma and Pais (2011), derived from cross-sectional data, could be suffering from endogeneity, few observations, and regression on clustered variables.[1] On the other hand, the results of Allen et al. (2012), also derived from a cross-sectional data set, report factors which explain the individual characteristics, not the aggregate level of financial inclusion.

This paper contributes to the financial inclusion literature in several respects. Firstly, we include government debt as one of the explanatory variables of financial inclusion. To our knowledge, no prior studies have taken account of the 'crowding out effect' government borrowing might have on financial inclusion. Secondly, we focus on African countries where the financial exclusion situation is believed to be severe but the phenomenon has not been conclusively investigated. Our robust generalized method of moments (GMM) dynamic estimation indicates that financial inclusion is positively related to its past level, GDP per capita and mobile access, and negatively related to government debt.

The rest of the chapter is structured as follows. Section 2 discusses relevant literature. Section 3 discusses the model specification. Section 4 presents and discusses the empirical results, and Section 5 concludes.

2. Theoretical and Empirical Literature Review

Goldsmith's (1969) pioneering study demonstrated an empirical association between economic growth and the increasing size and complexity of the financial system, i.e. the process of 'financial deepening'. The theoretical model underpinning the relationship between finance and economic growth is based on the ability of financial markets and institutions in (1) ameliorating the problem of information asymmetry (Blackburn, Bose, & Capasso, 2005; Blackburn & Hung, 1998; Bose & Cothren, 1996; Diamond 1984; Morales, 2003); (2) increasing the efficiency of investments (Greenwood & Jovanovic, 1990); (3) enhancing investment productivity (Saint-Paul, 1992); (4) providing liquidity, thereby allowing capital accumulation (Bencivenga & Smith, 1991); and (5) allowing human capital formation (De Gregorio & Kim, 2000).

---

[1]Instead of regressing financial inclusion (FI) on socio-economic, infrastructure, and banking (financial), it was specified phase by phase due to the small size sampling, which could not support the number of these variables.

Gertler and Gilchrist (1994) argue that economic growth and financial sector development are mutually dependent. Other authors have emphasized that financial sector policy can affect the pace of economic development. The dynamic link between financial innovation and economic development was empirically investigated by King and Levine (1993a, 1993b). They argue that financial institutions lower the social cost of investing in intangible capital through the evaluation, monitoring and provision of financing services. Montiel (1994) also noted that economic growth can be spurred by 'innovations' in financial development that improve the efficiency of intermediation, increase the marginal product of capital and raise the savings rate. All these studies and conclusions are based on a very simplistic assumption that financial development serves all segments of society. The rising number of financially excluded populations around the world is consistent with Patrick's (1966) and Galbis's (1977) argument that neither economic growth nor financial development may guarantee that the benefits of growth and financial system innovation will trickle-down equally to all segments of society, especially the poor.

According to UNDESA and UNCDF (2006), the concept of financial inclusion encompasses two primary dimensions, viz. (1) a person having access to a range of formal financial services, from simple credit and savings services to more complex ones such as insurance and pensions; and (2) having access to more than one financial services provider, which ensures a variety of competitive options. A corollary of this definition is that financial exclusion means the inability of the disadvantaged to access financial services. In the literature the range of barriers (price and non-price barriers) that could lead to financial exclusion include 'geography (limiting physical access), regulations (lack of formal identification proof or of appropriate products for poor households), psychology (fear of financial institution's staff, structures, complicated financial products, etc.), information (lack of knowledge regarding products and procedures), and low financial acumen (low income and poor financial discipline), among others' (Ramji, 2009; Dermiguc-Kunt & Klapper, 2012a).

Dermiguc-Kunt and Klapper (2012a) and (2012b) observe that without inclusive financial systems, poor people have to rely on their own limited savings to invest in their education or become entrepreneurs, and small enterprises must rely on their limited earnings to pursue promising growth opportunities. In various studies, it has been observed that the absence of inclusive financial systems contributes to persistent income inequality and slower economic growth (Beck, Demirguc-Kunt and Levine, 2007; Beck, Levine, & Loayza, 2000; Demirguc-Kunt and Levine, 2009; King & Levine, 1993a, 1993b; Klapper, Laeven and Rajan, 2006; World Bank, 2008). Kempson (2006) has also observed that levels of income inequality, as measured by Gini coefficients, are negatively correlated with levels of financial inclusion. For example, Scandinavian countries such as Denmark and Sweden, with very low Gini coefficients and thus low levels of inequality, have very high levels of financial inclusion, while mid-level Gini coefficient countries such as the UK and the USA show moderately high financial inclusion levels. Similarly, developing countries such as those in Africa that have high Gini coefficients and hence high levels of income inequality have high levels of financial exclusion.

Using descriptive statistics, Dermiguc-Kunt and Klapper (2012a) find that while GDP per capita explains much of the variation in having a formal account around the world, it only accounts for 22% of the variation among economies. Other factors that explain variations in financial inclusion include gender, education level, age and the rural–urban divide. The authors observe the use of formal accounts to be imperfectly correlated with the common measure of financial depth, namely credit to the private sector as a percentage of GDP. South Africa demonstrates this imperfection in a spectacular manner. While the country had a ratio of private credit to GDP of over 142% in 2010, only 54% of adults had a formal account and only 9% of adults have credit from regulated financial institutions; as well, points of access such as number of bank branches per 100,000 adults were low at just 10.1.

In the World Bank global survey, the most frequently cited reason for not having a formal account in sub-Saharan Africa (SSA) is poverty, i.e. lack of money to use one. This reason was given by more than 80% of adults without a formal account. Cost (e.g. high minimum account balance and high administrative burdens and fees), distance and documentation were also cited by more than 30% of non-account holders in SSA. Young adults cited insufficient documentation, while distance from a bank is an important barrier for adults living in rural areas. In Eastern and Southern Africa, fixed fees and high costs of opening and maintaining accounts were cited as important barriers. It is reported that maintaining a checking account in Uganda can cost the equivalent of 25% of GDP per capita annually, and 54% of adult non-account holders cited cost as a reason for not having a formal account (Dermiguc-Kunt and Klapper, 2012b).

Using data from the Global Findex database of the World Bank of 18,000 individuals from 18 SSA countries, Wale and Makina (2017) find account ownership and use to be higher amongst male, middle-aged, high-income and educated individuals. They further observe that the marginal effects of income and education are the most pronounced factors, suggesting that more policy attention is required with respect to the two factors.

While CGAP (2009) has observed that geographical expansion of bank branches into rural areas is restricted by poor infrastructure and telecommunications, Dermiguc-Kunt and Klapper's (2012b) descriptive statistics indicate that financial inclusion is positively and significantly correlated with access points measured as commercial branches per 100,000 people. Mobile phone infrastructure has rapidly taken off in Africa, enabling use of mobile money which has allowed financially excluded people to conduct financial transactions cheaply, securely and reliably. The global survey reports that in SSA, 16% of adults use mobile phones to perform financial transactions (e.g. pay bills or receive money). Kenya reported 68% of adults using mobile money, courtesy of the commercial launch of M-PESA service in 2007. It is noteworthy that 43% of respondents who reported using it do not have a formal account. Thus the mobile money infrastructure has become an important factor in facilitating financial inclusion. In a study of the impact of the mobile phone oneconomic growth in a sample of African countries from 1988 to 2007, Andrianaivo and Kpodar (2012) observed a positive impact.

Beyond descriptive statistics and simple correlation tests, few rigorous empirical works have investigated determinants of financial inclusion. From the literature review, we could only identify a few studies that utilized cross-sectional data analysis (Allen et al., 2012; Anzoategui, Demirguc-Kunt, & Peria, 2014; Sarma and Pais, 2011). Focussing on El Salvador, Anzoategui et al. (2014) employed cross-sectional data analysis on household data and observed financial inclusion to be positively related to real per capita income, house and land ownership, and education. Allen at al. (2012) employed the cross-sectional data of 123 countries and 124,000 individuals and observed that the cost of financial services, documentation and distance from intermediaries are important determinants of financial inclusion. Using a financial inclusion index coined from the formula of the HDI developed by Sarma (2008, 2010, 2012), Sarma and Pais (2011) regressed cross-sectional data of 49 countries and reported a significant positive relationship with factors such as income, human development, education and physical infrastructure for connectivity and information. They also reported significant negative relationships with factors such as non-performing loans, bank capital asset ratios, high share of foreign banks in total banking sector assets and the size of the rural population.

3. Empirical Strategy

3.1 Sources of Data

The data for this chapter were obtained from the World Bank database (*World Development Indicators*) and IMF database (*Financial Access Survey*). We used the data of 27 African countries (see Table 8.1) for a 10-year period (2004–13). The selection of countries was based on the availability of data for the three financial inclusion indicators (commercial bank branches per 100,000 adults; depositors with commercial banks per 1000 adults; and domestic credit to private sector as percentage of GDP). Explanatory variables were also limited to GDP per capita in constant (2005) US dollars, mobile phone infrastructure, government debt to GDP, and the size of the rural population, because of lack of data availability for a 10-year span. These data issues resulted in the exclusion of big African economies, viz. Egypt, Kenya, Nigeria and South Africa, from our sample.

3.2 Financial Inclusion Index Estimation

With some modifications, we adopt the approach of Sarma and Pais (2011) in using a financial inclusion index as the dependent variable in our model. Our index is constructed using three financial inclusion measures: commercial bank branches per 100,000 adults; depositors with commercial banks per 1000 adults and domestic credit to the private sector as percentage of GDP. The number of commercial bank branches variable is expected to capture the availability of financial services; the number of depositors captures the accessibility (in terms of convenience and cost of maintaining an account) of the banking system to the majority of the population. Finally, the amount of credit provided to the private sector (% of GDP) captures the usage dimension of financial inclusion. Following Sarma and Pais (2011), the financial inclusion index computed from the three dimensions lies between 0 and 1, where 0 denotes complete financial exclusion and 1 shows complete financial inclusion. Accordingly, the yearly index for each country is calculated as follows:

$$ifi = \frac{1}{2}\left[\frac{\sqrt{(I_b^2 + I_c^2 + I_d^2)}}{\sqrt{n}} + \left(1 - \frac{\sqrt{(1-I_b)^2 + (1-I_c)^2 + (1-I_d)^2}}{\sqrt{n}}\right)\right]$$

(8.1)

where ifi_i is the financial inclusion index, I_b number of bank branches per 100,000 adults; I_c private credit provided by the financial sector as % of GDP; I_d number of depositors with commercial banks per 1000 adults; n number of dimensions (variables used to construct the index).

We could not find any theoretical justification from the literature to give one dimension more weight over the others. Hence, we assigned equal weight for all the dimensions as in Sarma and Pais (2011). However, we acknowledge the subjective nature of such an approach.

3.3 Model Specification

We apply the dynamic GMM to the data panel. The dynamic GMM estimation using panel data has several advantages over purely cross-sectional estimation.

Assuming the explanatory variables to be only weakly exogenous, we specify a dynamic log-linear (ln) equation for financial inclusion index which includes a lagged dependent and lagged value of the explanatory variables. Our empirical model is therefore as follows:

$$\ln Fi_{it} = \beta_0 + \beta_1 \ln Fi_{it-1} + \beta_2 \ln y_{it-1} + \beta_3 \ln C_{it-1} + \beta_4 \ln M_{it-1}$$
$$+ \beta_5 \ln P_{it-1} + u_{it}$$

(8.2)

where Fi represents our dependent variable, y is GDP per capita in constant US dollar (2005), C is total domestic credit volume taken from the financial institutions by the government as percentage of GDP, M is mobile cellular subscriptions (per 100 people), P is percentage of rural population and u_{it} is an error term that contains country, time specific fixed effects and random error.

$$u_{it} = \mu_i + \varepsilon_t + \nu_{it}$$

(8.3)

where the ν_{it} are assumed to be independent and identically distributed with zero mean and variance $\sigma^2 \nu_{it}$. Hence, the most important errors terms need to be controlled in our specification are the country and time specific fixed effects.

In the context of cross-sectional regression, the unobserved country-specific effect is part of the error term. Therefore, a possible correlation between μ and the explanatory variables results in biased estimates. Furthermore, if the lagged dependent variable is included in the right side of the equation, then the country-specific effect would be correlated with the lagged variables. Another problem is the issue of endogeneity of some or all the explanatory variables, unless controlled, which leads to inappropriate inferences. Arellano and Bond (1991) suggest using first difference to eliminate the country-specific effect. Though differencing manages to solve the country-specific effect problem, it introduces a correlation between the new error term, $\varepsilon_{i,t} - \varepsilon_{i,t-1}$, and the lagged dependent, $fi_{i,t} - fi_{i,t-1}$, when it is included as additional explanatory variable (Beck et al., 2000; Levine et al., 2000; Roodman, 2009). To address this correlation and potential endogeneity problem, Arellano and Bond (1991) proposed the use of lagged values of the explanatory variables in levels as instruments.

Arellano and Bond (1991) propose a two-step GMM estimator. In the first step, the error terms are assumed to be both independent and homoscedastic across countries and over time. In the second step, the residuals obtained in the first step are used to construct a consistent estimate of the variance-covariance matrix, thus relaxing the assumptions of independence and homoscedasticity. They named this estimator as the difference estimator.

The difference estimator has several conceptual and econometric shortcomings. First, by first-differencing we lose the pure cross-country dimension of the data. Second, differencing may decrease the signal-to-noise ratio, thereby exacerbating measurement error biases (Griliches & Hausman, 1986). Finally, Alonso-Borrego and Arellano (1999) and Blundell and Bond (1998) showed that if the lagged dependent and the explanatory variables are persistent over time, lagged levels of these variables are weak instruments for the regressions in differences.

To address these conceptual and econometric problems, we follow the approach of Levine et al. (2000). We use an alternative method that estimates the regression in differences jointly with the regression in levels as proposed by Arellano and Bover (1995). Using Monte Carlo experiments, Blundell and Bond (1997) showed that this system estimator reduces the potential biases in finite samples and asymptotic imprecision associated with the difference estimator.

4. Results and Discussion

4.1 Descriptive Statistics

As shown in Table 8.1, when we observe the simple distribution of countries in terms of their achievements of financial inclusion index, taking an arbitrary cut-off value of the index below 0.3 as low, above 0.3 and below 0.5 as medium, and above 0.5 as highest, 33% of the countries fall in the lowest category. The remaining 52% and 15% are in the medium and high categories respectively.

The decomposed variance of the within and between variations is reported in Table 8.2. Except for mobile (dominated by within variations), in all the variables there is more variation across countries (between variations) than over time (within variation) so that within estimation may lead to considerable efficiency loss.

Correlation results are reported in Table 8.3. All the variables were found to have the expected direction of relation.

Finally, as reported in Fig. 8.1, in terms of the performance of countries according to the financial inclusion index (10-year average), Cape Verde leads with an average of 0.6 followed by Seychelles and Tunisia, while the poor-performing countries include Congo Democratic Republic, Congo Republic, Guinea and Guinea-Bissau with an average of 0.2.

4.2 Model Results

Based on our estimation, all variables have the expected coefficient sign, and four of the variables are significant (see Table 8.4). The coefficient of the lagged dependent variable is positive and significant, implying the beneficial effect of past achievement on current financial inclusion status. The positive and significant coefficient for GDP per capita (US$) is consistent with our expectation. Other things remaining constant, the higher the income level, the better the progress towards achieving financial inclusion. This result is consistent with the findings of Sarma and Pais (2011), who found a positive and significant for GDP per capita coefficient and financial inclusion index in their study for 47 countries; and Allen et al. (2012), using 123 countries and over 124,000 individuals.

The mobile infrastructure variable is found to be positive and significant at 1%, implying the profound effect mobile banking is bringing to underserved communities. The positive impact stems not just from the reduced cost of access to financial services, but also from providing communities access to a wider network of

Table 8.1 Summary Statistics of the Dependent Variable (Financial Inclusion Index) by Country.

s/n	Country	Observations	Mean	SD	Min	Max
Low Financial Inclusion						
1	Congo Dem Rep.	10	0.215	0.005	0.211	0.225
2	Congo Rep	10	0.236	0.012	0.22	0.259
3	Guinea	10	0.238	0.009	0.222	0.251
4	Guinea-Bissau	10	0.239	0.023	0.215	0.274
5	Niger	10	0.260	0.006	0.25	0.267
6	Madagascar	10	0.265	0.011	0.248	0.277
7	Cameroon	10	0.269	0.003	0.264	0.272
8	Comoros	10	0.287	0.015	0.269	0.307
9	Uganda	10	0.295	0.011	0.281	0.311
Medium Financial Inclusion						
10	Burundi	10	0.306	0.015	0.285	0.335
11	Cote D' Ivoire	10	0.315	0.004	0.308	0.322
12	Angola	10	0.325	0.06	0.25	0.427
13	Mali	10	0.329	0.012	0.313	0.351
14	Benin	10	0.331	0.010	0.310	0.345
15	Lesotho	10	0.334	0.017	0.316	0.368
16	Ghana	10	0.347	0.01	0.332	0.357
17	Togo	10	0.350	0.016	0.325	0.375
18	Algeria	10	0.354	0.029	0.318	0.397
19	Djibouti	10	0.360	0.014	0.343	0.392
20	Senegal	10	0.365	0.007	0.355	0.374
21	Swaziland	10	0.426	0.022	0.391	0.455
22	Botswana	10	0.451	0.018	0.424	0.487
23	Libya	10	0.478	0.035	0.43	0.543
High Financial Inclusion						
24	Namibia	10	0.549	0.018	0.520	0.574
25	Tunisia	10	0.708	0.012	0.693	0.728
26	Seychelles	10	0.725	0.033	0.682	0.795
27	Cape Verde	10	0.820	0.049	0.737	0.876
Total		270	0.377	0.004	0.372	0.385

Authors calculations from World Development Indicator *(World Bank); and* International Monetary Fund database *(Financial Access Survey).*

Table 8.2 Summary Statistics of Variables Used.

Variable		Mean	Std. Dev.	Min	Max	Observations
Ln Fi	Overall	0.314	0.104	0.191	0.629	N = 270
	Between		0.105	0.194	0.595	n = 27
	Within		0.014	0.257	0.389	T = 10
L. Fi	Overall	0.313	0.104	0.191	0.629	N = 243
	Between		0.105	0.194	0.597	n = 27
	Within		0.0137	0.264	0.381	T = 9
Ln y	Overall	6.926	1.154	4.968	9.564	N = 270
	Between		1.169	5.008	9.433	n = 27
	Within		0.094	6.170	7.183	T = 10
Ln c	Overall	2.871	0.948	−1.014	4.734	N = 231
	Between		0.946	0.484	4.312	n = 26
	Within		0.4651	0.119	4.060	T-bar = 8.88
Ln. M	Overall	3.421	1.089	0.291	5.195	N = 269
	Between		0.702	1.935	4.643	n = 27
	Within		0.843	0.993	4.971	T-bar = 9.96
Ln. p	Overall	3.983	0.358	3.083	4.509	N = 270
	Between		0.363	3.116	4.497	n = 27
	Within		0.029	3.887	4.079	T = 10

World Development Indicator *(World Bank); and International Monetary Fund database (*Financial Access Survey*); and own calculation.*

Table 8.3 Correlation Matrix of Covariates.

	Ln Fi	L. Fi	Ln y	Ln c	Ln. M	Ln.p
Ln Fi						
—	1.000					
L1.	0.995***	1.000				
Ln y	0.717***	0.716***	1.000			
Ln c	0.022	0.010	0.169***	1.000		
Ln. M	0.443***	0.415***	0.618***	−0.187***	1.000	
Ln. p	−0.140**	−0.135**	−0.192***	−0.028	−0.275***	1.000

Authors calculations from World Development Indicator *(World Bank); and International Monetary Fund database* (Financial Access Survey).

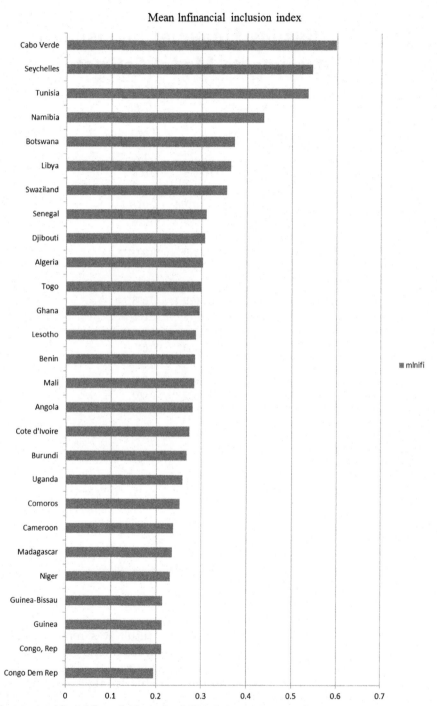

Figure 8.1 Mean natural log of financial inclusion index. Authors' calculations from data from World Development Indicator (World Bank); and International Monetary Fund database (Financial Access Survey).

Table 8.4 Results Financial Inclusion and Its Determinants Model Estimates.

	OLS		GMM		FE	
	β	Robust SE	β	Corrected SE	β	Robust SE
L1. Ln Fi	0.986	0.010***	0.878	0.144***	0.654	0.060***
Ln. y[a]			0.115	0.064*		
Ln. c						
L1.			−0.028	0.017*		
L2			0.009	0.010		
Ln. M						
L2			0.010	0.003***		
Ln. P						
D1			−0.582	1.721		
Time3			0.020	0.008***		
Time4			0.019	0.008**		
Time5			0.014	0.006**		
Time6			0.009	0.040**		
Time7			0.005	0.004		
Time8			0.000	0.003		
Time9			0.002	0.002		
_cons			0.073	0.073		
Number of countries			27			
Number of observations			214			
Number of instruments			24			
AR(1)			0.008			
AR(2)			0.933			
AR(3)			0.448			
AR(4)			0.148			
Sargan test			chi2(9) = 5.11			

[a]L2.ln y is included as additional control variables.
Authors estimation from World Development Indicator *(World Bank) and* International Monetary Fund database *(Financial Access Survey)* data.

service providers. A similar result was reported by Beck et al. (2010), that the ownership of a cell phone increased the likelihood of using financial services in Kenya.

The third important variable is credit amount given by the banking system to government as percentage of GDP. The regression result for credit was found to be negative and significant at

10%. In Africa, where there is substantial bank ownership by government, most of the credit service is expected to be channelled to government, crowding out the private sector. This in turn is expected to worsen the financial exclusion situation of the given country. This finding is not surprising, and it implies that as the volume of credit provided to the private sector increases, it opens the opportunity for more financial inclusion. To the best of our knowledge, the link between government borrowing and financial inclusion is a novel empirical finding.

The final variable in the model estimation is percentage of rural population. The coefficient is negative but not significant. However, consistent with expectations, as the percentage of rural population increases, financial inclusion declines. Thus, the rural population, who are the majority in Africa, suffers most from financial exclusion.

The consistency of GMM estimators depends both on the validity of the assumption that the error term, ε, does not exhibit serial correlation and on the validity of the instruments. We use two tests proposed by Arellano and Bond (1991) to test these assumptions. The first is a Sargan/Hanssen test of over-identifying restrictions, which tests the overall validity of the instruments. Under the null hypothesis of the validity of the instruments, this test has a χ_9^2 distribution with $J - K$ degrees of freedom, where J is the number of instruments and K the number of regressors. The second test examines the assumption of no serial correlation in the error terms. When the idiosyncratic errors are independently and identically distributed (i.i.d.), the first-differenced errors are first-order serially correlated (Arellano & Bond 1991). So as expected, our result (P-values $= 0.008$) presents strong evidence against the null hypothesis of zero autocorrelation in the first-differenced errors at order 1. However, our estimates show no significant evidence of serial correlation in the first-differenced errors at order 2 and even at deeper and higher orders (Table 8.4). Failure to reject the null hypothesis of both tests shows the proper specification (Beck et al., 2000).

For robustness checks, we first estimated both the naïve OLS regression and the GMM by including the lagged dependent variable (Roodman, 2009). The estimates for the coefficient of the lagged dependent variable (log of financial inclusion index) in the GMM model should lie in or near the range estimated by the naïve OLS model. Results of the estimated naïve OLS regression are not reported here but are available on request.

Secondly, in order to further check the robustness of our results, we estimated our dynamic GMM using the three components of financial inclusion comprising the index separately as dependent variables. The estimation results are shown in Appendices 8.1–8.3. In the first model, the number of depositors in commercial banks per 1000 adults is observed to be significantly and positively related to per capita income and negatively related to government debt, and positively and negatively related to mobile infrastructure and rural population, respectively, though not significant. In the second model, the number of depositors in commercial bank branches per 100,000 adults is observed to be significantly and positively related to per capita income and negatively related to government debt, and positively and negatively related to mobile infrastructure and rural population, respectively, though not significant. In the third model, private credit is observed to be significantly and positively related to per capita income and mobile infrastructure and negatively and positively related to government debt and rural population, respectively, though not significant. Save for the positive coefficient of the rural population in the third model, all three models give results with signs of coefficients that are consistent with those obtained using the composite financial index adopted from Sarma and Pais (2011).

5. Conclusion

The chapter has examined the determinants of financial inclusion across 27 African countries using GMM dynamic panel data analysis. The GMM dynamic panel estimators utilized are specifically designed to deal with the problems plaguing past studies of determinants of financial inclusion, namely simultaneity bias and omitted variable(s) bias, including unobserved country-specific effects. Our estimation shows that financial inclusion is significantly and positively related to its lagged value, GDP per capita and mobile infrastructure, and negatively related to government borrowing. These results are robust to alternative specifications of the model, namely using naïve OLS and the use of components of financial inclusion as dependent variables instead of the index.

The negative relationship between financial inclusion and government borrowing has important policy implications for African countries, which by and large have a low ratio of private sector credit to GDP. In this regard, the paper demonstrates that a large ratio of government debt to GDP hampers efforts to achieve financial inclusion.

On the other hand, the development of the mobile infrastructure is observed to have positive effects on financial inclusion. Thus, the upward trend of mobile penetration in Africa should lead to positive spinoff effects for both financial inclusion and economic growth.

Appendix 8.1: Determinants of Number of Depositors at Commercial Banks per 1000 Adults

	GMM	
	β	Corrected SE
Ln. GDP_Per capita (2005 $ US)	0.102	0.043**
Ln. Government credit		
L1.	−0.031	0.011***
Ln. Mobile		
L2	0.239	0.178
Ln. Rural_Population (%)		
D1	−21.93	16.25
Time3	0.109	0.222
Time4	0.105	0.179
Time5	0.099	0.135
Time6	0.079	0.085
Time7	0.015	0.037
Time8	0.015	0.023
Time9	0.005	0.016
_cons	−0.549	0.244**
Number of countries	27	
Number of observations	213	
Number of instruments	24	
AR(1)	0.679	
AR(2)	0.700	
Sargan test	chi2(9) = 6.69	

*10% level of significance
**5 % level of significance
***1 % level of significance
Authors estimation.

Appendix 8.2: Determinants of Commercial Bank Branches per 100,000 Adults

	GMM	
	β	Corrected SE
Ln. GDP_Per capita (2005 $ US)	0.120	0.0646**
Ln. Government credit		
L1.	−0.024	0.013*
Ln. Mobile		
L2	0.002	0.011
Ln. Rural_Population (%)		
D1	−2.293	7.413
Time3	0.020	0.036
Time4	0.005	0.031
Time5	−0.003	0.021
Time6	−0.001	0.016
Time7	0.003	0.013
Time8	0.004	0.010
Time9	0.002	0.005
_cons	−0.604	0.290
Number of countries	27	
Number of observations	214	
Number of instruments	24	
AR(1)	0.123	
AR(2)	0.171	
Sargan test	chi2(9) = 96.77	

*10% level of significance

**5 % level of significance

***1 % level of significance
Authors estimation.

Appendix 8.3: Determinants of Credit to the Private Sector

	GMM		FE	
	β	Corrected SE	β	Robust SE
Ln. GDP_per capita (2005 $ US)	0.434	0.230*		
Ln. Government credit				
L1.	−0.074	0.047		
Ln. Mobile				
L2	0.018	0.005***		
Ln. Rural_population (%)				
D1	1.269	1.311		
Time3	0.020	0.008***		
Time4	0.019	0.008**		
Time5	0.014	0.006**		
Time6	0.009	0.040**		
Time7	0.005	0.004		
Time8	0.000	0.003		
Time9	0.002	0.002		
_cons	0.073	0.073		
Number of countries	27			
Number of observations	214			
Number of instruments	24			
AR(1)	0.003			
AR(2)	0.807			
Sargan test	chi2(9) = 11.42			

*10% level of significance

**5 % level of significance

***1 % level of significance
Authors estimation.

References

Allen, F., Demirguc-Kunt, A., Klapper, L., Soledad, M., & Peria, M. (2012). *The foundations of financial inclusion: Understanding ownership and use of formal accounts. Policy research working paper 6290.* Washington DC: The World Bank.

Alonso-Borrego, C., & Arellano, M. (1999). Symmetrically normalized instrumental -variable estimation using panel data. *Journal of Business & Economic Statistics, 17,* 36–49.

Andrianaivo, M., & Kpodar, K. (2012). Mobile phones, financial inclusion, and growth. *Review of Economics and Institutions, 3*(2), 1–35.

Anzoategui, D., Demirguc-Kunt, A., & Peria, M. S. M. (2014). Remittances and financial inclusion: Evidence from El Salvador. *World Development, 54,* 338–349.

Ardic, O. P., Heimann, M., & Mylenko, N. (2011). *Access to financial services and the financial inclusion agenda around the world: A cross-country analysis with a new data set.* Washington, DC: The World Bank, Financial and Private Sector Development Consultative Group to Assist the Poor, The World Bank.

Arellano, M., & Bond, S. (1991). Some tests of specification for panel data: Monte Carlo evidence and an application to employment equations. *The Review of Economic Studies, 58*(2), 277–297.

Arellano, M., & Bover, O. (1995). Another look at the instrumental variable estimation of error-components models. *Journal of Econometrics, 68,* 29–51.

Beck, T., Cull, R., Fuchs, M., Getenga, J., Gatere, P., Randa, J., et al. (2010). *Banking sector stability, efficiency and outreach in Kenya. Policy research working paper series no. 5442.* Washington, DC: The World Bank.

Beck, T., Levine, R., & Loayza, N. (2000). Finance and the source of growth. *Journal of Financial Economics, 58,* 261–300.

Beck, T., Demirguc-Kunt, A., & Levine, R. (2007). Finance, inequality and the poor. *Journal of Economic Growth, 12,* 27–49.

Bencivenga, V. R., & Smith, B. D. (1991). Financial intermediation and endogenous growth. *The Review of Economic Studies, 58*(2), 195–209.

Blackburn, K., Bose, N., & Capasso, S. (2005). Financial development, financing choice and economic growth. *Review of Development Economics, 9*(2), 135–149.

Blackburn, K., & Hung, V. T. Y. (1998). A theory of growth, financial development and trade. *Economica, 65*(257), 107–124.

Blundell, R., & Bond, S. (1998). Initial Conditions and Moment Restrictions in Dynamic Panel Data Models. *Journal of Econometrics, 87,* 115–143.

Bose, N., & Cothren, R. (1996). Equilibrium loan contracts and endogenous growth in the presence of asymmetric information. *Journal of Monetary Economics, 38*(2), 363–376.

CGAP (Consultative Group to Assist the Poor). (2009). *Financial access 2009: Measuring access to financial services around the world.* Washington, DC: CGAP/World Bank.

Chibba, M. (2009). *Financial inclusion, poverty reduction and the millennium development goals, international centre for development effectiveness and poverty reduction, Canada.* Canada: Canadian International Development Consultants, Inc.

Demirguc-Kunt, A., & Klapper, L. (2012a). *Measuring financial inclusion: The global Findex database. Policy research working paper 6025.* Washington, DC: World Bank.

Demirguc-Kunt, A., & Klapper, L. (2012b). *Financial inclusion in Africa: An overview. Policy research working paper No. 6088*. Washington DC: World Bank.

Demirguc-Kunt, A., & Levine, R. (2009). Finance and inequality: Theory and evidence. *Annual Review of Financial Economics, 1*, 287–318.

De Gregorio, J., & Kim, S. (2000). Credit markets with differences in abilities: education, distribution, and growth. *International Economic Review, 41*(3), 579–607.

Diamond, D. W. (1984). Financial intermediation and delegated monitoring. *The Review of Economic Studies, 51*(3), 393–414.

Ellis, F., & Biggs, S. (2001). Evolving themes in rural development 1950s–2000s. *Development Policy Review, 19*(4), 437–448.

Galbis, V. (1977). Financial intermediation and economic growth in less developed countries: A theoretical approach. *Journal of Development Studies, 13*(2), 58–72.

Gertler, M., & Gilchrist, S. (1994). Monetary policy, business cycles, and the behavior of small manufacturing firms. *Quarterly Journal of Economics, 109*, 309–340.

Goldsmith, R. W. (1969). *Financial structure and development*. New Haven, CT: Yale University Press.

Griliches, Z., & Hausman, J. (1986). Errors in variables in panel data. *Journal of Econometrics, 31*, 93–118.

Greenwood, J., & Jovanovic, B. (1990). Financial development, growth, and the distribution of income. *Journal of Political Economy, 98*(5, Part 1), 1076–1107.

Honohan, P., & Beck, T. (2007). *Making finance work for Africa*. Washington DC: World Bank.

Kempson, E. (2006). *Policy level response to financial exclusion in developed economies: Lessons for developing countries. Paper for access to finance: Building inclusive financial systems, May 30–31, 2006*. Washington, DC: World Bank.

King, R. G., & Levine, R. (1993a). Finance and growth: Schumpeter might be right. *Quarterly Journal of Economics, 108*(3), 717–737.

King, R. G., & Levine, R. (1993b). Finance, entrepreneurship and growth. *Journal of Monetary Economics, 32*(3), 513–542.

Klapper, L., Laeven, L., & Rajan, R. (2006). Entry regulation as a barrier to entrepreneurship. *Journal of Financial Economics, 82*, 591–629.

Levine, R., Loayza, N., & Beck, T. (2000). Financial intermediation and growth: Causality and causes. *Journal of Monetary Economics, 46*, 31–77.

Montiel, P. (1994). Financial policies and economic growth: Theory, evidence and country-specific experience from sub-Saharan Africa. In *Paper presented at the African economic research consortium biannual workshop, Nairobi, May 1994*.

Morales, M. F. (2003). Financial intermediation in a model of growth through creative destruction. *Macroeconomic Dynamics, 7*(03), 363–393.

Nissanke, M., & Aryeetey, E. (2005). *Financial integration and development: Liberalization and reform in sub-Saharan Africa*. London and New York: Routledge Studies in Development Economics.

OECD. (2009). *Top Barriers and Drivers to SME Internationalisation, Report by the OECD Working Party on SMEs and Entrepreneurship*, OECD.

Patrick, H. (1966). Financial development and economic growth in developing countries. *Economic Development and Cultural Change, 14*(2), 174–189.

Ramji, M. (2009). *Financial inclusion in Gulbarga: Finding usage in access. Working paper series No. 26.* India: Institute for Financial Management and Research, Centre for Microfinance.

Roodman, D. (2009). How to do xtabond2: An introduction to difference and system GMM in Stata. *STATA Journal, 9*(1), 86–136.

Rousseau, P. L., & Wachtel, P. (1998). Financial intermediation and economic performance: Historical evidence from five industrialized countries. *Journal of Money, Credit, and Banking, 30*(4), 657–678.

Saint-Paul, G. (1992). Technological choice, financial markets and economic development. *European Economic Review, 36*(4), 763–781.

Sarma, M. (2008). *Index of financial inclusion. Working paper 215.* Indian Council for Research on International Economic Relations.

Sarma, M. (2010). *Index of financial inclusion. Discussion paper 10-05.* India: Centre on Money, Trade finance and Development.

Sarma, M. (2012). *Index of financial inclusion: A measure of financial sector inclusiveness. Working paper No. 07/2012.* India: Centre on Money, Trade finance and Development.

Sarma, M., & Pais, J. (2011). Financial inclusion and development. *Journal of International Development, 23*, 613–628.

Triki, T., & Faye, I. (Eds.). (2013). *Financial inclusion in Africa.* Tunis: African Development Bank.

UNDESA and UNCDF. (2006). *Building inclusive financial sectors for development.* New York: United Nations.

Wagle, U. R. (2012). The economic footing of the global poor, 1980-2005: The roles of economic growth, openness and political institutions. *Journal of International Development, 24*, S173–S197.

Wale, L. E., & Makina, D. (2017). Account ownership and use of financial services among individuals: Evidence from selected sub-Saharan African economies. *African Journal of Economic and Management Studies, 8*(1), 19–35.

World Bank. (2008). *Finance for all? Policies and pitfalls in expanding access.* Washington, DC: World Bank.

Further Reading

Adu, G., Marbuah, G., & Mensah, J. T. (2013). Financial development and economic growth in Ghana: Does the measure of financial development matter? *Review of Development Finance, 3*(4), 192–203.

Antonakis, J., Bendahan, S., Jacquart, P., & Lalive, R. (2010). On making causal claims: A review and recommendations. *The Leadership Quarterly, 21*(6), 1086–1120.

Atje, R., & Jovanovic, B. (1993). Stock markets and development. *European Economic Review, 37*(2–3), 632–640.

Beck, T., & Levine, R. (2004). Stock markets, banks, and growth: Panel evidence. *Journal of Banking & Finance, 28*(3), 423–442.

Benhabib, J., & Spiegel, M. M. (2000). The role of financial development in growth and investment. *Journal of Economic Growth, 5*(4), 341–360.

Benson, D. J. (2002). The effects of stock market development on growth and private investment in lower-income countries. *Emerging Markets Review, 3*(3), 211–232.

Blundell, R., & Bond, S. (1977). *Initial conditions and moment restrictions in dynamic panel data models. Discussion paper no. 97-07.* University College London.

Calderon, C., & Liu, L. (2003). The direction of causality between financial development and economic growth. *Journal of Development Economics, 72*(1), 321–334.

Cameron, A. C., & Trivedi, P. K. (2009). *Microeconometrics using stata.* College Station, Texas: A Stata Press Publication.

CGAP. (2006). *Access for all: Building inclusive financial systems.* Washington, DC: Consultative Group to Assist the Poor.

Chakrabarty, K. C. (2011). *Financial inclusion and banks: Issues and perspectives* (pp. 1831–1838). Monthly Bulletin of the Reserve Bank of India.

Chakraborty, I. (2008). Does financial development cause economic growth? The case of India. *South Asia Economic Journal, 9*(1), 109–139.

Chibba, M. (2008a). Poverty reduction in developing countries: No consensus but plenty of solutions. *World Economics, 9*(1), 197–200.

Chibba, M. (2008b). *Financial inclusion and development: Concepts, lessons learned and key pillars.* Mimeo.

Dev, M. S. (2006). Financial inclusion: Issues and challenges. *Economic and Political Weekly*, (October 14), 4310–4313.

Kirkpatrick, C. (2005). Finance and development: Overview and introduction. *Journal of Development Studies, 41*(4), 631–635.

Levine, R., & Zervos, S. (1998). Stock markets, banks, and economic growth. *The American Economic Review, 88*(3), 537–558.

Mayer, C., & Vives, X. (Eds.). (1993). *Capital markets and financial intermediation.* Cambridge University Press.

Robert, E.,C., & Bruce, C. P. (2002). Is the growth of small firms constrained by internal finance? *The Review of Economics and Statistics, 84*(2), 298–309.

9

FINANCIAL INCLUSION AND ECONOMIC GROWTH: EVIDENCE FROM A PANEL OF SELECTED AFRICAN COUNTRIES

Daniel Makina,[1] Yabibal M. Walle[2]

[1]*Department of Finance, Risk Management and Banking, University of South Africa, Pretoria, South Africa;* [2]*Department of Econometrics, Georg-August-University of Goettingen, Germany*

Extending Financial Inclusion in Africa. https://doi.org/10.1016/B978-0-12-814164-9.00009-8

1. Introduction

The literature generally acknowledges that financial inclusion – increasing the poor's access to financial services-is one effective tool that can assist to reduce poverty and lower income inequality (Beck, Demirguc-Kunt, & Levine, 2007; Dermirguc-Kunt & Levine, 2009). However, as pointed out by Demirguc-Kunt, Klapper, and Singer (2017), most of the evidence on the link between financial inclusion and growth exists at the individual and micro levels. There is still scant evidence on the relationship between financial inclusion and macroeconomic growth.

Theoretically, it can be demonstrated that financial inclusion has some relationship with macroeconomic growth and inequality. However, the World Bank (2008) observes that the relationship is not clear-cut. Theory postulates that in the absence of financial frictions, economic agents endowed with the most entrepreneurial ability would always have access to finance to fund their projects; in other words, entrepreneurial activity is a function of ability and not parental wealth (Banerjee & Newman, 1993; Dermirguc-Kunt & Levine, 2009). Researchers note direct and indirect channels through which access to finance by the poor can reduce poverty and income inequality. The direct channel manifests itself when the poor are able to have formal bank accounts for saving and building credit worthiness so that they are able to their smooth consumption and deal with adverse economic shocks. Savings or access to credit could then be utilized for the education of their children and micro-enterprise development and thus reduce poverty and income equality for present and future generations. The indirect effect occurs through the labour market channel. Increased access to finance increases competition among financial institutions, resulting in the reduction of intermediation costs and thus broadening access to credit to potential entrepreneurs. As new entrepreneurs expand their businesses, new jobs are created. One research observation using general equilibrium models on micro data from Thailand by Gine and Townsend (2004) demonstrated that the labour market channel had the most effect on income inequality compared with the direct channel.

At the macroeconomic level, we know that broader financial development – as measured by financial depth – influences economic growth (Goldsmith, 1969; McKinnon, 1973; Shaw, 1973). Extensive literature demonstrates a positive relationship between financial sector development and economic growth that runs bi-directionally with a mutually reinforcing effect (World Bank, 2007). In other words, financial sector development promotes economic growth while economic growth itself stimulates further financial sector development, and the two mutually influence each other. However, one researcher among others, Fung (2009), has observed that the mutually reinforcing relationship between financial sector development and economic growth is stronger in the early stage of economic development. When sustained economic growth gets underway, this relationship diminishes. Subsequent research has confirmed an inverted U-shaped effect of financial development. For instance, Cecchetti and Kharroubi (2012) demonstrate that financial development is beneficial to growth up to a point, after which it hampers it.

Notwithstanding the foregoing, it should be borne in mind that indicators of financial development are not the same as indicators of financial inclusion. Indicators of financial development include macroeconomic variables such as private credit as a ratio of GDP, money supply measures (M1, M2 and M3), stock market measures, among others. In contrast, indicators of financial inclusion are G20 Financial Inclusion Indicators measured in three dimensions: (1) access to financial services; (2) usage of financial services; and (3) the quality of the products and service delivery. Research on the relationship between financial inclusion and economic growth using these indicators is limited, for several reasons. First, national and global recognition of financial inclusion is fairly recent. The Millennium Development Goals which implicitly acknowledged its importance were only adopted in the 2000s. The first G20[1] Summit in Pittsburgh, USA, which specifically had an agenda item of financial inclusion, was only held in 2009. The G20 Pittsburgh Summit set the ball rolling by creating a Financial Inclusion Experts Group whose mandate was to facilitate strategies to expand access to finance to households, micro, small-sized and medium-sized enterprises. Second, analysis of factors that determine macroeconomic growth and inequality requires decades of data. However, such data on financial inclusion indicators only started to be collected in the 2000s. The IMF Financial Access Survey supply-side data first became available in 2004. Demand-side data on financial inclusion on individuals were first collected in 2011 when the first Global Findex database was launched. FinMark Trust, whose focus is Africa, only started collecting demand-side data in 2002.

Because of the lack of long-dated data on measures of financial inclusion, most studies that sought to elicit the impact of

---

[1]G20 refers to 'the group of 20', an international forum for governments and central bank governors whose membership comprises 19 individual countries plus the European Union.

financial inclusion have been undertaken at microeconomic and country levels. Few studies have been undertaken at macroeconomic levels. Some researchers like Sahay et al. (2015) attribute the lack of such empirical analysis to macroeconomists only taking the concept of financial inclusion seriously after the US subprime crisis.

Focussing on African countries using a decade of time-series data, this chapter investigates the relationship between financial inclusion and economic growth. The investigation is motivated by several factors. While in the past 2 decades sub- Saharan Africa (SSA) has experienced significant growth averaging 4.8% per year, the benefits of this growth have not been evenly distributed (AfDB, 2012). The *World Development Indicators 2014* reported that income inequality was actually rising, as the population living on less than $1.25 a day slightly decreased from 52.75% in 1981 to 46.85% in 2011. In other words, economic growth has been barely inclusive. Lack of financial inclusion is cited as one reason for the endemic poverty and income inequality (Devarajan & Fengler, 2013). Beck (2015) reports that despite financial liberalization, globalization and cross-border banking, the financial sector has largely remained the preserve of a few elites. The World Bank Findex 2014 shows that while account ownership in SSA increased from 24% in 2011% to 34% in 2014, access to credit increased moderately, from 4.8% to 6% over the same period (Demirguc-Kunt et al., 2014).

The rest of the chapter is organized as follows. Section 2 reviews literature. Section 3 describes the empirical strategy adopted. Section 4 presents and discuss empirical results, and the last section concludes.

2. Literature Review

While some literature finds a positive correlation between financial inclusion and poverty alleviation (e.g., Beck et al., 2007; Honohan, 2004, 2008), the researchers conducting this work do not explicitly determine a causal relationship between access to finance and economic outcomes. Bruhn and Love (2014) demonstrate that expanding access to finance to low-income individuals produces a sizeable positive effect on economic activity. They did this by studying a unique event, namely the opening of Banco Azteca in Mexico, a bank that catered to low —and middle-income groups largely excluded by the commercial banking sector. In October 2002, Banco Azteca opened more than 800 branches in all retail stores of Grupo Elektra, its parent company. Bruhn and Love's (2014) evaluation of the impact of increased access to financial services for low-income individuals showed a positive impact on poverty alleviation. They found that improving access to low-income households produces a significant impact on both the labour market and income levels.

In a different setting, Burgess and Pande (2005) have observed a similar and significant impact on poverty alleviation from the expansion of bank branches in rural India. However, Ayyagari, Beck, and Hoseini (2013), who used state-level indicators on financial depth, branch penetration and poverty for 1983 to 2005 across 15 Indian states, have observed mixed results. They show a negative relationship between financial deepening post-1991 (following financial liberalization) and rural poverty. They noted that the poverty reduction effects were more marked on the self-employed in rural areas.

On the other hand, the World Bank (2014) reports microeconomic evidence that access to basic payments and savings have beneficial results for poor households while access to finance by small and young firms is associated with innovation, job creation and growth. In contrast, randomized controlled trials and cross-country studies on the impact of access to microcredit have yielded mixed results. However, some microeconomic studies show that financial access by women is positive for society generally. For instance, Sanyal (2014) reports increasing evidence that the welfare of the family benefits when women are financially empowered.

Few country-level studies have looked at the linkages between financial inclusion, economic growth and poverty reduction. Sahay et al. (2015), who examined the linkages of financial inclusion with economic growth, financial inclusion and economic stability, and inequality, provide three key findings. First, they found that increased access to finance by firms and households increases economic growth, but up to a point, beyond which benefits of further inclusion start to be low or even negative in some developed economies. Second, they observe that unbridled broadening of access to credit without proper supervision can create financial stability risks. They further observe that the erosion of financial buffers is acute in countries with weaker supervision. On the other hand, in countries with strong supervision, the increase in access to credit results in financial stability gains. Third, expanding access to financial services other than credit was found to be beneficial to growth and not harmful to financial stability.

In another study, Park and Mercado (2015) investigated the impact of financial inclusion on poverty and income inequality on 37 selected developing economies. Their results showed that per capita income, rule of law, and demographic characteristics significantly affect financial inclusion. Furthermore, they found that financial inclusion also significantly reduces poverty and inequality.

Regarding the impact of microfinance, most studies are micro-evaluations that have produced mixed results. The study by Buera, Kaboski, and Shin (2012) is one of the few studies to attempt to investigate the macroeconomic impacts of microfinance. Their general equilibrium model results show that microfinance is a pro-poor redistributive policy that benefits the poor. It redistributes income from individuals with high saving rates to those with low saving rates, leading to lower aggregate saving and capital accumulation. During this process, marginal entrepreneurs benefit directly while workers benefit indirectly through higher wages. These higher factor prices adversely affect the established entrepreneurs. Notwithstanding these adverse effects, the lower capital accumulation and the higher total factor productivity have overall positive impacts on consumption and output.

In Africa, microfinance is the single most important development programme that has been the torchbearer in addressing financial inclusion. Microcredit has been seen as a financing tool for development, whose ultimate aim is to reduce poverty. Researchers have investigated both financial and non-financial impacts of microfinance. Financial impacts include those on income, savings, and expenditure and wealth accumulation, while non-financial impacts include those on health, nutrition, food security, education, child labour, women's empowerment, housing, job creation and social cohesion. Van Rooyen, Stewart, and de Wet (2012), who conducted a systematic review of evidence of the impact of microfinance in Sub-Saharan Africa, reported mixed results − positive, no impact and negative results. What follows are findings for selected countries obtained by various researchers.

2.1 Ethiopia

Doocy, Teffera, Norell, and Burnham (2005) conducted a study in a rural setting to investigate the coping capacity in drought and food insecure conditions for microfinance on two groups of clients − the treated (those who received credit) and the untreated (those who did not). They did not find any significant differences in coping capacity between those two groups. However, their findings suggested microfinance programmes could have an important impact on the nutritional status and health of female clients.

2.2 Ghana

Adjei, Arun, and Hossain (2009) investigated the impact of micro-credit and micro-savings on health and education in both rural and urban settings. The found a positive effect for enabling individual involuntary savings as well as positive effects on health and education. Furthermore, they found that microfinance programmes that are financial sustainable have greater impacts on participants. In another study, Nanor (2008) investigated the impact of microcredit on income, expenditure, food security and nutrition and education in a rural sample. They found mixed results for household and business income while the impact on expenditure was positive. The impact on education was mixed, being positive in some districts and negative in others. Overall microcredit did not contribute to poverty reduction.

2.3 Kenya

Ashraf, Gine, and Karlan (2008) conducted a randomized controlled trial in a rural setting to investigate the impact of microcredit on income. Provision of credit was accompanied by advice on export crops and facilitation of the export process. A positive impact on business income was found which could not be attributable solely to microcredit. In a similar randomized controlled trial, Dupas and Robinson (2008) found no impact on business income but a positive impact on individual savings, health and food security, and nutrition.

2.4 Madagascar

Analysing the impact of microcredit on income and education on an urban sample of those receiving credit and those not receiving, Gubert and Roubaud (2005) found positive impact for business income and no impact on education. Overall, they conclude that microenterprises that received microcredit performed better than informal enterprises that did not receive credit.

2.5 Malawi

Shimamura and Lastarria-Cornhiel (2010) evaluated the impact of agricultural credit on school attendance of children in the rural areas. Surprisingly, credit uptake decreased school attendance by young girls, raising the prospect of exploitation of child labour. However, that was not the case; rather there were simultaneous incidences between attending school and young children doing other household responsibilities. The finding can be viewed to be consistent with that of Wydick (1999), who observed that household enterprise capitalization through access to credit raises the marginal product of child labour and the opportunity cost, resulting in decreased school attendance.

2.6 Rwanda

Investigating the impact of microcredit on the accumulation of wealth, health, food security and nutrition, and education in rural Rwanda, Lacalle Calderon, Rico Garrido, and Duran Navarro (2008) found positive effects. Their results showed that microfinance clients' families are better off than the control group that did not receive microcredit. They also found evidence that microcredit increases the productive capacity and social status of families.

2.7 South Africa

Using a cluster or group randomized controlled trial, Pronyk et al. (2008) assessed the effects of a combined microfinance and training intervention on HIV risk behaviour among young female participants in rural South Africa. They found a positive impact on the health of young women and their wellbeing. However, these impacts could not be directly attributed to the microcredit element of the programme. In another randomized controlled trial, Karlan and Zinman (2010) found that expanded credit access increased economic self-sufficiency, food consumption and subjective wellbeing for the treated group, save for increasing depression and stress.

2.8 Tanzania

Brannen (2010) investigated the impact of microcredit on the accumulation of assets, health, food security and nutrition, and education in rural Zanzibar using a control group in which there was no intervention. The findings were positive for accumulation of assets, health, food security and nutrition, but neutral for education.

2.9 Uganda

Using a controlled trial in both rural and urban settings, Barnes, Gaile, and Kibombo (2001a) investigated the impact of microcredit on savings levels, accumulation of assets and education. They found negative impacts on education but positive impacts on individual savings, and the positive impact on accumulation of assets for households was not significant. In contrast, using a cluster randomized controlled trial, Ssewamala et al. (2010) found positive impacts on health, education, and individual savings. Though adolescent boys and girls saved similar amounts, the microfinance intervention benefitted girls in changing their attitudes towards sexual risk-taking behaviour.

2.10 Zimbabwe

Using a controlled trial in an urban setting, Barnes, Keogh, and Nemarundwe (2001b) investigated the impact of microcredit on income, accumulation of assets, health and education. Positive impacts were observed on household income, accumulation of business assets, health, food security and nutrition and education for boys (whilst negative for girls).

2.11 Sub-Saharan Africa

While micro-evaluations on the impact of microfinance have been relatively extensive in SSA, there is a huge research gap with regard to macroeconomic evaluations. The only attempt of a macroeconomic evaluation we could identify in the literature is a cross-sectional study by Tita and Aziakpono (2017) that examined the relationship between financial inclusion and income inequality in SSA. The results of the study show that formal account usage has a positive relationship with income inequality against the expectation of a negative relationship and in contradiction to evidence from other developing regions like Asia. The researchers attribute this contradictory evidence to low levels of financial inclusion in SSA. We also suspect that the problem could be data insufficiency as well as deficiencies inherent in cross-sectional analyses.

3. Empirical Strategy

The empirical research design is limited by the availability of time series on measures of financial inclusion. The IMF *Financial Access Survey* provided the first country-level information on commercial bank branches per 100,000 adults in 2004. Though not perfect, this measure presents us with at least a decade of time-series data of an indicator of financial inclusion and hence would give us an exploratory indication on the relationship between financial inclusion and growth. Using panel data of 42 African countries[2] obtained from *World Development Indicators* for the period 2004–14, we employ the approach of Sahay et al. (2015). This approach views economic growth to be a function of financial inclusion, financial depth, initial GDP per capita, trade openness, government consumption expenditure, among other factors. We estimate the following panel regression equation:

$$y_{i,t} = \beta_0 + \beta_1 FI_{i,t} + \beta_2 FD_{i,t} + \beta_3 FI_{i,t} * FD_{i,t} + \beta_4 X_{i,t} + \varepsilon_{it} \quad (9.1)$$

where y_{it}, FI_{it}, and FD_{it} denote real GDP per capita (GDPPC), financial inclusion (BBRANCH), and financial depth respectively. The vector X contains the control variables initial GDP per capita (lagged GDPPC), primary education (PRIM), trade openness (OPEN) and government consumption expenditure (GOV). Financial inclusion is measured using the number of commercial bank branches per 100,000 people, while financial development is measured as the ratio of credit to the private sector to GDP.

To estimate Eq. (9.1), we employ the *system* generalized method of moments (GMM) dynamic panel data estimator suggested by Arellano and Bover (1995) and Blundell and Bond (1998). This estimator is widely used in the finance-growth literature to account for unobserved country heterogeneity, omitted variable bias, and potential endogeneity that could arise from reverse-causality from growth determinants to economic growth (Beck et al., 2000). As a predecessor to system GMM, the difference GMM estimator employs a system of first differenced series (Arellano and Bond, 1991). While first differencing removes unobserved country-specific effects, it however introduces new correlations between the first differenced error terms and the lagged dependent variable. As a solution to this, and to account for potential endogeneity of other covariates, the difference GMM estimator uses lagged levels as instruments for the variables in levels. In addition to the difference GMM equations and instruments, the system GMM utilizes the equation in levels and instruments them by their first differences. Hence, the system-GMM estimator uses a system of two equations: one in first differences and the other in levels. These additional instruments of the system GMM estimator are found to reduce small sample biases

[2]These countries are Algeria, Benin, Botswana, Burkina Faso, Burundi, Cameroon, Cape Verde, C.A. Republic, Chad, Comoros, DR Congo, Egypt, Eq. Guinea, Gambia, Ghana, Guinea, Ivory Coast, Kenya, Lesotho, Liberia, Madagascar, Malawi, Mali, Mauritania, Mauritius, Morocco, Mozambique, Namibia, Niger, Nigeria, R. of Congo, Rwanda, Senegal, Seychelles, South Africa, Sudan, Swaziland, Tanzania, Togo, Tunisia, Uganda, Zambia.

associated with the difference-GMM estimator (Arellano and Bover, 1995 and Blundell and Bond, 1998).

On the empirical side, different issues must be considered in applying the system GMM estimator. First, as the number of instruments is quadratic in the time-series dimension, the proliferation of the number of instruments is a serious concern. Roodman (2009) shows that 'too many' instruments can make the instrument set invalid and weaken the Hansen test, often leading to implausibly high P-values. To reduce the instrument count, we restrict the number of lags to 1. The other important issue is the use of one-step vs. two-step GMM estimation. While both steps yield a consistent estimator, two-step GMM estimation yields an efficient one. Unfortunately, two-step GMM could result in downward-biased standard errors in small samples with a relatively large number of instruments. We report results using both methods.

4. Results and Discussion

In this section, we discuss empirical results on the role of financial inclusion on economic growth in Africa during the period 2004–14. Table 9.1 documents estimation results obtained by applying one-step system GMM estimation on (1). Results based on two-step GMM are qualitatively similar and are provided in Table 9.2.

Results documented in column 1 of Table 9.1 are based on a parsimonious growth model with lagged GDP per capita, financial development and financial inclusion included as determinants of growth. These results show that initial GDP per capita does not affect economic growth. The coefficient on the financial development index is negative and statistically insignificant. Though the latter result is not consistent with much of the empirical finance-growth nexus literature on Africa (see, for example, the survey of the literature in Walle, 2014), there are several plausible explanations for it. First, the study covers a recent decade, in which there has been a worldwide decline on the impact of finance on growth (Rousseau & Wachtel, 2011). Moreover, in the period under study African countries have not only seen rapid increases in financial development, but have also experienced a major global financial and economic crisis. A third explanation could be that our financial development measure is too broad, which incorporates both consumer and enterprise loans. Beck, Büyükkarabacak, Rioja, and Valev (2012) shows that credit to enterprises promotes economic growth while household credit does

Table 9.1 One-Step GMM Results.

Variables	1	2	3	4	5	6
Lag GDPPC	−0.016	−0.017	0.014**	−0.013	−0.011	0.009*
	(0.019)	(0.012)	(0.006)	(0.014)	(0.008)	(0.005)
PRIV	−0.069***	−0.053**	−0.051**	−0.065***	−0.047**	−0.039**
	(0.019)	(0.022)	(0.022)	(0.024)	(0.022)	(0.019)
BBRANCH	0.084***	0.054***	0.022*	0.036*	0.012	0.003
	(0.024)	(0.019)	(0.012)	(0.020)	(0.013)	(0.012)
GOV		0.050	0.041**		0.035	0.034**
		(0.035)	(0.020)		(0.029)	(0.016)
OPEN		0.020	0.006		0.016	0.002
		(0.018)	(0.012)		(0.014)	(0.011)
PRIM			0.030			0.026
			(0.023)			(0.021)
PRIV*BBRANCH				0.008	0.008	0.005
				(0.007)	(0.005)	(0.003)
Constant	0.215*	0.003	−0.225*	0.228**	0.033	−0.172
	(0.124)	(0.114)	(0.132)	(0.114)	(0.101)	(0.122)
Observations	420	400	370	420	400	370
Countries	42	40	37	42	40	37
Instruments	67	105	124	86	124	143
AR(1)	0.081	0.084	0.110	0.084	0.085	0.108
AR(2)	0.173	0.177	0.449	0.199	0.210	0.493
Sargan	0	0	0	0	0	0
Hansen	0.992	1	1	1	1	1

Notes: Estimation results are obtained by using one-step system GMM estimation. The dependent variable is the logarithmic growth rate of real per capita GDP. Lagged GDP is the first lag of the log of per capita GDP. PRIV is the ratio of credit to the private sector to GDP, which proxies financial development. BBRANCH is the number of bank branches per 100,000 people and is a proxy for financial inclusion. GOV denotes the ratio of general government consumption to GDP. PRIM represents primary school enrolment as a percent of all eligible children. OPEN denotes the ratio of imports plus exports to GDP. All variables are used in logarithmic forms. To reduce the instrument count, the maximum lag order is set to one. Standard errors are reported in parentheses and are robust to consistent any form of heteroskedasticity and autocorrelation within countries. In the model statistics AR(1), AR(2), Sargan and Hansen, only the P-values are presented. Asterisks denote the significance level (***$P < .01$, **$P < .05$, *$P < .1$).

not. It is plausible that most credit could be going towards consumption rather than investment that induces growth. A fourth explanation is emerging empirical evidence that is finding no positive relationship between financial development and economic growth (see for instance, Andersen & Tarp, 2003; Ductor & Grechyna, 2015). Ductor and Grechyna (2015), in particular, observe that the relationship between financial development

Table 9.2 Two-Step GMM Results.

Variables	1	2	3	4	5	6
Lag GDPPC	−0.016	−0.016	−0.172**	−0.008	−0.007	0.034
	(0.010)	(0.013)	(0.086)	(0.006)	(0.014)	(0.028)
PRIV	−0.067***	−0.029	−0.049**	−0.046***	−0.034***	−0.023
	(0.006)	(0.018)	(0.019)	(0.008)	(0.013)	(0.019)
BBRANCH	0.079***	0.036***	−0.025	0.014	0.008	−0.025
	(0.008)	(0.012)	(0.023)	(0.013)	(0.013)	(0.028)
GOV		0.044*	0.032		0.045***	0.036*
		(0.024)	(0.036)		(0.016)	(0.019)
OPEN		0.013	0.004		0.005	0.001
		(0.021)	(0.022)		(0.015)	(0.037)
PRIM			0.199*			0.142
			(0.107)			(0.133)
PRIV*BBRANCH				0.013***	0.009	0.008
				(0.004)	(0.006)	(0.013)
Constant	0.214***	−0.005	0.372	0.149***	−0.006	−0.920
	(0.070)	(0.180)	(0.808)	(0.051)	(0.085)	(0.713)
Observations	420	400	370	420	400	370
Countries	42	40	37	42	40	37
Instruments	67	105	124	86	124	143
AR(1)	0.091	0.096	0.204	0.091	0.098	0.116
AR(2)	0.179	0.221	0.737	0.231	0.237	0.616
Sargan	0	0	0	0	0	0
Hansen	0.992	1	1	1	1	1

Notes: Estimation results are obtained by using two-step system GMM estimation. In the model statistics AR(1), AR(2), Sargan and Hansen, only the P-values are presented. Asterisks denote the significance level (***$P < .01$, **$P < .05$, *$P < .1$). For further notes, see Table 9.1.

and economic can be negative in a situation where the rate of economic growth lags the rate of growth of private credit.

Turning to our variable of interest, results documented in Table 9.1 generally show a positive effect of financial inclusion on economic growth in Africa in the period 2004−14. In particular, this effect is positive and statistically significant in specifications 1, 2 and 3, where the interaction between financial inclusion and financial development is not included. Even when the interaction is included (columns 4, 5 and 6), financial inclusion has a significantly positive effect in the parsimonious model where government expenditure, openness to trade and primary education are not included. Given that financial development and financial inclusion have opposite effects on economic growth, it is not surprising that the interaction between the two does not have a significant effect on economic growth and that its presence renders the coefficient on financial inclusion insignificant although positive in specifications 5 and 6. Accordingly, the models without the interaction terms appear to be more appropriate, leading us to conclude that financial inclusion has a significantly positive effect on economic growth in Africa. This result is robust to the inclusion of other growth determinants government expenditure, openness to trade and primary education.

Estimated coefficients on other control variables carry expected signs, though they are often not statistically significant. As an exception to this, government size is positively associated with economic growth in the most comprehensive specifications, (3) and (6). This is consistent with the fact that most African economies are low-income economies, and governments play a crucial role in their early stages of economic development. The insignificance of coefficients for trade openness and primary school enrolment rate could be explained by the small size of our sample.

Model diagnostics are presented in the bottom rows of Table 9.1. The autocorrelation test results indicate the presence of autoregression of order one in the first-differenced residuals, which is expected by construction. Failure to reject the null hypothesis of an AR (2) representation for first-differenced residuals justifies our use of the first lagged levels as instruments for first differenced variables. The Sargan and Hansen tests test the validity of GMM instruments. Unfortunately, the Sargan test is not robust to autocorrelation and heteroscedasticity, while the Hansen test gets weaker as the number of instruments increases. Hence, the Sargan test is not reliable in our data, which are very likely to be heteroskedastic, nor is the implausibly high P-value of the Hansen test a strong evidence of instrument validity. Nevertheless, the high P-value of the Hansen test even when the number of instruments is much lower than the number of countries suggests that the GMM internal instruments are valid.

As discussed before, our dynamic panel data model could be estimated using one-step or two-step GMM estimation. It is noteworthy that while the two-step GMM estimation is efficient, it could however result in standard errors that are downward biased in small samples, especially when the number of instruments is relatively large in comparison with the cross-sectional dimension. To check the robustness of our baseline results (Table 9.1), we re-estimate (1) using the two-step GMM estimation. The corresponding results are presented in Table 9.2. The results generally confirm the robustness of main results from Table 9.1: financial inclusion promotes economic growth while financial development hinders it. The only difference between one-step and two-step results is that the impact of financial inclusion on economic growth becomes statistically insignificant in the most comprehensive specification (3) of Table 9.2. This fact is likely to have been driven by the relatively small size of our sample in comparison with the large number of instruments being used for the GMM estimation.

5. Concluding Remarks

The study is one of the few to investigate the relationship between financial inclusion and macroeconomic growth against the odds of non-availability of long-dated time-series data on indicators of financial inclusion. Unlike other studies, it is unique in that it solely focusses on Africa, a continent with the lowest financial inclusion level in the world. Despite long-dated time-series data constraints, the study finds that financial inclusion – as measured by the dimension of access – has a significantly positive effect on economic growth in Africa. The finding reinforces the need for greater efforts to pursue the financial inclusion agenda as one of the most effective tools for realizing inclusive growth.

References

Adjei, J. K., Arun, T., & Hossain, F. (2009). *The role of microfinance in asset building and poverty reduction: The case of Sinapi Aba Trust of Ghana.* Manchester: Brooks World Poverty Institute.

AfDB. (2012). *Briefing notes for AfDB long term strategy. Briefing note 5: Income inequality in Africa.*

Andersen, T. B., & Tarp, F. (2003). Financial liberalization, financial development and economic growth in LDCs. *Journal of International Development, 15*(2), 189–209.

Ashraf, N., Gine, X., & Karlan, D. (2008). *Finding missing markets (and a disturbing epilogue): Evidence from an export crop adoption and marketing intervention in Kenya.* Washington, DC: World Bank.

Ayyagari, M., Beck, T., & Hoseini, M. (2013). *Finance and poverty: Evidence from India.* Discussion Paper No. 9497. CEPR Series.

Banerjee, A., & Newman, A. F. (1993). Occupational choice and the process of development. *Journal of Political Economy, 101*(2), 274–298.

Barnes, C., Gaile, G., & Kibombo, R. (2001a). *The impact of three microfinance programs in Uganda.* Washington, DC: Development Experience Clearinghouse, USAID.

Barnes, C., Keogh, E., & Nemarundwe, N. (2001b). *Microfinance program clients and impact: An assessment of Zambuko Trust Zimbabwe.* Washington, DC: Assessing the Impact of Microenterprise Services (AIMS).

Beck, T. (2015). Cross-border banking and financial deepening: The African experience. *Journal of African Economies, 24*(Suppl. 1), i32−i45. AERC.

Beck, T., Büyükkarabacak, B., Rioja, F. K., & Valev, N. T. (2012). Who gets the credit? And does it matter? Household vs. firm lending across countries. *The B.E. Journal of Macroeconomics, 12*(1), 1−46.

Beck, T., Demirguc-Kunt, A., & Levine, R. (2007). Finance, inequality and the poor. *Journal of Economic Growth, 12*, 27−49.

Brannen, C. (2010). *An impact study of the village savings and loan association (VSLA) program in Zanzibar, Tanzania.* BA Dissertation. Wesleyan University.

Bruhn, M., & Love, I. (2014). The real impact of improved access to finance: Evidence from Mexico. *The Journal of Finance, 69*(3), 1347−1376.

Buera, F. J., Kaboski, J. P., & Shin, Y. (2012). *The macroeconomics of microfinance.* NBER Working Paper 17905. Cambridge, Massachusetts: National Bureau of Economic Research.

Burgess, R., & Pande, R. (2005). Do rural banks matter? Evidence from the Indian social banking experiment. *The American Economic Review, 95*, 780−795.

Cecchetti, S. G., & Kharroubi, E. (2012). *Reassessing the impact of finance on growth.* BIS Working Paper No. 381. Monetary and Economic Department, Bank for International Settlements.

Demirguc-Kunt, A., Klapper, L., & Singer, D. (2017). *Financial inclusion and inclusive growth: A review of recent empirical evidence.* Policy Research Paper WPS8040. Washington D. C: World Bank, Development Research Group.

Dermirguc-Kunt, A., & Levine, R. (2009). *Finance and inequality: Theory and evidence.* Washington D. C: The World Bank Policy Research Paper No. 4967.

Demirguc-Kunt, A., Klapper, L., Singer, D., & Van Oudheusden, P. (2014). *Global Findex Database 2014: Measuring Financial Inclusion around the World.* Washington D.C: World Bank.

Devarajan, S., & Fengler, W. (2013). *Africa's economic boom: Why the pessimists and the optimists are both right.* Available: http://www.foreignaffairs.com/articles/139109/shantayayan-devarajanand-wolfgang-fengler/africa-economic-boom.

Doocy, S., Teffera, S., Norell, D., & Burnham, G. (2005). Credit program outcomes: Coping capacity and nutritional status in the food insecure context of Ethiopia. *Social Science & Medicine, 60*(10), 2371−2382.

Ductor, L., & Grechyna, D. (2015). Financial development, real sector, and economic growth. *International Review of Economics & Finance, 37*, 393−405.

Dupas, P., & Robinson, J. (2008). *Savings constraints and microenterprise development: Evidence from a field experiment in Kenya (Working paper no 14693).* Cambridge, MA: National Bureau of Economic Research.

Fung, M. K. (2009). Financial development and economic growth: Convergence or divergence? *Journal of International Money and Finance, 28*, 56−67.

Gine, X., & Townsend, R. M. (2004). Evaluation of financial liberalization: A general equilibrium model with constrained occupation choice. *Journal of Development Economics, 74*, 269−307.

Goldsmith, R. (1969). *Financial structure and development.* Yale Uinversity Press.

Gubert, F., & Roubaud, F. (2005). *Analyser l'impact d'un projet de microfinance: l'exemple d'ADe'FI a` Madagascar.* Paris: DIAL (Developpement, Institutions et Analyses de Long terme).

Karlan, D., & Zinman, J. (2010). Expanding credit access: Using randomized supply decisions to estimate the impacts. *The Review of Financial Studies, 23*(1), 433−464.

Lacalle Calderon, M., Rico Garrido, S., & Duran Navarro, J. (2008). Estudio piloto de evaluacion de impacto del programa de microcreditos de Cruz Roja Espanola en Ruanda. *Revista de Economia Mundial, 19*, 83–104.

McKinnon, R. (1973). *Money and capital in economic development.* Washington D. C: Brookings Institution.

Nanor, M. A. (2008). *Microfinance and its impact on selected districts in Eastern region of Ghana. College of art and social sciences.* Kumasi: Kwame Nkrumah University of Science and Technology.

Park, C.-Y., & Mercado, R. V. (2015). *Financial inclusion, poverty, income inequality in developing asia.* Asian Development Bank Economics Working Paper 426.

Pronyk, P. M., Kim, J. C., Abramsky, T., Phetl, G., Hargreaves, J. R., Morison, L. A., et al. (2008). A combined microfinance and training intervention can reduce HIV risk behavior in young female participants. *AIDS, 22*(13), 1659–1665.

Rousseau, P., & Wachtel, P. (2011). What is happening to the impact of financial deepening on economic growth? *Economic Inquiry, 49*(1), 276–288.

Sahay, R., Cihak, M., N'Diaye, P., Barajas, A., Mitra, S., Kyobe, A., et al. (2015). *Financial inclusion: Can it meet multiple macroeconomic Goals?.* IMF Staff Discussion Note 15/17, September.

Sanyal, P. (2014). *Credit to capabilities: A sociological study of microcredit groups in India.* Cambridge: Cambridge University Press.

Shaw, E. (1973). *Financial deepening and economic development.* New York: Oxford University Press.

Shimamura, Y., & Lastarria-Cornhiel, S. (2010). Credit program participation and child schooling in rural Malawi. *World Development, 38*(4), 567–580.

Ssewamala, F. M., Ismayilova, L., McKay, M., Sperber, E., Bannon, W., & Alice, S. (2010). Gender and the effects of an economic empowerment program on attitudes toward sexual risk-taking among AIDS orphaned adolescent youth in Uganda. *Journal of Adolescent Health, 46*, 372–378.

Tita, A. F., & Aziakpono, M. J. (2017). *The effect of financial inclusion on welfare in Sub-Saharan Africa: Evidence from disaggregated data.* Working Paper No. 679. South Africa: Economic Research Southern Africa (ERSA), National Treasury.

Van Rooyen, C., Stewart, R., & de Wet, T. (2012). The impact of microfinance in Sub-Saharan Africa: A systematic review of the evidence. *World Development, 40*(11), 2249–2262.

Walle, Y. M. (2014). Revisiting the finance–growth nexus in Sub-Saharan Africa: Results from error correction-based panel cointegration tests. *African Development Review, 26*(2), 310–321.

World Bank. (2007). *Making finance work for Africa.* Washington D.C: World Bank.

World Bank. (2008). *Finance for all? Policies and pitfalls in expanding access.* World Bank Policy Report. Washington D.C: World Bank.

World Bank. (2014). *Global financial development report: Financial inclusion.* Washington D. C: The World Bank.

Wydick, B. (1999). The effect of microenterprise lending on child schooling in Guatemala. *Economic Development and Cultural Change, 47*(4), 853–869.

Further Reading

Cull, R., Ehrbeck, T., & Holle, N. (2014). *Financial inclusion and development: Recent impact evidence.* CGAP (Consultative Group to Assist the Poor). Focus Note 9/2014.

Morduch, J. (1998). *Does microfinance really help the poor? Evidence from flagship programs in Bangladesh.* Working Paper. Stanford University.

Morduch, J. (1999). The microfinance promise. *Journal of Economic Literature, XXXVII*, 1569–1614.

Pitt, M. M. (1999). *Reply to Jonathan Morduch's "does microfinance really help the poor? New evidence from flagship programs in Bangladesh.* Mimeo, Brown University.

Pitt, M. M. (2014). Response to "the impact of microcredit on the poor in Bangladesh: Revisiting the evidence". *Journal of Development Studies, 50*(4), 605–610.

Pitt, M. M., & Khandker, S. R. (1998). The impact of group-based credit programs on poor households in Bangladesh: Does the gender of participants matter? *Journal of Political Economy, 106*(9), 58–96.

Pitt, M. M., & Khandker, S. R. (2012). *Replicating replication: Due diligence in Roodman and Morduch's replication of Pitt and Khandker (1998).* Working Paper 6273. Washington D.C: World Bank.

THE RELATIONSHIP BETWEEN TECHNOLOGY AND FINANCIAL INCLUSION: CROSS-SECTIONAL EVIDENCE

Ashenafi Beyene Fanta,[1] Daniel Makina[2]

[1]University of Stellenbosch Business School, Cape Town, South Africa;
[2]Department of Finance, Risk Management and Banking, University of South Africa, Pretoria, South Africa

1. Introduction

An overwhelming body of empirical evidence shows a causal relationship between financial development and economic growth through three linkages: (1) financial deepening promotes economic growth; (2) economic growth stimulates financial development; and (3) financial development and economic growth influence each other (Beck & Levine, 2002; Demirguc-Kunt & Maksimovic, 2002; Levine, 2002; World Bank, 2007)). However,

Extending Financial Inclusion in Africa. https://doi.org/10.1016/B978-0-12-814164-9.00010-4

for there to be inclusive growth in an economy, there should be inclusive financial systems that ensure accessibility, availability and usage of formal financial services for the entire population. According to the United Nations (2006), financial inclusion encompasses two primary dimensions, viz. (1) a customer having access to a range of formal financial services, from simple credit and savings services to more complex services such as insurance and pensions; and (2) a customer having access to more than one financial services provider, which ensures a variety of competitive options.

Why is financial inclusion so important? Financial inclusion reduces poverty (Ayyagari, Beck, & Hoseini, 2013) and enables the poor to pay for their children's educations (Jacoby, 1994). Ayyagari et al. (2013) argue that the poorest of the poor can directly benefit from financial inclusion and indirectly from the structural effects of financial deepening. Explaining the role of financial inclusion on education, Jacoby (1994) reported that children from financially constrained families are more likely to withdraw early. In general, as is reported by Diniz, Birochi, and Pozzebon (2012), based on a study in a Brazilian township, financial inclusion positively contributes to socio-economic development.

Dermiguc-Kunt and Klapper (2012) have argued that without inclusive financial systems, poor people have to rely on their own limited savings to invest in their education or become entrepreneurs—and small enterprises must rely on their limited earnings to pursue promising growth opportunities. Financial inclusion allows low-income individuals to pay for education and health care and facilitates entrepreneurship by people with promising ideas but little collateral and income (Demirguc-Kunt & Levine, 2009). Also as reported by Kempson (2006) and World Bank (2008), the absence of inclusive financial systems contributes to persistent income inequality and slower economic growth. In particular, Kempson (2006) has reported that levels of income inequality, as measured by Gini coefficients, are negatively correlated with levels of financial inclusion. For instance, developing countries such as those in Africa that have high levels of income inequality have high levels of financial exclusion.

The prevalence of financial exclusion in developing countries is highlighted by Kendall, Mylenko, and Ponce (2010) who reported that despite an approximately 6.2 billion bank accounts in the world, more than one per adult, a disproportionate number of the accounts — 3.2 per adult — are located in the developed-world economies, compared with approximately 0.9 per adult in developing countries. They also estimated that while roughly 19% of developed-world adults do not have bank accounts, closer to 72% of adults in the developing world do not have accounts. In Africa, for instance, less than a quarter of adults have an account with a formal financial institution, and many adults use informal methods to save and borrow (Demirgüç-Kunt and Klapper, 2012). A key constraint cited for achieving financial inclusion that has been cited is the cost of servicing small-value customers or providing credit to those with irregular incomes.

The advent of mobile phones and their wider accessibility is believed to reduce the cost of information processing. As reported by the World Bank (2012), three-quarters of the world population have access to mobile phones. Mobile phones are also widely accessed by the poor in developing countries. In some developing countries, more people have access to a mobile phone than to clean water, a bank account or even electricity (World Bank, 2012). The wider prevalence of mobile phones in developing countries can be explained by the fact that people in those countries have no access to alternative modes of communication such as the internet and fixed-line telephones. Consequently, as argued by James (2014), it is more difficult and expensive to communicate by means other than mobile phones. This leads to the prediction that mobile phones will be most intensively used in relatively poor countries which are especially lacking in technological infrastructure such as paved roads, post offices, taxis, public phones, rail transport and so on.

The combination of IT and mobile telephony has emerged as a viable solution for greater financial inclusion because it minimises the need for setting up physical branches by banks. Increased mobile phone penetration increases financial access (Andrianaivo & Kpodar, 2012; Beck, Faye, Maimbo, & Triki, 2011; Mbiti & Weil, 2011). The combination allows servicing banks to improve efficiency through using multiple channels that work together as an inter-connected system.

This study contributes to the strand of emerging literature on the relationship between technology and financial inclusion. In the literature, we identify three studies that have attempted to elicit this relationship (Andrianaivo & Kpodar, 2012; Kendall et al., 2010; Sarma & Pais, 2008). However, our study differs in several respects. Firstly, we use two dimensions of financial inclusion — access and usage — whilst Sarma and Pais (2008) use a composite index that is amenable to criticism with respect to weights of financial inclusion measures included in the index. Secondly, Kendall et al. (2010) and Andrianaivo and Kpodar (2012) utilizes only one dimension of financial inclusion — usage. Thirdly, we expand the variables of usage of banking services by including electronic payments, whose use is a consequence of technology. Fourthly, our study utilize financial inclusion as the dependent variable while in prior studies it is an explanatory variable.

The rest of the chapter is structured as follows. Section 2 discusses key issues regarding information and communication technologies (ICT) adoption and empirical evidence on the technology–finance nexus. Section 3 describe the source of data and the methodology utilized. Section 4 presents and discusses the empirical results. Finally, Section 5 concludes.

2. Key Issues and Empirical Evidence

Though the literature gives a variety of definitions of ICT, in general the term means the use of computers, telecommunications, office systems and technologies for the collection, processing, storing and dissemination of information. Telecommunications would include devices such as fixed telephones and mobile phones, whereas office systems would include automated teller machines, electronic funds transfer systems, and software applications. Other technologies comprise the internet and mobile technology. ICT is a network technology because the more people and firms use the network, the more benefits the network generates.

While it is common knowledge that technological developments such as the internet and mobile technology foster wider access and use of financial services, very few studies have attempted to measure the relationships empirically. One reason is that the wider adoption of these technologies is recent, whereas the measurement of causal relationships requires decades of time-series data. Another reason, as pointed out by Birch and Young (1997, p. 120), is that the response of the retail financial services sector to the rapid development of new computer and communication technologies has been cautious. This has been so despite the fact that new technologies provide banks with low-cost electronic delivery channels that would enable them to become more efficient and effective. Furthermore, the new technologies have the potential to break entry barriers to the financial services market, which was once the preserve of banks.

In essence, technology has enabled branchless banking which is the delivery of financial services without using conventional bank branches but using information and communications technologies and non-bank retail agents. Key to the adoption of financial innovations are communication technologies such as the telephone and/or mobile phone, and internet penetration. The developing world, especially Africa, has lagged behind other regions with regard to the development of communication infrastructure. Fortunately, the advent of mobile phones is propelling communications in Africa. As described by Donovan (2012), mobile phones are multifunctional devices that enable a variety of communication methods ranging from ubiquitous voice and SMS channels to more sophisticated means such as software applications and web browsers.

An examination of the adoption of ICT across the regions of the world shows an interesting picture. Table 10.1 illustrates how technologies have been adopted over time; these are in respect of fixed telephone subscriptions per 100 people, mobile phone subscriptions per 100 people, ATMs per 100,000 adults and individuals using the internet as a percentage of the population.

With regard to the uptake of the fixed telephone, the biggest laggard has been sub-Saharan Africa (SSA) followed by South Asia. Across all regions, however, fixed telephone subscriptions are on the decline while mobile phone subscriptions are on the rise. The fixed telephone is slowly being replaced by mobile communication. Despite SSA having the highest increase in mobile subscriptions which rose from 1.72 subscriptions per 100 people in 2000 to 74.36 subscriptions in 2016 (an increase of 4323% over 16 years), it lags all other regions in absolute terms, with the exception of South Asia. Nevertheless, mobile phone subscriptions have exponentially increased over the last decade in all regions of the world, indicating a high appetite for mobile communication. In contrast, though automated teller machines (ATMs) were invented in the 1960s, their adoption in the provision of financial services only became marked in the 2000s. ATMs foster financial inclusion because their availability

Table 10.1 ICT and ATM Adoption.

Technology	Fixed Telephone			Mobile Subscriptions			ATMs			Internet Access		
Year	2000	2010	2016	2000	2010	2016	2000	2010	2016	2000	2010	2016
Sub-Saharan Africa	1.38	1.47	1.00	1.72	44.40	74.36	....	3.20	5.82	0.50	7.15	19.99
Latin America & Caribbean	13.98	17.70	16.66	11.66	95.51	108.32	....	29.34	41.12	3.40	34.20	55.81
South Asia	2.68	2.92	1.83	0.33	59.55	84.82	....	4.40	9.64	0.47	7.21	26.47
East Asia & Pacific	9.20	18.47	11.50	5.72	69.92	107.22	....	15.12	37.63	1.90	28.96	48.39
Middle East & North Africa	8.63	16.17	14.66	2.21	82.05	102.84	....	11.85	27.12	0.84	20.62	42.47
Europe and Central Asia	20.73	25.51	19.73	6.65	122.44	128.99	....	42.25	59.99	2.02	35.88	63.67
OECD members	50.73	43.94	37.75	45.24	101.36	118.02	....	89.48	75.25	27.88	67.62	78.59

Note: the reported figures exclude high-income countries in each region.
Source: World Development Indicators (2018).

facilitates easy access to financial services. In terms of access to ATMs, SSA is the biggest laggard followed by South Asia; the two regions happen to have the lowest levels of financial inclusion.

The internet is increasingly becoming an important channel for communication as well as for offering financial services. Individuals using the internet as a percentage of the population are on the increase in all regions of the world. SSA is again the biggest laggard, followed by South Asia. By way of facilitating financial inclusion, mobile phones are making a significant impact through enabling mobile money, which is the provision of financial services via a mobile device. The 2017 Global Findex survey estimates that globally, there are about 1.1 billion adults who have a mobile phone but unbanked; that is, about two-thirds of all unbanked adults.

Mobile money is now the leading payment platform for the digital economy in the developing world. The GSMA reports that in 2017 there were 690 million registered mobile money accounts worldwide, for which aggregate daily transactions processed averaged $1 billion. African countries are in the top in world usage, as 66% of the combined population of Kenya, Rwanda, Tanzania and Uganda are reported to be using mobile money on active basis. Table 10.2 shows the regional spread of registered mobile money customers for the period 2012–17. Noteworthy is that South Asia has overtaken SSA as the fastest-growing region in terms of new mobile money accounts, though SSA still maintains its pole position.

SSA accounts for the majority of mobile money accounts with a total of 338 million in 2017 (compared with 75 million in 2012),

Table 10.2 Regional Spread of Mobile Money Accounts 2012–17.

Year	2012	2017
Region	**% Share of 136 Million Accounts**	**% Share of 690 Million Accounts**
Sub-saharan Africa	54.9	49.1
Middle East & North Africa	24.9	6.8
East Asia & Pacific	10.4	5.3
South Asia	5.6	34.0
Latin America & Caribbean	2.7	3.1
Europe & Central Asia	1.5	1.7

Source: GSMA (2018b)

Table 10.3 Mobile Money Accounts in Sub-Saharan Africa 2012–17.

Region	2012, % Share	2017, % Share
East Africa	76.1	56.4
West Africa	16.7	30.9
Central Africa	3.6	9.7
Southern Africa	3.5	3.0

Source: GSMA (2018)

which is nearly half the caught up in mobile money adoption to significantly raise its percentage share (Table 10.3).

Globally, the number of people connected to mobile services surpassed five billion in 2017 and the GSMA estimates that by 2025, there will be five billion mobile internet users. It acknowledges that mobile internet adoption will soon become the key metric that will be used to measure the reach and value that the mobile industry is creating. Thus, mobile internet users will represent the market for e-commerce and digital solutions as well as financial technology (FinTech).

While just a few studies have attempted to directly measure the relationship between financial inclusion and technology, many have investigated the link between economic growth and technology. Studies by Norton (1992) and Alleman et al. (1994), for instance, report causal effects in both directions between GDP and telecommunications. Similarly, Quiana and Rossotto (2009) observed that a 10% increase in high-speed internet connections could lead to an increase of up to 1.3% in overall economic growth. Furthermore, a study covering Serbia, Bangladesh, Ukraine, Malaysia, Thailand and Pakistan by Deloitte and Touche (2008) reported that the contribution of mobile technology to national income amounted to between 4.5% and 6%. To underscore reverse causality, growth in GDP has in turn been found to have a positive causal effect on ICT investment and growth. For example, a study of OECD countries for the period 1985–97 observed that a 1% change in GDP produces an 8% increase in telecommunications investment (OECD, 2009).

Since economic growth has also been empirically found to cause financial development, this should in turn foster financial inclusion. A study by Andrianaivo and Kpodar (2012) investigated whether mobile phone development fostered economic growth via increased financial inclusion in African countries. Financial inclusion measures — private credit as a ratio of GDP and deposits per head — were entered as some of the explanatory variables with income per capita as the dependent variable. The results indicated that mobile phone development significantly contributes to economic growth and that the positive effect comes from increased financial inclusion.

In another similar study, Sarma and Pais (2008) investigated the relationship between financial inclusion and development. They utilized an index of financial inclusion constructed using the three dimensions of financial inclusion, viz. accessibility, availability and usage of banking services. Accessibility was measured by the number of bank accounts per 1000 population. Availability was measured by the number of bank branches and number of ATMs per 100,000 people, and the usage of banking services was measured by the volume of credit plus deposits relative to GDP. They observed a significant impact of telephone and internet variables on financial inclusion. The mobile phone variable was not factored into this study.

A number of studies have directly examined the relationship between specific technologies, mobile money in particular, and financial inclusion. The success of mobile money, M-Pesa, in East Africa in facilitating financial inclusion is a celebrated example being imitated throughout Africa and elsewhere in the developing world.

3. Empirical Strategy

Our study investigates the relationship between ICT and financial inclusion. Financial inclusion is taken as a dependent variable and is seen as a function of ICT components — telephone, mobile phone, internet and ATMs — and other control variables. The three measures of financial inclusion used are ownership of a bank account, electronic funds transfer and deposits as a percentage of GDP. The study is a cross-sectional study that accounts for insufficient time-series data regarding mobile technology and internet penetration rates as well as the Gini coefficients of countries.

3.1 Data

Data were obtained from the *World Development Indicators* database of the World Bank. Although the database contains data for

219 countries, our sample is limited to 168 countries, of which 48 are African, based on data availability. The list of countries is shown as Appendix 10.1. To avoid missing-value bias, we carried out a multiple-imputation procedure using SPSS after finding that missing values occur randomly and that they constitute only 15% of the data. As shown by Acock (2005), multiple imputation is robust over traditional missing-value approaches.

3.2 Estimation Model

The estimation model is based on that of Andrianaivo and Kpodar (2012). The difference is that our model is a cross-sectional analysis and the dependent variable is financial inclusion, whereas that of the latter is a panel data analysis, and their dependent variable is income per capita. We specify three models based on measures of financial inclusion:

$$Bankacct_i = \alpha_0 + \alpha_1 s_i + \alpha_2 dens_i + \alpha_3 mob_i + \alpha_4 tele + \alpha_5 \text{int}$$
$$+ \sum_{k=1}^{n} X_i^k + \varepsilon_i \quad \quad (10.1)$$

$$EFT_i = \alpha_0 + \alpha_1 s_i + \alpha_2 dens_i + \alpha_3 tele_i + \alpha_4 \text{int} + \sum_{k=1}^{n} X_i^k + \varepsilon_i \quad (10.2)$$

$$Dep_i = \alpha_0 + \alpha_1 s_i + \alpha_2 dens_i + \alpha_3 mob_i + \alpha_4 tele + \alpha_5 \text{int}_i + \sum_{k=1}^{n} X_i^k + \varepsilon_i$$
$$(10.3)$$

We measure financial inclusion using two dimensions, viz. accessibility and usage. *BankAcct* is a dependent variable used to measure accessibility of financial services using bank accounts per 1000 adults. *EFT* and *Dep* measure usage of financial service and represent electronic funds transfers and deposits as a percentage of GDP, respectively. Andrianaivo and Kpodar (2012) used only one dimension of usage as measured by number of deposits and loans per head. In terms of explanatory variables, *s* denotes the gross savings to GDP ratio; *dens* denotes population density; *mob* denotes mobile phone penetration rate; *tele* denotes telephone infrastructure; *int* denotes internet penetration rate; *X* is a set of other control variables such as ATM per 100,000 adults, bank branches per 100,000 adults, secondary school enrolment, inflation, and population density, and ε is the error term.

4. Empirical Results

4.1 Technology and Financial Inclusion: Preliminary Results

As shown in Table 10.4, while North America has the highest number of bank accounts per 1000 people, sub-Saharan Africa has the least. This is consistent with reports by the World Bank (2012). Lower financial inclusion may be partly explained by the fact that the region has underdeveloped financial systems. This is evident from the fact that while sub-Saharan Africa has a financial system deposits to GDP ratio of only 31.22%; the comparable figures for Asia and Latin America are 59.62% and 45.03%, respectively. The region also has the lowest internet penetration in the world, which partly explains the low level of electronic funds transfers. In contrast, Europe has the highest mobile, telephone and internet penetration among all the regions. In general, one can argue that financial inclusion and technology penetration are correlated with income because high-income economies have the highest mean value for all the parameters used to gauge financial inclusion and technology penetration.

Table 10.4 Mean Value of Selected Variables Grouped by Region.

Region	Bank Accounts per 1000 Adults	EFT	Deposit	Mobile per 100 People	Telephone Lines per 100 People	Internet per 100 People
Sub Saharan Africa	390.4	7.36	31.22	69.21	4.74	13.35
Middle East and North Africa	895.23	11.36	86.3	108.05	17.61	46.68
Asia[a]	918.03	16.46	59.62	89.49	16.45	31.02
Europe	1428.1	55.03	99.04	122.65	43.23	77.45
North America	1449.8	46.3	70.08	87.75	25.26	40.34
Latin America and the Caribbean	740.87	9.37	45.03	110.23	17.51	37.46
Middle East	608.58	2.33	34.72	100.44	13.25	44
Eastern Europe	1229.89	7.1	47.14	119.41	29.36	45.64

[a]includes Australia and Japan.

Table 10.5 Descriptive Statistics of Variables in the Dataset.

Variable	Description	Min	Max	Mean	Std. Dev
Bank accounts	Bank accounts per 1000 adults	5	3373.74	859.54	685.51
Electronic funds transfers	Electronic payments used to make payments (% of people reporting)	0.04	91.46	18.31	23.6
Deposit	Financial system deposits to GDP	0.5	325.18	55.67	47.74
Mobile	Mobile cellular subscription per 100 people	2.38	215.5	96.57	40.24
Tele line	Telephone lines per 100 people	0.02	119.41	19.12	18.89
Internet	Internet users per 100 people	0.9	94.82	37.24	28.13
Deposit interest rate	Deposit interest rate	0	20	4.73	3.77
Inflation	Inflation-consumer prices annual	−3.7	53.23	6.61	6.22
ATM	Automated teller machines (ATMs) (per 100,000 adults)	0.01	208.96	42.28	39.96
Bank branch	Bank branches per 100,000 adults	0.2	103.86	19.17	18.07
Gross savings	Gross savings to GDP	0.05	326.66	22.79	25.44
School enrolment	Gross secondary school enrolment	14.68	153.07	79.42	27.24
Pop. Density	Population density	0.5	18,630.5	320.57	1600.38

The descriptive statistics of variables (see Table 10.5) show that there is in fact some high degree of variation in most of the factors that can be explained by the high heterogeneity of countries in the sample. Variation is very high for electronic funds transfers, gross savings and population density because the standard deviation of the variables exceeds their respective means. Divergence in financial inclusion across countries is evident from the fact that bank accounts per 1000 adults ranges from a minimum of 5 to a maximum of 3373. Similarly, measures of technology penetration exhibit the same pattern. Mobile subscription ranges from a minimum of 2.38 to a maximum of 215.5. Internet users per 100 people ranges from a minimum of 0.9 to a maximum of 94.82. These high variations indicate the differences in the level of development of information technology and financial inclusion of economies in the sample of 168 countries. Ideally, the sample should have been divided into sub-samples representing, say, low-income, middle-income and high-income countries. However, this could not be done because the lack of enough available data resulted in a small-sized sample.

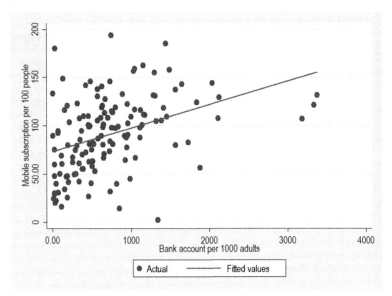

Figure 10.1 Bank accounts vs mobile subscriptions.

The most important question is whether technology penetration enhances financial inclusion. We make a preliminary examination by plotting bank accounts per 1000 adults against mobile subscriptions per 100 people. As depicted in Fig. 10.1, mobile subscriptions appear to be correlated with bank account ownership in a slightly positive manner, though a negative correlation cannot be ruled out, judging from the evident scatter across countries. Countries such as Singapore, the Netherlands and Chile, with higher bank account ownership also have a higher mobile subscription rate. Countries such as Ethiopia, Mozambique and Rwanda, with lower bank account ownership, also have lower mobile subscription rates. However, this is not a consistent trend, as countries such as Canada have higher bank account ownership rates but low mobile subscription rates. Similarly, countries such as Peru and the Russian Federation that have higher mobile subscription rates but lower bank account ownership rates. This suggests that the relationship between bank account ownership and mobile subscription may not be that strong.

As depicted in Fig. 10.2, bank account ownership is also positively related to internet usage, and the relationship is seemingly stronger than it is with mobile subscription. While countries such as Australia, Spain and Singapore, which have high bank account ownership, also have high internet penetration, while countries such as Zambia and Gabon have low internet penetration as well

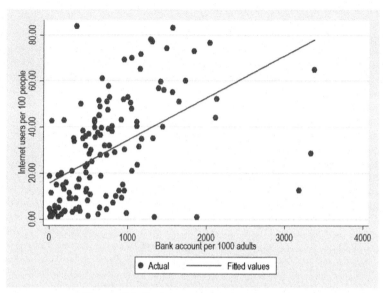

Figure 10.2 Bank accounts vs internet users.

as bank account ownership. However, the existence of countries with a high value of one variable with a lower value for the corresponding variable casts doubt on the robustness of the positive relationship between bank account ownership and internet penetration.

Bank accounts per 100 people appears positively related to telephone lines, though the relationship does not appear strong. As depicted in Fig. 10.3, countries with a higher telephone penetration, such as Australia, Spain, Japan and Singapore, have a higher bank account ratio. Those with a lower telephone penetration, such as Panama and Yemen, have a lower bank account ratio. However, the existence of countries with higher value of one variable without a commensurate value of the other cast doubt on the robustness of the relationship between telephone penetration and financial inclusion.

We also examine financial inclusion from the dimension of usage employing electronic funds transfers. As depicted in Fig. 10.4, electronic funds transfers and internet penetration have a strong positive relationship. While countries such as Switzerland, Ireland and Denmark have a higher internet penetration and higher number of people using electronic funds transfers, others such as Paraguay, Rwanda and Angola have a lower level of both electronic funds transfers and internet penetration.

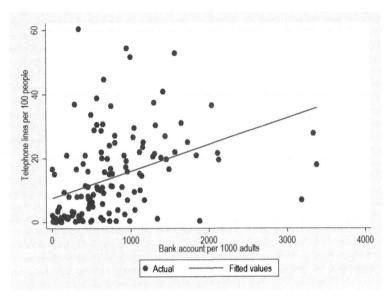

Figure 10.3 Bank accounts vs telephone lines.

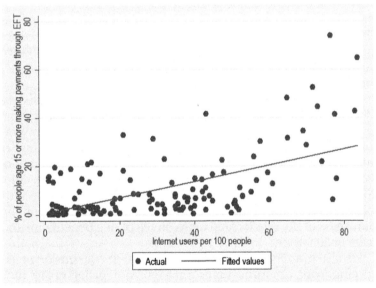

Figure 10.4 Electronic funds transfers vs internet users.

4.2 Technology and Financial Inclusion: Regression Results

The results of our cross-sectional regressions are reported in Table 10.6, and diagnostic tests of multicollinearity are reported

Table 10.6 Regression Results.

Variables	Model 1:Bank acct	Model 2: EFT	Model 3: Deposit
Mobile subscription rate	-0.145^b		0.017
Telephone line subs	-0.329^c	0.023	0.097
Internet	0.084	0.539^c	0.237^a
Bank acts		0.077	-0.092
ATM	0.678^c	0.246^c	0.064
Inflation	-0.102		-0.083
Deposit interest rate	0.092		
Gross savings	0.196^c		0.065
School enrol	0.439^c		
Pop. Density	0.149^b		0.087
Bank branches		-0.042	0.407^c
F-stat(P-value)	28.929(0.000)	49.023(0.000)	16.405(0.000)
R-squared	0.594	0.583	0.446
D-W statistic	1.984	1.834	2.144
Observations	173	173	173

[a]significant at 10%.

[b]significant at 1%.

[c]significant at 5%.

in Appendix 10.2. In the first model, both mobile subscription rate and fixed-line telephone subscription have a significant negative relationship with bank account ownership. This implies that a higher mobile and fixed-line telephone penetration corresponds to lower bank account ownership. The fact that higher mobile penetration is related to lower bank account ownership can be suggestive of the recent trend of a rapid increase in mobile penetration in developing countries compared with advanced economies. This confirms a report by the World Bank (2012) that the developing world is 'more mobile' than the developed world, possibly replacing bank accounts with mobile money accounts.

Many innovations related to mobile phones such as multi-SIM phones, low-value recharges, and mobile payments originated in developing countries and spread to the rest of the world. The internet user rate, the other measure of technology penetration, has a positive but statistically insignificant relation with bank account ownership. However other variables such as ATMs, gross savings, school enrolment and population density have a statistically significant positive relationship with bank account ownership. While inflation is seen to discourage bank account ownership, deposit interest rate encourages it, but neither have a statistically significant relationship with bank account ownership.

In the second model, where we measure financial inclusion from the dimension of usage of electronic funds transfers (EFTs), the telephone subscription rate is positive but not significant, but internet penetration has a positive and a statistically significant relationship with EFT, implying that EFT increases with increase in internet access. Furthermore, the ATM variable is positive and significant, suggesting that people use EFT in countries where there are wider ATM access which in fact corresponds to a higher internet penetration.

In the third model, the deposits-to-GDP ratio is used as a dependent variable. We find that neither mobile nor fixed-line telephone has a statistically significant relationship with deposits. However, internet penetration has a statistically significant positive relationship with deposits. We think that people's decision to keep a deposit is not related to their having either a mobile or fixed-line phone. However, a positive relationship between the internet and deposits may be because countries with a highly developed financial sector also have a higher internet penetration rate. For instance, while Switzerland has a private credit-to-GDP ratio (a measure of financial development) of 167% and internet usage-per-100 people of 85, Cameroon has a private credit-to-GDP ratio of 12.2% and internet user per 100 people ratio of 3.1.

In general, our cross-sectional analysis shows that while internet penetration seems to have a strong relationship with usage of financial services, it does not have a significant relationship with financial access (account ownership). Mobile phone and telephone lines are found to have no effect on usage of financial services, and they are negatively related to access. The 2017 Global Findex survey corroborates the increasing use of the internet to pay bills or buy goods or services online. It found that globally, 29% of adults had used the internet for digital payments in 2016. When percentage is disaggregated, 68% of adults used it in high-income countries, and only 11% of adults used it in developing countries excluding China, where 49% used it.

5. Concluding Remarks

The most significant driver of financial inclusion today is technology. Its potent effect is its ability to deliver financial services to people wherever they are and when they need them. The results of our study clearly show how the ATM and internet technologies affects financial access and usage of financial services. On the other hand, mobile and telephone subscriptions are positively related to the usage of financial services, although the relationship is not significant. Thus, overall, we observe a significant positive relationship between financial inclusion and technology. Thus, technology is seen to be fostering both access and usage of financial services.

Research on the link between technology and financial inclusion could be said to be in its infancy. This is due to several factors. First, there are limited time-series data on both financial inclusion and technology measures for rigorous analysis to be undertaken. Hence this study had to settle with a cross-sectional analysis for which it is difficult to infer causality. Second, there is a rapid development of technologies being tailored to deliver financial services, and the motives of the developers are not financial inclusion but rather for profits. Financial inclusion has arisen as a by-product of these technologies now commonly known as FinTech. Since financial technology lowers the costs of financial intermediation, it enables profitable intermediation of the unbanked poor.

References

Acock, A. C. (2005). Working with missing values. *Journal of Marriage and Family, 67*(4), 1012–1028.

Alleman, J., Hunt, C., Michaels, D., Mueller, M., Rappoport, P., & Taylor, L. (1994). *Telecommunications and economic development: Empirical evidence from Southern Africa.* Sydney, Australia: International Telecommunications Society.

Andrianaivo, M., & Kpodar, K. (2012). Mobile phones, financial inclusion, and growth. *Review of Economics and Institutions, 3*(2), 1–30.

Ayyagari, M., Beck, T., & Hoseini, M. (2013). *Finance and poverty: Evidence from India.* CEPR Discussion. Paper No. DP9497.

Beck, T., Faye, I., Maimbo, S. M., & Triki, T. (2011). *Financing Africa through the crisis and beyond.* Washington, DC: World Bank.

Beck, T., & Levine, R. (2002). Industry growth and capital allocation: Dose having a market- or bank-based system matter? *Journal of Financial Economics, 64*(2), 147–180.

Birch, D., & Young, M. A. (1997). Financial services and the Internet - what does cyberspace mean for the financial services industry? *Internet Research, 7*(2), 120–128.

Deloitte, & Touche. (2008). *Economic impact of mobile in Serbia.* Ukraine, Malaysia, Thailand, Bangladesh, and Pakistan. Report prepared for Telenor.

Demirguc-Kunt, A., & Klapper, L. (2012a). *Measuring financial inclusion: The global Findex database.* Washington, DC: World Bank. Policy Research Working Paper 6025.

Demirguc-Kunt, A., & Klapper, L. (2012b). *Financial inclusion in Africa: An overview. Policy research working Paper No. 6088*. Washington, DC: World Bank.

Demirguc-Kunt, A., & Levine, R. (2009). Finance and inequality: Theory and evidence. *Annual Review of Financial Economics, 1*, 287–318.

Demirguc-Kunt, A., & Maksimovic, V. (2002). Funding growth in bank-based and market-based financial system: Evidence from firm-level data. *Journal of Financial Economics, 65*(3), 337–363.

Diniz, E., Birochi, R., & Pozzebon, M. (2012). Triggers and barriers to financial inclusion: The use of ICT-based branchless banking in an Amazon county. *Electronic Commerce Research and Applications, 11*(5), 484–494.

Donovan, K. (2012). Mobile money for financial inclusion. In *2012 information and communications for development*. Washington, DC: World Bank.

GSMA. (2018). *The mobile economy 2018*. GSM Association. https://www.gsma.com/mobileeconomy/wp-content/uploads/2018/02/The-Mobile-Economy-Global-2018.pdf.

GSMA. (2018). *2017 state of the industry report on mobile money*. GSMA. https://www.gsma.com/mobilefordevelopment/wp-content/uploads/2018/02/GSMA_State_Industry_Report_2018_FINAL_WEBv4.pdf.

Jacoby, H. G. (1994). Borrowing constraints and progress through school: Evidence from Peru. *The Review of Economics and Statistics*, 151–160.

James, J. (2014). Patterns of mobile phone use in developing countries: Evidence from Africa. *Social Indicators Research, 119*(2), 687–704.

Kempson, E. (2006). Policy level response to financial exclusion in developed economies: Lessons for developing countries. In *Paper for access to finance: Building inclusive financial systems conference, May 30–31, 2006*. Washington, DC: World Bank.

Kendall, J., Mylenko, N., & Ponce, A. (2010). *Measuring financial access around the world*. (Washington, DC: World Bank). Policy Research Working Paper No. 5253.

Levine, R. (2002). Bank-based or market-based financial systems: Which is better? *Journal of Financial Intermediation, 11*(4), 398–428.

Mbiti, I., & Weil, D. N. (2011). *Mobile banking: The impact of M-Pesa in Kenya*. NBER. Working Paper No. 17129.

Norton, S. (1992). Transaction costs, telecommunications, and the micro-economics of macro-economic growth. *Economic Development and Cultural Change, 41*(1), 175–196.

OECD. (2009). *The role of communication infrastructure investment in economic recovery*. OECD. DSTI/CCP/CISP(2009)1/FINAL, 19 May.

Qiang, C., & Rossotto, C. (2009). Economic impacts of broadband. In World Bank (Ed.), *Information and communications for development 2009: Extending reach and increasing impact*. Washington, DC: The World Bank.

Sarma, M., & Pais, J. (2008). *Financial inclusion and development: A cross country analysis*. Indian Council for Research in International Economic Relations. Working Paper.

United Nations. (2006). *Building inclusive financial sectors for development*. New York: United Nations, 2006.

World Bank. (2007). *Making finance work for Africa*. Washington, DC: World Bank.

World Bank. (2008). *Finance for all? Policies and pitfalls in expanding access*. Washington, DC: World Bank.

World Bank. (2012). *Information and communications for development 2012: Maximizing mobile*. World Bank Publications.

Further Reading

Beck, T., Demirgüç-Kunt, A., Laeven, L., & Maksimovic, V. (2006). The determinants of financing obstacles. *Journal of International Money and Finance, 25*, 932–952.

World Bank. (2017). *The global Findex database: Measuring financial inclusion and the fintech revolution.* Washington, DC: World Bank.

Appendix 10.1 Countries Included in Sample

Afghanistan	Central African Rep	Germany	Latvia	Nigeria	St Lucia
Albania	Chad	Ghana	Lebanon	Norway	St Vincent
Algeria	Chile	Greece	Lesotho	Oman	Sudan
Angola	China	Grenada	Liberia	Pakistan	Suriname
Argentina	Colombia	Guatemala	Lithuania	Palau	Swaziland
Armenia	Comoros	Guinea	Luxembourg	Panama	Sweden
Australia	Congo, Dem Rep	Guinea-Bissau	Macedonia, FYR	Papua New Guinea	Switzerland
Austria	Congo, Rep	Haiti	Madagascar	Paraguay	Tajikistan
Azerbaijan	Costa Rica	Honduras	Malawi	Peru	Tanzania
Bahrain	Cote dIvoire	Hong Kong SAR	Malaysia	Philippines	Thailand
Bangladesh	Croatia	Hungary	Mali	Poland	Timor-Leste
Belarus	Cyprus	Iceland	Malta	Portugal	Togo
Belgium	Czech Republic	India	Mauritania	Romania	Tonga
Belize	Denmark	Indonesia	Mauritius	Russian Federation	Trinidad and Tobago
Benin	Dominica	Iran, Islamic Rep	Mexico	Rwanda	Tunisia
Bhutan	Dominican Rep	Iraq	Micronesia, Fed	Sao Tome and Principe	Turkey
Bolivia	Ecuador	Ireland	Monaco	Saudi Arabia	Uganda
Bosnia and Herz	Egypt, Arab Rep	Israel	Mongolia	Senegal	Ukraine
Botswana	El Salvador	Italy	Montenegro	Serbia	United Arab Emirates
Brazil	Equatorial Guinea	Jamaica	Morocco	Seychelles	United Kingdom
Brunei Darussal	Estonia	Japan	Mozambique	Sierra Leone	United States
Bulgaria	Ethiopia	Jordan	Myanmar	Singapore	Uruguay
Burkina Faso	Fiji	Kazakhstan	Namibia	Slovak Republic	Uzbekistan
Burundi	Finland	Kenya	Nepal	Slovenia	Vanuatu
Cambodia	France	Kiribati	Netherlands	South Africa	Venezuela, Boliv Rep
Cameroon	Gabon	Korea, Rep	New Zealand	Spain	Vietnam
Canada	Gambia	Kuwait	Nicaragua	Sri Lanka	Yemen, Rep
Cape Verde	The Georgia	Kyrgyz Republic	Niger	St Kitts	Zambia

Appendix 10.2 Collinearity Results

Variables	Model 1: Bank Account		Model 2: EFT		Model 3: Deposit	
	Tolerance	VIF	Tolerance	VIF	Tolerance	VIF
Mobile Subscription	0.525	1.904			0.58	1.725
Telephone Line Subscription	0.194	5.16	0.318	3.143	0.199	5.017
Deposit Interest Rate	0.607	1.647				
Internet	0.174	5.736	0.267	3.74	0.194	5.143
Inflation	0.604	1.656			0.831	1.204
Bank Acts			0.495	2.022	0.444	2.251
ATM	0.504	1.986	0.323	3.092	0.297	3.368
Gross Savings	0.933	1.071			0.895	1.117
School Enrolment	0.28	3.569				
Population Density	0.621	1.612			0.593	1.686
Bank Branches			0.564	1.772	0.539	1.855

11

UNINTENDED CONSEQUENCES OF FINANCIAL INCLUSION

Ashenafi Beyene Fanta,[1] Daniel Makina[2]

[1]University of Stellenbosch Business School, Cape Town, South Africa;
[2]Department of Finance, Risk Management and Banking, University of South Africa, Pretoria, South Africa

1. Introduction

It is now a generally accepted axiom that in order to achieve inclusive development, there should be inclusive financial systems that ensure accessibility, availability and usage of formal financial services by the entire population. In other words, financial inclusion is considered one of every country's strategies for spreading opportunity and fighting poverty. Having the poverty dimension

Extending Financial Inclusion in Africa. https://doi.org/10.1016/B978-0-12-814164-9.00011-6

in mind, Ramji (2009) defined financial inclusion as the timely delivery of financial services to disadvantaged sections of society. The corollary – financial exclusion – would mean the inability of the disadvantaged to access financial services. Ramji (2009: 6) goes on to list a range of price and non-price barriers to financial inclusion as 'geography (limiting physical access), regulations (lack of formal identification proof or of appropriate products for poor households), psychology (fear of financial institution's staff, structures, complicated financial products, etc.), information (lack of knowledge regarding products and procedures), and low financial acumen (low income and poor financial discipline), among others'.

In the absence of inclusive financial systems, poor and marginalized segments of the population must rely on only their own limited savings to invest in their education, while small enterprises have to rely on their limited earnings to pursue growth opportunities (Dermiguc-Kunt and Klapper, 2012). The World Bank (2008) and Kempson (2006) have reported that the absence of inclusive financial systems contributes to persistent income inequality and slower economic growth. Levels of income inequality, as measured by Gini coefficients, have been reported to be negatively correlated with levels of financial inclusion. For instance, Scandinavian countries such as Denmark and Sweden, which have low levels of inequality, also show very high levels of financial inclusion, whereas mid-level Gini coefficient countries such as the UK and the USA show moderately high financial inclusion levels. On the contrary, developing countries such as those in Africa that have high levels of income inequality exhibit low levels of financial inclusion.

Cognizant of the critical role played by inclusive financial systems, the G20 world leaders at their Pittsburgh Summit in 2009 committed to improve access to financial services for the poor by creating a Financial Inclusion Experts Group (FIEG) whose mandate was to facilitate strategies to expand access to finance to households as well as micro and small- and medium-sized enterprises. The group developed nine principles for innovative financial inclusion reflecting the experiences and lessons learned from policymakers worldwide. The nine principles, namely leadership, diversity, innovation, protection, empowerment, cooperation, knowledge, proportionality and framework were endorsed during the G20's Toronto Summit in June 2010. They formed the basis of the Financial Inclusion Action Plan endorsed by the subsequent summit in Korea in November 2010. This G20's Korean Summit in November 2010 created the Global Partnership for Financial Inclusion as an instrument to execute its commitment.

Before the efforts of the G20, the United Nations (UN) had long recognized the role that financial inclusion played in poverty reduction when 147 countries adopted Millennium Development Goals (MDGs) in 2000, set to be achieved by 2015. These MDGs have since been superseded by 17 Sustainable Development Goals (SDGs) adopted in September 2015. None of the UN's new 17 SDGs explicitly focus on financial inclusion as a stand-alone goal. However, SDG 10 – promoting economic inclusion – implicitly embraces financial inclusion. In addition, SDG 8, which focuses on promoting shared economic growth, includes sub-goal 8.10, with a specific financial inclusion target. This sub-goal states: 'Strengthen the capacity of domestic financial institutions to encourage and expand access to banking, insurance and financial services for all'. It further provides two indicators of financial inclusion – (1) number of commercial bank branches and automated teller machines (ATMs) per 100,000 adults, and (2) proportion of adults (15 years and older) with an account at a bank or other financial institution or with a mobile money service provider. Thus, at both national and global levels there continue to be concerted efforts to break the barriers to financial inclusion.

In this chapter we hypothesize that breaking some barriers, particularly access to credit, may have unintended consequences contrary to the virtues espoused of financial inclusion. We investigate this phenomenon using a sample of selected African countries for which data are available from FinScope consumer surveys.

FinMark Trust, which conducted FinScope[1] consumer surveys on some African countries, gives a trend of increasing financial inclusion as shown in Table 11.1.

It is evident that the majority of countries have had a remarkable increase in financial inclusion over the years. The research question therefore is whether this increase in financial inclusion has always been beneficial as envisaged by both theory and stakeholders. Thus, the chapter sets out to investigate the hypothesis that access to credit by households can have the unintended effects of causing over-indebtedness and poverty among households. In particular, it examines factors affecting indebtedness and over-indebtedness, and assesses the link between over-indebtedness and poverty.

---

[1]The FinScope survey tool developed by FinMark Trust of South Africa is a nationally representative survey of consumer perceptions about financial services and issues that provides insights into how people source their income and manage their financial lives.

Table 11.1 Trends of Financial Inclusion in Selected African Countries.

Country & Year of Earliest and Latest FinScope Survey	% Adult Population Banked		% with Non-formal Products		% Financially Excluded	
	First FinScope Survey	Latest FinScope Survey	First FinScope Survey	Latest FinScope Survey	First FinScope Survey	Latest FinScope Survey
Botswana (2009 and 2014)	41	50	7	8	31	24
Ghana (2010 and 2015)	41	58[a]	15	17	44	25
Kenya (2006 and 2016)	27	75	32	7	41	17
Malawi (2008 and 2014)	26	34	19	15	55	51
Mozambique (2009 and 2014)	13	24	9	16	78	60
Rwanda (2008 and 2016)	21	68	26	21	52	11
South Africa (2003 and 2016)	50	88	4	3	50	11
Swaziland (2011 and 2014)	50	64	13	9	37	27
Tanzania (2009 and 2013)	16	65	29	7	55	28
Uganda (2009 and 2013)	28	54	42	31	30	15
Zambia (2009 and 2015)	23	38	14	21	63	41
Zimbabwe (2011 and 2014)	38	69	22	8	40	23

[a]Financial Inclusion Insight(FII) survey.

The rest of the chapter is structured as follows. Section 2 reviews both theoretical and empirical literature on the subject matter. Section 3 discusses case studies of observed unintended consequences of financial inclusion. Section 4 describes the research methodology employed to investigate the phenomenon using a sample of selected African countries. Section 5 presents and discusses the empirical results. Finally, Section 6 concludes and offers policy implications.

2. Literature Review

According to the life cycle theory of consumption as propagated by Modigliani and Brumberg (1954) and the permanent income hypothesis of Friedman (1957), access to credit enables households to smooth their consumption over their lifetimes. The life cycle theory states that people make rational choices about how much they would like to spend at each stage of their lives, which decision is only limited by the resources available over their lifespan. As they earn income, people tailor their consumption patterns to their needs at different ages, and such decisions are made independently of their incomes at each age. Similarly, the permanent income hypothesis stipulates that individuals base their consumption and savings decisions not on their current income, but on the total expected stream of future income from various sources (employment, business, investments, inheritances, etc) during their lifespan.

In essence, the life cycle and permanent income theories treat current and future consumption as a function of expected future income and current income. These theories are based on the notion that people's consumption in the current period would be higher if they expect to receive higher income in the future. On the converse, their consumption in the current period is reduced, and their saving increased, if their future income is expected to decline. In addition to the theories' emphasis on demographic trends and consumption smoothing, a basic feature is that an individual can borrow and lend in order to have relatively stable consumption as income fluctuates over the lifespan. When income is low early in life, an individual can borrow because of the prospects of higher income in the future. Thus, low income may not constrain consumption because financial intermediation ensures there is no shortage of funds. Theories assume that liquidity constraints do not exist (hypothetical world), so that everybody can borrow or lend at the interest rate set by equilibrium in the credit market.

However, in the real world there are liquidity constraints that restrict borrowing. Individuals may not be able to borrow when their current income is low compared with their expected future income. Though there may be many financial institutions in an economy, they are likely to compete on lending to the same creditworthy customers because of asymmetric information and transaction costs. As a result, low-income and unemployed people would not gain access to credit in the formal sector at all. Therefore, because there are constraints on individuals' abilities to borrow, their consumption and saving behaviours are affected. In other words, in an economy, some segments of the population face barriers to accessing credit. Such segments of the population are in abundance in Africa, where the ratio of private credit to GDP averages about 24%, the lowest in the world.

Yet in modern society, credit plays a critical role in consumption smoothing and in maintaining a desired lifestyle even when earnings fall short of expenditures. Credit allows people to respond to unexpected events such as illness, job loss, and emergencies; it enables individuals and firms to finance start-ups and existing businesses, and it allows individuals to finance their education and skills development (De Gregorio & Kim, 2000; Hodson, Dwyer, & Neilson, 2014; Kilborn, 2005). In general, expansion of credit fuels household consumption and hence drives economic growth.

In recent years, rising financial inclusion and what Kus (2015) terms 'democratization of credit' and a 'culture of consumption' hav led to easier access to credit in many countries across the globe. This in turn has led to significant indebtedness and some stress when people are unable to service their debt. In OECD countries, household debt as a proportion of disposable income has been on an upward trend since the mid-1990s as a result of falling interest rates and innovations in mortgage markets (Andre, 2016).

Increased availability of credit coupled with pressure to spend on consumer goods is responsible for over-indebtedness, which has become a serious concern in many countries. The term over-indebtedness has various definitions. According to the European Union (EU) (2013), households are considered over-indebted if they are having − on an on-going basis − difficulties meeting (or falling behind with) their commitments, whether these relate to servicing secured or unsecured borrowing or payment of rent, utilities or other household bills. The *Report to the UK Department for Business* compiled by Disney, Bridges, and Gathergood (2008) classifies individuals as over-indebted if they are spending more than 25% of their gross monthly income on unsecured repayments; more than 50% of their gross monthly income on total borrowing repayments; have four or more credit commitments; are in arrears on a credit commitment for more than 3 months; and declare their household's borrowing repayments to be a 'heavy burden'. However, subjectivity in determining the cut-off point makes the definition less amenable to wider adoption in research. A practical definition is one from the Bank of Italy's occasional paper by d'Alessio and Iezzi (2013) which uses the debt−poverty indicator. According to this definition, a household is over-indebted if its total borrowing repayments bring its income below the poverty line.

In this chapter the definition of indebtedness is guided by available data. The questionnaire that elicited the data we utilize considers a person to be over-indebted if the person is borrowing to repay another debt, or does not want to borrow or had a loan application turned down because of too much debt, or had debt restructured, or defaulted on a debt obligation, or has a garnishee or emolument order, or has been garnished.

There are many causes of over-indebtedness, and the literature broadly classify them into four categories, viz. behavioural factors, occurrence of risky events, supply-side factors and demographic factors. Behavioural sciences attribute over-indebtedness to 'impulsivity' and 'overconfidence bias'. As Anderloni, Bacchiocchi, and Vandone (2012: 294) aptly puts it: 'over-indebtedness is likely to happen to impulsive individuals, who may adopt impatient, short-sighted behaviour patterns which make it difficult for them to be fully aware of the consequences of their financial and spending decisions'. On the other hand, Kilborn (2005) reports that individuals may exhibit 'overconfidence bias', in which they tend to be overly optimistic about their susceptibility to problems of over-indebtedness, which overconfidence is aggravated by an 'illusion of control' that results in individuals overestimating their ability to avoid negative events. Anderloni and Vandone (2010) have observed that such behaviour leads to the decision to purchase, using debt if necessary, regardless of the effect this choice may have on the sustainability of future debt levels.

Over-indebtedness has also been observed to increase emotional distress, deterioration of general health including mental health and higher divorce rate (see for detailed discussions by Angel (2016); Bridges and Disney (2016); Cuesta (2015); Gathergood (2012); Shen, Sam, and Jones (2014); Sweet et al. (2013); among others). Wang (2010) further reports that over-indebtedness decreases self-esteem and social relationships. One shocking observation by McIntyre and Lacombe (2012) is that it explained the observed pattern of robberies and thefts in Ireland. Furthermore, over-indebtedness has been reported to be one of the factors that creates and sustains poverty, particularly among the low-income population, old-age households and single-parent households with young children (d'Alessio & Iezzi, 2013; Betti et al., 2007).

Risky events have the potential to cause over-indebtedness. Such events include loss of employment (including the failure of a business), marital breakdown, an unforeseen expense such as expensive medical care, economic downturns that erode an individual's income, and poor financial management by households that modify the initial conditions in the contract between creditor and debtor (Disney et al., 2008; Hodson et al., 2014; Keese, 2009).

Supply-side factors can also contribute to over-indebtedness of individuals. Kilborn (2005) has reported that intense competitive pressures are forcing lenders to advertise and structure their products in a manner that would take advantage of the psychological biases and weaknesses of their customers. In support of this observation, Ironfield et al. (2005) reported that the financial services industry in the UK is partly to blame for over-indebtedness. Similarly, in South Africa Hurwitz and Luiz (2007) attribute the increased household debt burden to a political and legislative stance that encouraged wider access to the formal financial sector.

Demographic factors such as age, gender, number of independents, work status, marital status (Aristei & Gallo, 2016; Du Caju, Rycx, & Tojerow, 2016; Ottaviani & Vandone, 2011; Schicks, 2014; Worthington, 2006), illness or disability (Patel, Balmer, & Pleasence, 2012), and financial literacy (Gathergood, 2012; Lusardi & Tufano, 2015; French & McKillop, 2016; Ironfield-Smith, Keasey, Summers, Duxbury, & Hudson, 2005) are important factors explaining over-indebtedness. Over-indebtedness can also be caused by the cross-borrowing that happens when one lender fails to satisfy the borrower's needs (Haile, Osman, Shuib, & Oon, 2015). In addition, Brunetti, Giarda, and Torricelli (2015) reported that homeownership increases the likelihood of over-indebtedness.

Some scholars have observed that macroeconomic variables such as changes in interest rates, general inflation and house price increases are likely to lead to over-indebtedness (Kim, Lee, Son, & Son, 2014; Meng, Hoang, & Siriwardana, 2013; Miango et al., 2013). Over-indebtedness is observed to hamper consumption over business cycles and amplify recessions (Kukk, 2016). It also leads to increase in non-performing loans and weakens bank balance sheets, which may cause a credit crunch. The EU (2013) has reported that household over-indebtedness adversely affects the overall health of the economy by curtailing aggregate demand, employment and growth.

The multifaceted causes and consequences of over-indebtedness justify studies that would guide formulation of policy. However, studies on over-indebtedness in Africa are scant. In the literature, we could only identify one exploratory study by Fanta et al. (2017), which examined the phenomenon on 11 Southern African countries.

3. Case Studies of Adverse Effects of Financial Inclusion

Although the ultimate objective of extending access to financial services is to enable individuals to get value by managing their

Box 11.1 The Curse of Owning a Bank Account Where There is no Bank Branch: A Mozambican Teachers Story.

Fatima Cugala is a teacher working at a school a few hours by bus north of Maputo, Mozambique. For most of her working career, Fatima received her salary in cash at the school, but in 2011 the government introduced an initiative to pay salaries directly into bank accounts and opened accounts for all teachers on their payroll. A few days before payday Fatima now takes leave from school to make the bus trip to the northernmost part of Maputo to the bank branch where she is a customer. When she arrives at the bank she waits in a long queue, and by the time she gets to the ATM, typically the system is down. Usually she must wait until the next day to try again. On the next day, if she arrives at the ATM early, she is usually able to withdraw her money. She then starts the trip home where she plans to save the cash that she has withdrawn in the community Xitique (an informal savings group). Fatima repeats the same trip every month, receiving one deposit into her account and making one withdrawal to access her income. The time away from school means that valuable tuition time is lost. While Fatima is now considered a `banked' adult, and thus `financially included', the additional costs incurred to use her bank account outweigh the value she derives from it and she uses it only when she must.

Source: UNCDF. (2016) Lost in the mail: Why bank account access is not translating into usage. http://www.uncdf.org/sites/default/files//Documents/insight_note_04.pdf

financial resources more efficiently, this is often overlooked in some cases due to a drive for increases in account ownership. Increasing account ownership per se does not bring the intended benefit, and it may instead lead to loss of value as illustrated in Box 11.1. Similarly, unfettered access to credit may contribute to accumulation of debt by households and a loss of welfare.

The collapse of the mortgage market in the US that triggered the 2007/8 global financial crisis was a consequence of extending mortgage loans to sub-prime borrowers – individuals with a questionable financial capability to service their debt (Acharya & Richardson, 2009). Sub-prime mortgages were close to USD 15 billion in 2000, but massive expansion of credit fuelled by securitization of sub-prime mortgages led to a significant hike in sub-prime mortgages to USD150 billion in 2006, just before the financial crisis (ibid). The crisis led to a loss of value by all market participants including borrowers, mortgage originating banks and investors in mortgage-backed securities. The lesson that emerged after the financial crisis is consistent with our argument that financial inclusion may at times lead to unintended consequences.

With regard to the impact of microfinance, there are divergent opinions regarding the contribution of microcredit. A study by Buera, Kaboski, and Shin (2012) have come up with results which show that broader access to microcredit is simply redistributive, with a small gain in per capita income. The reason given is that increases in total factor productivity are counter-balanced by the lower capital accumulation resulting from the distribution of income from high savers to low savers while raising some risks for financial stability. Similarly, Sahay et al. (2015) observed that unchecked broadening of access to financial services can result in financial instability. The World Bank (2014) observes that the redistribution of credit towards new borrower segments may lead to losses in the efficiency of financial intermediation due to higher screening and information costs and the change in the risk profile of bank lending as banks make loans to new borrowers who are on average riskier and poorer clients.

4. Research Methodology

4.1 Data

Data for the study were obtained from nationally representative FinScope consumer surveys conducted in different years in 15 African countries listed in Table 11.2. Although FinScope survey data were available for 23 African countries, we only found valid data for our analysis only for the 15 countries.

4.2 Estimation Model

We use a logistic regression technique. Logistic regression enables us to predict a discrete outcome from a set of variables that may be continuous, dichotomous or a mix of these. Logistic regression is best suited for handling dichotomous outcomes (Cabrera, 1994; Cox and Snell, 1989). We use two sets of models, where the first model determines factors affecting over-indebtedness. The second model examines the relationship between poverty and over-indebtedness. The dependent variable in each model is binary and hence a binary logistic regression model.

The dependent variable for each model can take the value 1 with a probability for each variable, q, or otherwise zero (1-q), while the predictors or independent variables can take any form. No assumption about the distribution of the independent variables is made and hence they need not be normally distributed or linearly related to the dependent variable or of equal

Table 11.2 Sample Size and Year Survey Was Conducted.

No	Country	Year of Survey	Sample Size
1	Botswana	2014	1503
2	Burkina Faso	2016	5066
3	DRC	2014	5000
4	Lesotho	2011	2000
5	Madagascar	2016	5040
6	Malawi	2014	3005
7	Mauritius	2014	4000
8	Mozambique	2014	3905
9	Namibia	2011	1200
10	Rwanda	2016	12,480
11	South Africa	2015	5000
12	Swaziland	2014	3440
13	Tanzania	2013	7987
14	Zambia	2015	8479
15	Zimbabwe	2014	4000
	Total		72,105

variance within each other. Because the relationship between the dependent and independent variables is not a linear function, the logistic regression function that is utilized is the logit transformation of q represented as follows:

$$\theta = \frac{e^{(\alpha + \beta_1 x_1 + \beta_2 x_2 + \ldots + \beta_i x_i)}}{1 + e^{(\alpha + \beta_1 x_1 + \beta_2 x_2 + \ldots + \beta_i x_i)}} \qquad (11.1)$$

where a = the constant of the equation and, b = the coefficient of the predictor variables entered into the model, viz: β1 … βn for coefficients of predictor variables.

The alternative form of the logistic regression equation which is estimated is as follows:

$$\text{logit}[\theta(\text{x})] = \log\left[\frac{\theta(x)}{1 - \theta(x)}\right] = \alpha + \beta_1 x_1 + \beta_2 x_2 + \ldots + \beta_i x_i \quad (11.2)$$

For the first model: Y (1, 0) = α + β1 credit literacy + β2 home-ownership + β3 household size + β4 age + β5 marital status + β6 gender + β7 level of education + β8 employment status + β9 income level $+ \beta 10$ location$+ \beta 11$ no. of institutions $+ \beta 12$ institution, where Y represents the probability of over-indebtedness, with one representing a person who is over-indebted and 0 otherwise.

The second model: Y $(1, 0) = \alpha + \beta 1$ credit literacy$+\beta 2$ home-ownership$+ \beta 3$ household size $+ \beta 4$ age $+ \beta 5$ marital status $+ \beta 6$ gender $+ \beta 7$ level of education $+ \beta 8$ employment status $+ \beta 9$ income level $+ \beta 10$ location$+ \beta 11$ no. of institutions $+ \beta 12$ institution$+ \beta 13$ over-indebtedness, where Y represents the probability of poverty (as measured by going without food due to lack of money), with one representing a person who has gone without food and 0 otherwise.

5. Results and Discussion

The results are presented in two parts where the results of descriptive analysis are presented first, followed by results of the binary logistic regression analysis.

5.1 Descriptive Analysis

The first sub-section of the descriptive analysis comprises cross-country comparisons of over-indebtedness as well as cross-borrowing patterns across the countries. The second sub-section focuses on description of variables used in the study using mean comparisons.

5.1.1 Cross-Country Comparison

The cross-country comparison of over-indebtedness shows variations across countries. South Africa and Tanzania are at the top of the over-indebtedness ranking with nearly a third of adults reporting that they experienced over-indebtedness, while Mauritius and DRC are at the bottom with only 1% or less reporting being over-indebted (see Fig. 11.1). Given that 45% of adults borrow from the formal market, the over-indebtedness in South Africa might be related to conduct of the formal credit market that can be tackled through regulation. In contrast, the over-indebtedness problem in Tanzania is related to informal market activity that is not amenable to regulatory intervention. It can in fact be addressed through credit literacy.

Mozambique, Botswana, Mauritius and DRC exhibit lower levels of over-indebtedness than the rest of the countries in the region. However, the low level of over-indebtedness might be due to varying reasons. For instance, the low levels of over-

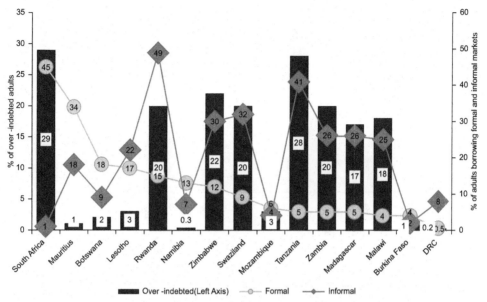

Figure 11.1 Source of credit and over-indebtedness.

indebtedness in Mozambique and DRC may be due to lower credit penetration (both countries have the lowest credit penetration record in the region), while prudent market conduct might explain the trend in Botswana and Mauritius (both have a high level of formal credit usage). In general, the comparison shows that over-indebtedness is not necessarily linked to either formal or informal credit.

Over-indebtedness might also be caused by a person's ability to access credit from multiple sources. As a result, we grouped adults into three categories. The first group comprises those who borrowed either from a bank, non-bank formal institution or informal institution. The second group comprises individuals who borrowed from two sources (for instance, bank and non-bank formal institution or bank and informal or non-bank formal institution and informal institution). The third group comprises those who access credit from all three sources simultaneously.

As shown in Fig. 11.2, cross-country variation is evident in the number of institutions used to access credit. The countries can be fairly grouped into two categories. The first category comprises countries where adults accessed credit from two types of institutions. The second includes countries in which adults sourced credit from three types of institutions. While DRC, Mozambique and Madagascar are in the first category, the rest are in the second

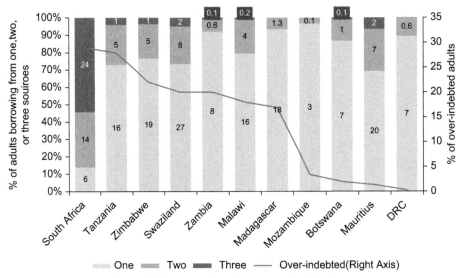

Figure 11.2 Source of credit and over-indebtedness.

category. South Africa stands out as an outlier among the countries wherein adults accessed credit from three types of institutions because a quarter of adults in the country reported to have accessed credit from three sources simultaneously. This actually confirms our statement in the earlier section that in South Africa credit is easy to come by. Furthermore, one can observe that competition in the credit market may not be confined within firms in the same institutional category but across institutions – i.e. across banks as well as other formal and informal lenders.

To get insights on factors that are likely to affect over-indebtedness, a comparison of mean values of variables is made based on whether an individual is over-indebted. Disparity between the two groups is analysed using either an independent sample t-test or Cramer's V test. The t-test is employed to test statistical significance of mean values of continuous variables and a Cramer's V test is used to test the significance of nominal variables.

As reported in Tables 11.3 and 11.4, the incidence of over-indebtedness is related to increased tendency to access credit from multiple sources and is observed among individuals with a higher level of credit literacy. Interestingly, over-indebtedness is observed for both formal and informal credit, suggesting that both formal and informal markets are to blame for accumulation of debt. The other interesting observation is a higher incidence of

Table 11.3 Variables With Descriptive Statistics.

Variable Name	Description	Over-Indebted		Mean Difference	Test of Significance
		Yes	No		
Institutions	Number of institutions(formal and or informal) from which credit was obtained	0.63	0.4	0.223***	T-test
Credit literate	A person chooses a lender using at least two criterion (%)	0.3	0.23	0.061***	Cramers V
Gone without food	A person gone without food due to lack of money (%)	27	25	0.021***	
Household size	Number of people living in the household	4.5	5	−0.627***	T-test
Own home	A person owns a residential property (%)	0.27	0.22	0.055***	Cramers V
Formal credit	A person obtained credit from a bank (%)	0.3	0.24	0.053***	
Informal credit	A person obtained credit from an informal lender (%)	0.38	0.24	0.081***	
Age	Age of respondent	37	40	−3.168***	T-test
Gender(Male = 1)	Respondents gender	0.48	0.48	0.003***	Cramers V
Low income	A person has low monthly income (%)	0.63	0.69	−0.06***	
Middle income	A person has medium monthly income (%)	0.25	0.21	0.04***	
High income	A person has high monthly income (%)	0.11	0.10	0.01***	
Employed	A person is employed (%)	0.36	0.32	0.04***	
Urban	A person lives in urban area (%)	0.45	0.38	0.07***	
No education	A person has no education (%)	0.09	0.15	−0.06***	
Primary	A person has primary education (%)	0.35	0.31	0.04***	
Secondary	A person has secondary education	0.48	0.46	0.02***	
Post-secondary	A person has post-secondary education	0.08	0.08	0.004***	

Note: ***significant at 1% level.

Table 11.4 Logistic Regression Output: Determinants of Over-indebtedness.

	South Africa	Botswana	DRC	Malawi	Mauritius	Mozambique	Swaziland	Tanzania	Zambia	Zimbabwe	Madagascar	Namibia	Lesotho	Rwanda	Burkina Faso
Credit literate	0.040***	0.41***	−0.224***	1.13***	17.06	−0.463***	−0.209***	0.004*	−0.202***	0.041***	−0.473***	−0.599***	–	−0.262***	0.440***
No of institutions	0.087***	3.182***	−14.111	0.856***	0.024	1.374***	0.625***	0.045***	−0.066***	1.578***	0.819***	2.810***	0.514***	0.651***	2.224***
Formal credit	0.024***	−1.905***	−11.058	−1.013***	0.913***	0.356***	0.243***	−0.203***	0.351***	−0.599***	−0.182***	7.266***	−0.266***	−0.149***	−2.995***
Informal credit	0.377***	1.398***	−13.615	−0.167***	−16.521	−17.985	0.325***	−0.308***	−0.110***	−0.121***	−0.213***	4.524***	−1.279***	0.157***	−18.286
Own home	0.031***	−0.115***	−0.711***	0.379***	0.464***	0.167***	0.053***	−0.153***	−0.211***	−0.161***	0.349***	−4.655***	0.230***	−0.056***	0.200***
Household size	−0.050***		0.231***	–	−0.022	0.008***	−0.096***	−0.009***	−0.012***	−0.020***	−0.005***	−0.089***	−0.129***	−0.034***	0.016***
Age of respondent	−0.008***	0.020***	0.036***	−0.002***	−0.057***	0.000***	−0.009***	−0.001***	0.016***	0.001***	−0.009***	0.259***	−0.037***	−0.001***	−0.012***
Respondent gender	0.126***	−0.125***	0.284***	0.270***	−1.095***	−0.226***	−0.005	0.429***	−0.292***	0.180***	0.066***	−3.504***	0.037***	−0.078***	−0.078***
Personal monthly income (=low income)	Ref	Ref	Ref	Ref	Ref	Ref	Ref	Ref	Ref	Ref	Ref	Ref	Ref	Ref	Ref
Personal monthly income (=middle income)	0.190***	19.586	15.655	−0.689***	0.963***	−0.395***	0.086***	−0.287***	−0.007	−0.309***	−0.036***	17.372	0.605***	0.354***	−1.240***
Personal monthly income (=high income)	0.268***	18.992	0.038	−0.219***	0.005	−0.182***	0.216***	−0.099***	−0.096***	−0.322***	−0.157***	15.119	0.641***	0.706***	−17.464
Marital status (=Widowed)	Ref	Ref	Ref	–	Ref	Ref	Ref	Ref	Ref	Ref	Ref	Ref	Ref	Ref	Ref
Marital status (=Divorced)	0.017***	−16.896	−14.953	–	−13.909	−0.218***	0.375***	0.072***	−0.634***	−0.211***	−0.377***	18.880	0.076***	0.323***	−15.917
Marital status (=Married)	0.149***	−17.499	−2.519***	–	2.240***	−0.503***	0.482***	−0.474***	−0.478***	−0.056***	−0.176***	4.549	−1.867***	0.184***	−16.430
Marital status (=Single)	−0.037***	−0.158***	−0.338***	–	1.010***	−0.037***	0.311***	0.073***	−0.354***	−0.048***	−0.145***	15.735	−0.238***	0.174***	0.243***
Level of education (=No education)	Ref	Ref	Ref	Ref	Ref	Ref	Ref	Ref	Ref	Ref	Ref	Ref	Ref	Ref	Ref
Level of education (=Primary schooling1)	0.399***	−15.482	−15.568	0.916***	−16.884	0.386***	0.300***	0.302***	0.082***	−0.545***	0.037***	−22.318	−0.620***	0.024***	0.951***

Level of education (=Secondary schooling2)	0.067***	1.475***	−3.252***	0.751***	−1.160***	0.366***	0.480***	0.017***	−0.239***	0.073***	0.034***	−7.094***	−0.245***	−0.083***	0.071***
Level of education (=post secondary schooling)	0.051***	1.476***	−1.481***	1.023***	−1.363***	0.617***	0.192***	−0.009**	0.018***	−0.090***	−0.457***	−4.390***	−0.061***	0.076***	0.388***
Employment status (=Unemployed)	Ref	Ref	Ref	Ref	Ref	Ref	Ref	Ref	Ref	Ref	Ref	Ref	Ref	Ref	Ref
Employment status (=Employed)	0.270***	17.06	−0.285***	−1.883***	1.045***	−0.835***	−0.377***	1.194***	19.817	−0.156***	0.059***	−12.277	−1.163***	−0.606***	16.187
Employment status (=Retired)	0.410***	16.4	—	−2.452***	−0.127*	−0.258***	−0.594***	1.117***	19.681	−0.522***	−0.221***	−3.573***	−2.118***	−0.398***	16.005
Place of residence (=Urban)	−0.357***	0.903***	1.439***	−0.090***	−17.540	−0.375***	0.200***	0.214***	−0.386***	0.161***	0.126***	0.524***	18.616	−0.217***	1.381***
−2 log likelihood	43,213,968	107,390	368,285	5,078,230	24,032	3,438,362	406,587	8,235,125	2,350,574	3,586,560	7,499,382	13,588	199,385	1,793,175	572,539
Cox & Snell R square	0.017	0.036	0.007	0.070	0.04	0.011	0.068	0.026	0.027	0.139	0.032	0.028	0.094	0.043	0.005
Nagelkerke R square	0.024	0.242	0.235	0.114	0.278	0.042	0.105	0.035	0.042	0.215	0.053	0.699	0.387	0.068	0.068

Note: ***significant at 1% level.

over-indebtedness among urbanites, which might be due to a higher level of financial inclusion in urban areas across all countries in the study. However, it should be noted that mean comparisons can only provide a rough picture of how over-indebtedness is related to different variables at a sub-national level; otherwise it is difficult to draw a valid conclusion, because the analysis is done using aggregated data. Important variations across countries are not revealed at this stage. A more valid conclusion can be drawn only from a more robust analysis that involves a binary logistic regression.

5.2 Econometric Results

5.2.1 Drivers of Over-Indebtedness

Over-indebtedness can be triggered by a combination of supply-side factors, personal characteristics and risk factors. However, our analysis in this section focuses on personal characteristics of adults such as credit literacy, number of institutions from which credit is obtained, source of credit, homeownership and socio-demographic characteristics. As reported in Table 11.5, credit literacy is negatively related to over-indebtedness in most countries, implying that credit-literate individuals are less likely to be over-indebted. However, credit-literate individuals in South Africa, Botswana, Tanzania and Zimbabwe are still more likely to be over-indebted.

Cross-borrowing, measured using the number of institutions from which credit is obtained, increases the chance of over-indebtedness in the majority of cases. A higher incidence of cross-borrowing can be observed when countries do not have credit registries, as in the case of Malawi, or have irresponsible lending practices, as in the case of South Africa (Hurwitz & Luiz, 2007; Schicks, 2014).

To examine the relationship between over-indebtedness and each source of credit, we introduce both formal (i.e. bank and non-bank formal credit) and informal credit. We do not observe any unique relationship between source of credit and over-indebtedness, implying that over-indebtedness is not linked to any single source of credit and that individuals can rather experience over-indebtedness when borrowing from either formal or informal institutions.

Homeownership is positively related with over-indebtedness, suggesting that homeowners are more likely to experience over-indebtedness. In markets where mortgage loan penetration is high, this might be explained based on the possibility that

Table 11.5 Outputs of the Logistic Regression Analysis on the Link Between Over-indebtedness and Poverty.

Variable	South Africa	Botswana	DRC	Malawi	Mauritius	Swaziland	Tanzania	Zimbabwe	Madagascar	Namibia	Lesotho	Rwanda	Burkina Faso
Over-Indebtedness	0.280***	1.018***	-2.743***	0.154***	0.903***	0.121***	0.130***	0.124***	-0.154***	2.687***	-0.445***	0.748***	-0.958***
No of institutions	0.030***	0.217***	0.164***	0.207***	0.013	0.073***	-0.085***	-0.099***	0.163***	0.621***	0.154***	-0.370***	0.828***
Formal credit	-0.153***	0.353***	0.703***	0.046***	-0.256***	-0.036***	0.111***	-0.051***	-0.192***	-1.599***	-0.252***	-0.249***	-1.070***
Informal credit	-0.513***	0.492***	0.407***	-0.062***	0.300***	-0.052***	-0.022***	-0.052***	0.050***	-0.106***	-0.405***	0.231***	-0.574***
Own home	-0.181***	0.195***	-0.303***	0.394***	-0.574***	0.069***	-0.008***	0.373***	-0.115***	-0.150***	-0.035***	-0.050***	-0.007***
Household size	-0.011***	—	0.006***	0.060***	0.024***	-0.025***	0.013***	-0.008***	0.011***	0.079***	0.045***	-0.025***	0.002***
Age of rrespondent	0.007***	0.002***	0.007***	0.005***	-0.003***	0.005***	-0.003***	0.003***	-0.013***	0.025***	-0.011***	0.001***	0.005***
Respondent gender	0.059***	-0.319***	-0.143***	0.055***	1.154***	-0.066***	-0.001	-0.011***	-0.154***	0.438***	0.023***	0.097***	-0.267***
Personal monthly income	-0.423***	-1.490***	-0.330***	-0.342***	0.192***	-0.718***	0.008***	-0.155***	0.096***	1.798***	-1.494***	-1.084***	-1.005***
Marital status (=Widowed)	Ref	Ref	Ref	Ref	Ref	Ref	Ref	Ref	Ref	Ref	Ref	Ref	Ref
Marital status (=Divorced)	0.019***	0.799***	0.476***	—	-0.164***	0.162***	0.387***	-0.236***	-0.251***	-0.919***	0.559***	0.065***	0.080***
Marital status (=Married)	-0.240***	-18.564	0.417***	—	0.531***	0.024	-0.446***	-0.049***	-0.485***	0.386***	-0.033***	1.318***	-0.006***
Marital status (=Single)	-0.355***	0.278***	-0.038***	—	0.618***	-0.170***	0.099***	-0.102***	-0.260***	-0.312***	-0.022***	0.063***	-0.211***
Level of education (=No education)	Ref	Ref	Ref	Ref	Ref	Ref	Ref	Ref	Ref	Ref	Ref	Ref	Ref
Level of education (=Primary schooling1)	1.131***	-0.257***	0.486***	0.388***	0.348***	1.413***	-0.216***	0.896***	0.461***	4.167***	0.819***	0.697***	1.725***
Level of education (=Secondary schooling2)	0.917***	-0.067***	0.707***	0.055***	0.214***	0.972***	-0.205***	0.451***	0.400***	3.758***	0.624***	0.513***	1.595***
Level of education (=post-secondary schooling)	0.518***	-0.147***	0.480***	-0.224***	-0.079***	0.411***	-0.317***	0.317***	0.300***	3.524***	-0.016***	0.341***	1.106***
Employment status (=Unemployed)	Ref	Ref	Ref	Ref	Ref	Ref	Ref	Ref	Ref	Ref	Ref	Ref	Ref
Employment status (=Employed)	0.468***	0.804***	0.106***	1.005***	1.025***	0.532***	-0.280***	-0.078***	-0.153***	1.139***	-0.613***	0.746***	-0.823***
Employment status (=Retired)	0.248***	0.929***	—	0.916***	0.504***	0.352***	-0.174***	-0.239***	-0.027***	0.222***	-0.663***	0.682***	-0.995***
Place of residence (=Urban)	-0.736***	-0.633***	0.109***	-0.286***	0.203***	-0.338***	-0.245***	-0.098***	-0.210***	-0.362***	-0.115***	-0.411***	0.051***
-2 log likelihood	41,239,515	477,909.00	21,053,414	611,773	197,290	488,048	7,913,597	5,412,392	10,691,185	554,457	1,261,548	1,693,522	9,394,842
Cox & Snell R square	0.089	0.034	0.033	0.04	0.015	0.118	0.009	0.034	0.021	0.062	0.089	0.085	0.047
Nagelkerke R square	0.127	0.081	0.045	0.06	0.063	0.169	0.013	0.046	0.029	0.143	0.125	0.133	0.066

Note: ***significant at 1% level.

homeowners are likely to be over-indebted due to outstanding home loans, as is the case in Germany (Keese, 2009). However, with less than 10% of GDP as mortgage loans, penetration is low in sub-Saharan Africa except in South Africa and Namibia (Nguena, Tchana, & Zeufack, 2016), and hence an alternative explanation is needed. The alternative explanation might be increased loan acquisition capacity using a home as a collateral. While homeowners are more likely to access and accumulate debt, this may not happen with those who do not own a house.

Despite earlier reports by Ottaviani and Vandone (2011) that increased household size is positively related to over-indebtedness due to the financial burden caused by the increased number of dependents, our result suggests that increased household size decreases the chance of over-indebtedness. This might be due to a possible correlation between household size and household income contributors. This can further be supported by the scale economies hypothesis, which suggests a fall in per capita consumption in a household commensurate with an increase in household size (Deaton and Paxson, 1998).

Income is the other important predictor of over-indebtedness. Consistent with expectation, an increase in income decreases the chance of over-indebtedness in countries except in South Africa, Swaziland, Lesotho and Rwanda. A negative link between over-indebtedness and income suggests that people at a lower income quintile are more likely to suffer from the strains of over-indebtedness.

While employment is related to a lower chance of indebtedness in most countries, it increases over-indebtedness in South Africa and Tanzania; both countries have a higher level of over-indebtedness, albeit with different triggers. In South Africa, where penetration of formal credit is very high, over-indebtedness seems to be rooted in the conduct of the formal market, whereas in Tanzania the informal market is the culprit.

In general, seven factors stand out as useful in explaining over-indebtedness. These are credit literacy, the number of institutions from which credit is obtained, homeownership, household size, income, employment and the rural—urban divide.

5.2.2 Over-Indebtedness and Poverty: Is There a Link?

Over-indebtedness has many negative consequences for the lives of people, including health problems, loss of self-esteem, marital breakdown, poverty, etc. However, we could not assess all the possible adverse consequences that over-indebtedness can inflict upon individuals due to limited data and hence examined only the relationship between over-indebtedness and poverty. We measured poverty using the question 'gone without food'. As reported in Table 11.5, over-indebtedness increases the chance of poverty in most countries. This is consistent with the observation in a study by d'Alessio and Iezzi (2013), who reported that over-indebtedness can erode income to the extent that people are unable to afford basic needs of life.

Cross-borrowing can theoretically be expected to decrease the chance of poverty because individuals can withstand poverty by using borrowed money to pay for basic necessities such as food. It is also possible that living beyond one's means can lead to a significant portion of income going to service debt and hence result in poverty. Our analysis shows that borrowing from multiple sources is related to an increased chance of poverty in most countries, which confirms the second hypothesis. As a caveat, a positive link between borrowing from multiple sources and poverty might be due to reverse causality, where the poor tend to look for credit from multiple sources to sustain life.

Results of the model show that homeownership is related to lower chances of experiencing poverty. Obviously, income decreases the chance of poverty across all countries, and the same is true for employment. Contrary to what has been reported by Ravallion and Sangraula (2007), the incidence of poverty is lower in urban areas than in rural areas, implying that the brunt of poverty increasingly rests on the shoulders of rural people.

In general, over-indebtedness is likely to impoverish the indebted. Our control variables revealed interesting insights into other correlates of poverty that include cross-borrowing and place of residence. Both cross-borrowing and living in rural areas are related to a higher chance of poverty. On the other hand, the likelihood of over-indebtedness decreases with increases in income and homeownership.

6. Conclusions and Policy Implications

Financial inclusion is believed to improve household welfare by allowing individuals to manage liquidity and to invest in activities such as education, which can potentially enhance future earning capacity. However, expansion of financial services to the hitherto excluded can also lead to unintended consequences such as accumulation of debt that can aggravate poverty. This chapter analyses the unintended consequences of financial inclusion in the form of over-indebtedness and its links with poverty using survey data from 15 sub-Saharan African countries.

We compare the mean difference between variables related to the over-indebted and the rest using independent sample t-test and Cramer's V test. To get better insight into the determinants of over-indebtedness and its relationship with poverty, we utilize a binary logistic regression technique. Our results show that while over-indebtedness can be triggered by cross-borrowing and a lack of credit literacy, it can be curbed by increased income and employment.

We observe that over-indebtedness is likely to aggravate rather than alleviate poverty. The policy implication of our results is clear. Because unfettered access to financial services, particularly that of credit, has the potential to further impoverish the poor, financial sector policies aimed at regulating credit extension to people with questionable repayment capacity should be promoted in each country.

Acknowledgments

The preparation of this chapter was made possible by FinScope survey data provided by FinMark Trust.

References

d'Alessio, G., & Iezzi, S. (2013). *Household over-indebtedness: Definition and measurement with Italian data.* Bank of Italy Occasional Paper, (149).

Acharya, V. V., & Richardson, M. (2009). Causes of the financial crisis. *Critical Review, 21*(2–3), 195–210.

Anderloni, L., Bacchiocchi, E., & Vandone, D. (2012). Household financial vulnerability: An empirical analysis. *Research in Economics, 66*(3), 284–296.

Anderloni, L., & Vandone, D. (2010). *Risk of over-indebtedness and behavioural factors.* Working Paper n. 2010-25.

Andre, C. (2016). *Household Debt in OECD countries: Stylised Facts and Policy Issues.* Economics Department Working Paper No. 1277. Paris: OECD.

Angel, S. (2016). The effect of over-indebtedness on health: Comparative analyses for Europe. *Kyklos, 69*(2), 208–227.

Aristei, D., & Gallo, M. (2016). The determinants of households' repayment difficulties on mortgage loans: Evidence from Italian microdata. *International Journal of Consumer Studies, 40,* 453–465.

Betti, G., Dourmashkin, N., Rossi, M., & Ping Yin, Y. (2007). Consumer over-indebtedness in the EU: Measurement and characteristics. *Journal of Economics Studies, 34*(2), 136–156.

Bridges, S., & Disney, R. (2016). Household finances, income shocks, and family separation in Britain. *Economic Inquiry, 54*(1), 698–718.

Brunetti, M., Giarda, E., & Torricelli, C. (2015). Is financial fragility a matter of illiquidity? An appraisal for Italian households. *Review of Income and Wealth, 62*(4), 628–649.

Buera, F. J., Kaboski, J. P., & Shin, Y. (2012). *The macroeconomics of microfinance*. Cambridge, MA: National Bureau of Economic Research. NBER Working Paper 19705.

Cabrera, A. F. (1994). Logistic regression analysis in Higher Education: An applied perspective. In John C. Smart (Ed.), *Higher Education: Handbook of Theory and Research* (*Vol.* 10, pp. 225–256). New York: Agathon Press.

Cox, D. R., & Snell, E. J. (1989). *Analysis of Binary Data* (2nd ed). London: Chapman and Hall/CRC.

Cuesta, M. B. (2015). *The effects of over-indebtedness on individual health*. Institute for the Study of Labor. Discussion Paper No. 8912.

De Gregorio, J., & KIM, S. (2000). Credit markets with differences in abilities: Education, distribution, and growth. *International Economic Review, 41*(3), 579–607.

Demirguc-Kunt, A., & Klapper, L. (2012a). *Financial inclusion in Africa: An overview*. Washington, DC: World Bank. Policy Research Working paper No. 6088.

Demirguc-Kunt, A., & Klapper, L. (2012b). *Measuring financial inclusion: The global findex database*. Washington, DC: World Bank. Policy Research Working Paper 6025.

Deaton, A. S., & Paxson, C. H. (1998). Aging and inequality in income and health. *The American Economic Review, 88*(2), 248–253.

Disney, R., Bridges, S., & Gathergood, J. (2008). *Drivers of over-indebtedness*. Report to the UK Department for Business.

Du Caju, P., Rycx, F., & Tojerow, I. (2016). *Unemployment risk and over-indebtedness. A micro-econometric perspective*. European Central Bank. ECB Working Paper 1908.

EU. (2013). *The over-indebtedness of European households: Updated mapping of the situation, nature and causes, effects and initiatives for alleviating its impact − Part 1: Synthesis of findings*.

Fanta, A., Mutsonziwa, K., Berkowitz, B., & Goosen, R. (2017). *Credit is good, but not good when too much. Analysis of indebtedness and over-indebtedness in the SADC region using FinScope Surveys*. Johannesburg: FinMark Trust. Policy Research Paper No. 04/2017.

French, D., & McKillop, D. G. (2016). Financial literacy and over-indebtedness in low-income households. *International Review of Financial Analysis, 48*, 1–11.

Friedman, M. (1957). *A theory of the consumption function*. Princeton, N. J.: Princeton University Press.

Gathergood, J. (2012). Debt and depression: Causal links and social norm effects. *The Economic Journal, 122*(563), 1094–1114.

Haile, H. B., Osman, I., Shuib, R., & Oon, S. W. (2015). Is there a convergence or divergence between feminist empowerment and microfinance institutions' success indicators? *Journal of International Development, 27*(7), 1042–1057.

Hodson, R., Dwyer, R. E., & Neilson, L. A. (2014). Credit card blues: The middle class and the hidden costs of easy credit. *The Sociological Quarterly, 55*(2), 315–340.

Hurwitz, I., & Luiz, J. (2007). Urban working class credit usage and over-indebtedness in South Africa. *Journal of Southern African Studies, 33*(1), 107–131.

Ironfield-Smith, C., Keasey, K., Summers, B., Duxbury, D., & Hudson, R. (2005). Consumer debt in the UK: Attitudes and implications. *Journal of Financial Regulation and Compliance, 13*(2), 132–141.

Keese, M. (2009). *Triggers and determinants of severe household indebtedness in Germany*. DIW Berlin: The German Socio-Economic Panel (SOEP). SOEP papers 239.

Kempson, E. (2006). Policy level response to financial exclusion in developed economies: Lessons for developing countries. In *Paper for access to finance: Building inclusive financial systems, May 30–31, 2006*. Washington, DC: World Bank.

Kilborn, J. J. (2005). Behavioral economics, overindebtedness and comparative consumer bankruptcy: Searching for causes and evaluating solutions. *Bankruptcy Developments Journal, 22*, 13.

Kim, H. J., Lee, D., Son, J. C., & Son, M. K. (2014). Household indebtedness in Korea: Its causes and sustainability. *Japan and the World Economy, 29*, 59–76.

Kukk, M. (2016). How did household indebtedness hamper consumption during the recession? Evidence from micro data. *Journal of Comparative Economics, 44*, 764–786.

Kus, B. (2015). Sociology of debt: States, credit markets, and indebted citizens. *Sociology Compass, 9*(3), 212–223.

Lusardi, A., & Tufano, P. (2015). Debt literacy, financial experiences, and overindebtedness. *Journal of Pension Economics and Finance, 14*(04), 332–368.

McIntyre, S. G., & Lacombe, D. J. (2012). Personal indebtedness, spatial effects and crime. *Economics Letters, 117*(2), 455–459.

Meng, X., Hoang, N., & Siriwardana, M. (2013). The determinants of Australian household debt: A macro level study. *Journal of Asian Economics, 29*, 80–90.

Meniago, C., Mukuddem-Petersen, J., Petersen, M. A., & Mongale, I. P. (2013). What causes household debt to increase in South Africa? *Economic Modelling, 33*, 482–492.

Modigliani, F., & Brumberg, R. H. (1954). Utility analysis and the consumption function: An interpretation of cross-section data. In K. K. Kurihara (Ed.), *Post- Keynesian economics* (pp. 388–436). New Brunswick, NJ: Rutgers University Press.

Nguena, C. L., Tchana, F. T., & Zeufack, A. (2016). Housing finance and inclusive growth in Africa: Benchmarking, determinants, and effects. In *Article submitted for African economic conference (AEC) 2015 on "addressing poverty and inequality in the post 2015 development Agenda" Kinshasa, democratic republic of Congo, November 2-4, 2015*. Available at: https://www.afdb.org/uploads/tx_llafdbpapers/HOUSING_FINANCE_and_INCLUSIVE_GROWTH_in_Africa._Benchmarking__Determinants_and_Effects.pdf.

Ottaviani, C., & Vandone, D. (2011). Impulsivity and household indebtedness: Evidence from real life. *Journal of Economic Psychology, 32*(5), 754–761.

Patel, A., Balmer, N. J., & Pleasence, P. (2012). Debt and disadvantage: The experience of unmanageable debt and financial difficulty in England and Wales. *International Journal of Consumer Studies, 36*(5), 556–565.

Ramji, M. (2009). *Financial inclusion in Gulbarga: Finding usage in access*. Institute for Financial Management and Research, Centre for Microfinance. Working Paper Series No. 26.

Ravallion, M., Chen, S., & Sangraula, P. (2007). New evidence on the urbanization of global poverty. *Population and Development Review, 33*(4), 667–701.

Sahay, R., Cihak, M., N'Diaye, P., Barajas, A., Mitra, S., Kyobe, A., et al. (2015). *Financial inclusion: Can it meet multiple macroeconomic goals?* IMF Staff Discussion Note 15/17, September.

Schicks, J. (2014). Over-indebtedness in Microfinance—an empirical analysis of related factors on the borrower level. *World Development, 54*, 301–324.

Shen, S., Sam, A. G., & Jones, E. (2014). Credit card indebtedness and psychological well-being over time: Empirical evidence from a household survey. *Journal of Consumer Affairs, 48*(3), 431–456.

Sweet, E., Nandi, A., Adam, E. K., and McDade, T. W. (2013) The high price of debt: Household financial debt and its impact on mental and physical health. Social Science & Medicine, 91, 94–100.

The World Bank. (2014). *Global financial development report 2014: Financial inclusion.* Washington, DC: World Bank.

UNCDF. (2016). *Lost in the mail: Why bank account access is not translating into usage.* http://www.uncdf.org/sites/default/files//Documents/insight_note_04.pdf.

Wang, J. J. (2010). Credit counselling to help debtors regain footing. *Journal of Consumer Affairs, 44*(1), 44–69.

World Bank. (2008). *Finance for all? Policies and pitfalls in expanding access.* Washington, DC: World Bank.

Worthington, A. C. (2006). Debt as a source of financial stress in Australian households. *International Journal of Consumer Studies, 30*(1), 2–15.

Further Reading

Awanis, S., & Chi Cui, C. (2014). Consumer susceptibility to credit card misuse and indebtedness. *Asia Pacific Journal of Marketing & Logistics, 26*(3), 408–429.

Dattasharma, A., Kamath, R., & Ramanathan, S. (2016). The burden of microfinance debt: Lessons from the Ramanagaram financial diaries. *Development and Change, 47*(1), 130–156.

Dickerson, A. M. (2008). Consumer over-indebtedness: A US perspective. *Texas International Law Journal, 43*, 135.

Dwyer, R. E., McCloud, L., & Hodson, R. (2011). Youth debt, mastery, and self-esteem: Class-stratified effects of indebtedness on self-concept. *Social Science Research, 40*(3), 727–741.

Fitch, C., Hamilton, S., Bassett, P., & Davey, R. (2011). The relationship between personal debt and mental health: A systematic review. *Mental Health Review Journal, 16*(4), 153–166.

Flores, S. A. M., & Vieira, K. M. (2014). Propensity toward indebtedness: An analysis using behavioral factors. *Journal of Behavioral and Experimental Finance, 3*, 1–10.

Howley, P., & Dillon, E. (2012). Modelling the effect of farming attitudes on farm credit use: A case study from Ireland. *Agricultural Finance Review, 72*(3), 456–470.

Keese, M. (2012). Who feels constrained by high debt burdens? Subjective vs. objective measures of household debt. *Journal of Economic Psychology, 33*(1), 125–141.

McCarthy, Y., & McQuinn, K. (2015). Deleveraging in a highly indebted property market: Who does it and are there implications for household consumption? *Review of Income and Wealth, 63*(1), 95–117.

Nakajima, M. (2012). Rising indebtedness and temptation: A welfare analysis. *Quantitative Economics, 3*, 257–288.

Nettleton, S., & Burrows, R. (1998). Mortgage debt, insecure home ownership and health: An exploratory analysis. *Sociology of Health and Illness, 20*(5), 731–753.

Pavlíková, E. A., & Rozbořil, B. (2014). Consumerism and indebtedness. *Procedia Economics and Finance, 12,* 516–522.

Ramsay, I. (2012). A tale of two debtors: Responding to the shock of over-indebtedness in France and England—a story from the trente piteuses. *The Modern Law Review, 75*(2), 212–248.

Ryoo, S., & Kim, Y. K. (2014). Income distribution, consumer debt and keeping up with the Joneses. *Metroeconomica, 65*(4), 585–618.

Van Heerden, C., & Renke, S. (2015). Perspectives on the South African responsible lending regime and the duty to conduct pre-agreement assessment as a responsible lending practice. *International Insolvency Review, 24*(2), 67–95.

Walks, A. (2014). Canada's housing bubble story: Mortgage securitization, the state, and the global financial crisis. *International Journal of Urban and Regional Research, 38*(1), 256–284.

5

THE TRAJECTORY OF FUTURE DEVELOPMENTS

12

FINANCIAL INCLUSION AND THE SUSTAINABLE DEVELOPMENT GOALS

John Kuada

Department of Business and Management, Aalborg University, Aalborg, Denmark

1.   Introduction

The financial sectors in sub-Saharan African (SSA) countries have generally been described as underdeveloped, risk averse, highly concentrated in urban areas, and skewed against the poor, women and youth (Allen, Demirgüç-Kunt, Klapper, & Pería, 2016; Aterido, Beck, & Iacovone, 2013; Kuada, 2016). The banking sector in particular has been found to be unwilling or unable to tap into the large 'under/unbanked' segments of populations across the sub-continent, thereby keeping parts of the economies non-monetized and less productive (Andrianaivo & Yartey, 2009, pp. 1–40; European Investment Bank, 2016; Makina, 2017). The current thinking is that the more financially inclusive the SSA economies become, the more able they will be in reducing

Extending Financial Inclusion in Africa. https://doi.org/10.1016/B978-0-12-814164-9.00012-8

poverty. The main argument runs as follows: Financial inclusion enhances poor families' ability to increase their capacity to absorb financial shocks, smooth consumption, accumulate assets and invest in such components of human capital as health and education and/or take advantage of promising investment opportunities in their economies (Beck, Demirgüç-Kunt, & Honohan, 2009; Brune, Giné, Goldberg, & Yang, 2011). As a result, countries with well-functioning and inclusive financial systems tend to see poverty levels drop more rapidly than those with weak and non-inclusive financial systems (Beck, Maimbo, Faye, & Triki, 2011). For this reason, the design of policies aimed at improving access to finance in key economic sectors and to unbanked segments of populations remains a key challenge in SSA.

Arguably, the above understanding is in line with the Sustainable Development Goals (SDGs) adopted by the UN in 2015. Scholars are therefore calling on SSA governments and policymakers to discuss how they can explicitly factor the development of inclusive financial sectors into policies and plans aimed at achieving the SDGs. This is the task initiated in this chapter. The chapter draws on different strands of research to provide a synthesis of the currently available theoretical and empirical knowledge in SSA on the role of inclusive finance in economic development processes and to concurrently discuss policy choices that will enhance the development of inclusive financial sectors on the sub-continent.

The chapter is structured as follows: The next section provides an overview of the theoretical rationale underlying financial inclusion and poverty alleviation in the economic development literature. I then discuss the roles that financial inclusion can play in achieving the SDGs. This is followed by discussions of contemporary policies and strategies of financial inclusion as well as issues that remain unsettled in the existing literature and require further research.

2. Contrasting Perspectives on Poverty and Financial Inclusion

2.1 The Theoretical Arguments

The contemporary financial inclusion debate is predicated on the understanding that inclusive financial systems tend to alleviate poverty through the stimulation of economic growth within communities and nations (Beck et al., 2009; Makina, 2017; Tita & Aziakpono, 2017). Since poverty is a central construct in the debate and in policy prescriptions, an understanding of the theoretical viewpoints related to poverty is crucial in predicting the policy directions that are likely to guide financial inclusion efforts.[1]

Views on poverty reduction policies have traditionally fallen between two extremes: structural/institutional and welfare/behavioural. The structural/institutional perspective promotes the view that a capitalist economic system may be structured in such a way that it disables the poor from pulling themselves out of poverty regardless of how competent they may be. One structural barrier to social mobility is financial exclusion. Structural changes that ensure financial inclusion can unleash resources embedded in individuals and provide them with a pathway to socio-economic mobility.

Building on this perspective, the 'structuralists' appear to be more interested in issues relating to the supply side of finance (i.e. access to finance). Scholars subscribing to this perspective endorse the view that people are generally rational decision-makers, and if financial services are available and affordable to all, poor people will rationally access these services. For this reason, the responsibility for financial inclusion has at least partially been laid at the doors of the formal financial service providers, including banks.

The 'structuralists' argue that there is no shortage of funds within the global economy, but it is the ability to move money from the sender to the receiver (the so-called 'velocity of money') that is the stumbling block in SSA's financial sector development process. In other words, if the velocity of money can increase, the general access to finance in an economy will increase as well. Institutional voids, rigid regulations, bureaucratic bottlenecks and weak contract enforcement mechanisms have been listed among the factors that constrain the velocity of money (Leão, 2005; Ramsaran, 1992). Thus, the establishment of high-quality institutions, efficient legal rules, strong contract enforcement and political stability can improve the supply of money through the supply chain and improve financial inclusion.

It has also been argued that improvement in access to financial services will encourage talented but poor entrepreneurs to start their own businesses—e.g. microenterprises. As the fortunes of the micro-business-owners increase, they will be able to grow

---

[1]Distinction is usually drawn in the literature between the 'transient poor' — i.e. those households who suffer from extreme volatility in terms of regularly moving above and then dipping below the poverty line on the one hand, and the 'chronically poor' or long-term poor — i.e. households who spend extended periods of time below the poverty line. The discussions in the section will draw on this distinction.

the businesses by ploughing part of their profits back, thereby creating sustainable income for themselves and their employees (Klapper, Laeven, & Rajan, 2006). In sum, the structuralists believe that microenterprise development can be facilitated by the financial market, and this can lead to substantial poverty reduction.

In contrast, scholars subscribing to the welfare/behavioural perspective argue that poverty has an all-encompassing characteristic, concurrently having an impact on individuals, households and communities. It is more than just a lack of income. It also connotes lack of respect, self-worth, dignity, inclusion, choice and security for an individual and his/her family (especially, the long-term poor people). This strand of research draws distinction between 'transient poor' – i.e. those households who suffer from extreme volatility in terms of regularly moving above and then dipping below the poverty line on the one hand; and the 'chronically poor' – i.e. long-term poor households who spend extended periods of time below the poverty line and rarely exit poverty. Chronically poor people, in particular, resign to their living conditions, and this holds their creativity in check. This means any effort made to pull the chronically poor out of poverty can unleash hitherto untapped psychological and physical human resources within a community and thereby help transform a negative spiral into a positive one. In other words, financial inclusion has the potential to shape people's worldviews, expand their perspectives and allow them to engage in future thinking (Kane, 1987).

The welfare perspective therefore tends to be more concerned with the impact of specific projects and interventions on poverty reduction. Scholars endorsing this perspective argue that economic growth by itself does not provide a sufficient condition for poverty alleviation. In their view, growth must be regulated and directed through proficient welfare programmes that support health, education and social security for it to support development (Kuada, 2015). For this to happen, development-oriented societies must be encouraged to engage in internal criticism of local values and practices that hamper social progress (Nussbaum & Sen, 1989). Financial inclusion may have a role in the process if it relates to the provision of affordable financial services – i.e. access to payments and remittance facilities, savings, loans and insurance services to those who tend to be excluded.

Although the positions championed in each of the two contrasting perspectives contain significant strengths, reality appears to suggest a blend of structural and welfare perspectives. Some scholars have argued that structural barriers that limit access to financial resources do not only constrain economic growth. They can also create what Kane (1987) describes as the culture of learned helplessness—i.e. loss of control over one's own situation in life. It is therefore now acknowledged in the development economics literature that the opportunities that individuals are likely to be exposed to during their life course and their capacity to take advantage of these opportunities are influenced by the socio-economic contexts within which they have been born. For example, human capital formation of household members and the dynamic capabilities that they develop depend on their initial household resource endowments (Kuada, 2015). Thus, a poor child is most likely to become a poor adult—i.e. the incidence of inter-generational transmission of poverty (See UNICEF, 2000). Fortunately, life is not entirely path-dependent or destiny-bound. Other factors can operate independently to affect well-being of individuals over their life-course and thereby re-shape the course of their destinies. But the fact remains that any removal of structural barriers will tend to concurrently promote welfare advantages and economic growth. Similarly, the reduction of psychological deficits through welfare programmes will inevitably be growth-propelling. However, pure redistributive policies have been found to create disincentives to work and save (Aghion & Bolton, 1997). Thus, prudent financial inclusion policies must consider a judicious blend of welfare programmes and financial access policies and strategies.

2.2 Some Empirical Evidence

The empirical literature on the relationship between financial inclusion and poverty alleviation is rather sparse (Tita & Aziakpono, 2017). But the available evidence suggests a positive impact of financial inclusion on poverty. Beck, Demirgüç-Kunt and Levine's study (2007) found that 60% of income growth was due to the impact of financial development on aggregate economic growth, and about 40% was due to the long-run impact of financial development on the income growth of the poorest quintile as the result of reductions in income inequality. Brune et al. (2011) found that increased financial access through commitment savings accounts in rural Malawi has improved the wellbeing of poor households as it helps them improve their farm output. Similarly, a study in Ghana by Karlan, Osei-Akoto, Osei, and Udry (2014) showed that insured farmers were able to buy more fertilizers, plant more acreage, hire more labour and have higher yields and income, which have led to fewer missed meals and fewer missed school days for their children. A South African study that looked at expanding access to consumer credit found increased borrower wellbeing in terms of increased income and food consumption, improved health and improved status of borrowers in the community (Karlan & Zinman, 2010). There is also evidence from a range of countries indicating that financial access increases the share of household income controlled by women—either through their own earnings or cash transfers (World Bank, 2014).

But some studies have not been able to document improvements in welfare as a result of access to finance through microfinance outlets (Cull, Ehrbeck, and Holle. 2014). Some scholars therefore warn against blind faith in financial-inclusion policies as harbingers of total poverty eradication. It has also been suggested that access to financial services does not necessarily imply the actual use of these services. Some individuals may voluntarily exclude themselves from the use of these services for religious and/or personal reasons (Tita & Aziakpono, 2017).

In sum, the current level of theoretical and empirical knowledge on financial inclusion conveys the understanding that institutional structure and policy environment that exists in a particular country will determine the extent to which financial inclusion efforts will affect poverty levels in the country (Kirkpatrick, 2000). For example, policies that promote welfare gains at the same time as they promote pro-poor growth will tend to reduce poverty a lot more and a lot faster than policies that focus on either welfare or economic growth alone (Goudie & Ladd, 1999).[2]

3. Potential Contributions of Financial Inclusion to the SDGs

The arguments above seem to be reflected in the thinking underlying the UN Sustainable Development Goals (SDGs), which aim at ending poverty, protecting the planet and ensuring prosperity for all. The UN policy document contains 17 main goals with 169 specific targets to be achieved by 2030. The impact of inclusive financial services on some of the SDGs is direct (e.g. SDGs 1, 2, 5 and 8), while their impact on others is not immediately evident.[3] But there was no doubt in the minds of the expert groups that worked on the SDGs that financial inclusion will contribute to

---

[2]Some scholars suggest that for a robust pro-poor growth to take place, incomes of the poor must rise at a faster rate than the increase in average incomes, with positive effects in terms of reduced income inequality.

[3]In the run-up to the finalization of the SDGs, financial inclusion was included as a specific target in a number of the SDGs, while no agreement was reached among the expert groups on its relevance to the achievement of other goals.

enterprise development and poverty eradication. For example, as noted above, having access to financial instruments opens up opportunities for starting one's own business and improving household incomes for some segments of poor populations. Thus, Asongu and De Moor (2015) argue that the more inclusive the financial systems in a country, the more able the poorer segments of that country will be in pursuing their economic ambitions, such as starting new businesses and improving the development of their children in terms of non-cognitive and cognitive abilities. Again, as noted above, financial inclusion of farmers can lead to bigger investments in the planting season, resulting in higher yields and improved food security (SDG 2). There are also expectations that microfinance institutions will develop products such as insurance to small farmers to protect their asset base from exogenous shocks and encourage them to undertake relatively risky investments. Furthermore, microenterprise development will tend to increase household welfare by providing more ample possibilities for the smoothing of consumption and investment in human capital—e.g. education and health services (SDGs 3 and 4). The development literature also acknowledges the link between poverty and good health in the sense that poorer households tend to buy poorer quality food items and spend less on fresh fruits and vegetables.

The gender equality goal (SDG 5) is also partially linked to financial inclusion. Some empirical evidence suggests that women face greater barriers than men in accessing finance because of poor credit history or lack of collateral. Not only are they more likely to be denied bank loans than men; they often pay higher interest rates than men on formal bank loans (World Bank, 2014). This means that in the absence of inclusive financial systems, women will rely a lot more on internal resources or support from family members to invest in their educations or take advantage of promising growth opportunities (Kuada, 2009). Previous studies also suggest that women are more likely than men to be self-employed in developing countries and thus are in greater need of access to financial services (Demirguc-Kunt, Klapper, & Singer, 2013). Thus, providing women with direct financial services will enable them to have greater control over their finances and investing in their children's health and education. This will result in general improvements in household welfare (Sanyal, 2014).

It is apparent from the discussions above that the attainment of most of the SDGs rests, to a large extent, on sustainable economic growth and a faith that microenterprise development will lift many poor people out of poverty. This assumption ties well with the decent work goal as well as the innovation goals (SDGs 8 and 9). For example, innovation demands substantial psychological resources that poor individuals may find hard to leverage without general welfare improvements that are expected to be driven by microenterprise growth. In other words, microenterprise development (with the support of inclusive finance) may create enabling conditions for innovation.

Furthermore, previous research suggests that financial inclusion may do more for the poor than simply helping them achieve greater economic stability. It may provide them with greater cognitive resources (i.e. psychological capital) that enable them to reduce the anxieties associated with not being able to efficiently manage their household finances (McLoyd, 1998) and thereby focus on important and previously neglected life outcomes such as the education of their children (Mullainathan & Shafir, 2013). Table 12.1 provides an overview of the SDGs and how financial inclusion may be expected to have an impact on their achievement.

However, it is important to bear in mind that people's decisions to engage in entrepreneurial activities depend not only on the availability of financial resources. For example, the extent to which a society perceives entrepreneurial activities to be desirable has a tremendous influence on such decisions (Shapero, 1984). That is, if a society considers entrepreneurial drive as a value on its own, entrepreneurs will emerge in that society. But if the society encourages individuals to see themselves as being entitled to the wealth of others through birth or ascription (rather than to create their own wealth), very few within that society will choose the tortuous entrepreneurial path. Furthermore, scholars of entrepreneurship remind us that not all potential and actual entrepreneurs can make good use of support. A vast majority of African entrepreneurs may be classified as necessity-driven, while a few of them are growth-oriented (Kuada, 2016). Microenterprise owners who enter business due to necessity (i.e. lack of alternative sources of income) do not often see any clear economic path out of poverty. They may see their businesses as temporary occupations. With such an attitude, the dedication and sacrifice required to grow a business are usually lacking in their everyday business decisions and actions. Those who start these businesses therefore require some guidance, mentoring and support to change their mindsets from having survival as their main goal in business and in order to develop the courage to grow these businesses. We need to take this observation on board when we assess the potential impact of financial inclusion on the SDGs.

Table 12.1 Potential Contributions of Financial Inclusion to the Attainment of the Sustainable Development Goals.

No.	Goals	Expected Impact of Financial Inclusion
1	No poverty — end poverty in all its forms everywhere	Access to financial services by all, especially the poor and vulnerable by 2030; this will help them smooth consumption and accumulate assets
2	No hunger — end hunger, achieve food security and improved nutrition, and promote sustainable agriculture	Access to financial services should double the agricultural productivity and incomes of small-scale producers by 2030
3	Good health and wellbeing — ensure healthy lives and promote wellbeing for all at all ages	Reduce delays in seeking medical services and advice for members of the household; reduce poverty-related stress and depression in households
4	Quality education — ensure inclusive and equitable quality education and promote lifelong learning for all	Increases household income that, in turn, encourages investments in education
5	Gender equality — achieve gender equality and empower all women and girls	Reforms must be undertaken to give women equal rights to economic resources and access to finance in particular
6	Clean water and sanitation — ensure availability and sustainable management of water and sanitation for all	Improvements in household income impact household-level sanitation
7	Affordable and clean energy — ensure access to affordable, reliable, sustainable, and clean energy for all	Improvements in income impact the use of cleaner energy at household-levels
8	Decent work and economic growth — promote sustained, inclusive and sustainable economic growth, full and productive employment, and decent work for all	Strengthen the capacity of domestic financial institutions to encourage and expand access to banking, insurance and financial services for all
9	Industry, innovation and infrastructure — build resilient infrastructure, promote inclusive and sustainable industrialization, and foster innovation	Microenterprise development may improve innovation within certain industries
10	Reduced inequalities — reduce inequality within and among countries	Impacts economic growth in rural and poor communities through enterprise development

Continued

Table 12.1 Potential Contributions of Financial Inclusion to the Attainment of the Sustainable Development Goals.—*continued*

No.	Goals	Expected Impact of Financial Inclusion
11	Sustainable cities and communities — make cities and human settlements inclusive, safe, resilient and sustainable	No immediate impact
12	Responsible consumption and production — ensure sustainable consumption and production patterns	Impacts economic growth in rural and poor communities through enterprise development
13	Climate action — take urgent action to combat climate change and its impacts	No immediate and direct impact
14	Life below water — conserve and sustainably use the oceans, seas and marine resources for sustainable development	No immediate and direct impact
15	Life on land — protect, restore, and promote sustainable use of terrestrial ecosystems, sustainably manage forests, combat desertification, stop and reverse land degradation and halt biodiversity loss	No immediate and direct impact
16	Peace and justice — promote peaceful and inclusive societies for sustainable development, provide access to justice for all, and build effective, accountable, and inclusive institutions at all levels	No immediate and direct impact
17	Partnerships for the goals — strengthen the means of implementation and revitalize the global partnership for sustainable development	No immediate and direct impact

4. Financial Inclusion Policies and Strategies

If we accept the view that microenterprise creation by talented poor individuals in Africa is a prerequisite for poverty alleviation, there is a need to design policies and strategies that ensure the accessibility of finance to these groups of people. This has been the goal of the financial liberalization policies initiated in several

African countries since the beginning of the 1980s (Ndikumana, 2001, pp. 1–50). In spite of the dismantling of restrictive financial regulations and the adoption of innovative financial delivery systems (including mobile banking) in several countries, the hitherto 'unbanked' segments of the population remain excluded from financial services.

Several policy options have surfaced during the past decade to address this need. For example, Chibba (2009) argues that tackling financial inclusion challenges in developing countries requires a focus on four key pillars: private (financial and non-financial) sector development, financial literacy, extending microfinance outreach, and public sector support. Similarly, Asongu and De Moor (2015) suggest that financial products targeting the rural communities in Africa must include farmer-specific features that allow for the spreading of agricultural credit risks and provide special poor-farmer loans and rural low interest policy funds. They also endorse the development of financial and non-financial institutions that encourage and support funds for elementary schools 'by providing guarantees for rural elementary education and providing more incentives for teachers to take positions in rural areas' (p. 12). Others have suggested the use of 'correspondent' or 'agent' banking in which people can deposit into and withdraw from their bank accounts using non-bank agents such as retail stores.

Many of these suggestions have merit, and their appropriateness must be examined in specific countries, communities and contexts. In assessing their appropriateness, it is important to make sure that the usage of these financial services and the delivery mechanisms adopted do not overstretch the comfort zones of their potential users. It is advisable to adopt financial inclusion mechanisms that are consistent with the users' financial skills. Furthermore, these services must be concurrently supported by policies that strengthen their users' beliefs in their personal efficacy to exercise control over their life situations. It is under such conditions that they can be empowered to leverage the resources to create their individual pathways out of poverty.

It is in light of the above discussions that we may reconsider the role of financial service delivery mechanisms such as informal financial associations (IFAs) including savings and credit cooperatives, village savings and loans associations, and rotating savings and credit associations (RASCOs) in any future policy framework. The RASCO system works in this way: each member contributes the same amount at each meeting, and one member takes the whole sum once (Kimuyu, 1999). As a result, each member is able to access a relatively larger sum of money during the life of the association and use it for whatever purpose she or he wishes. The transactions are trust-based; no records are kept and no money is retained inside the group.[4] Recent developments indicate an increasing reliance on these services to cover financial commitments such as paying children's school fees, hospital bills, and funeral or other occasional expenses in many rural communities in Africa. They therefore contribute to the fulfilment of several SDGs. Their strength and competitive advantage lies in their context-specificity—i.e. their ability to use community-based methods to monitor the financial activities of the clients they serve and thereby minimize the incidence of default among them (Thomas, 1992). It has been argued that the social structures that characterize informal and quasi-formal financial associations enable the associations to be better informed about the financial needs and creditworthiness of their members. They therefore serve as a proxy for the distribution of information (Gugerty, 2007). In addition to this, the delivery mechanisms allow their members to have greater control over their financial experiences. Arguably, a modernization of the IFAs and their integration into the formal financial systems is worth serious attention in financial inclusive policy and strategy considerations.

The emergence of ICT-enabled financial services innovation through the use of digital interfaces such as mobile phones is another development with the potential of fast-tracking the financial inclusion process in SSA. Using a mobile phone rather than cash saves considerable travel time, reduces the risk of theft and boosts convenience. An example of a mobile phone financial delivery system frequently cited in the policy literature is the rapid evolution of the M-Pesa system in Kenya, which has grown rapidly since its inception in 2007, reaching approximately 38% of Kenya's adult population in 2015.

The general knowledge from the operations of mobile phone-enabled financial services in Africa is that they have created a new and easier entry point into the financial system and have introduced a large measure of convenience into domestic remittance transactions. People living in the urban centres can now transfer money to their relatives in the rural areas a lot more easily, allowing recipients to get fairly regular incomes to finance health and educational expenses. Mobile money also provides opportunities for the 'microtization' of transactions—i.e. transacting in smaller amounts and more frequently than has otherwise

---

[4]This method of saving and borrowing has also been variously described as peer-to-peer banking or peer-to-peer lending and serves as an alternative to saving at home, with the risk of family and relatives demanding access to the savings.

been possible. Health bills, electricity bills and school tuition fees can then be broken into small, frequent payments. This will make such services accessible to even the long-term poor segments of populations.

Digital financial transactions also have cost advantages that reinforce their growing popularity among the poorer segments of the African population. A study by McKay and Pickens (2010)[,5] found that branchless banking (including mobile money) was 19% cheaper on average than alternative services. It also provides opportunities for the development of other financial products that may be tailor-made to rural communities without basic infrastructural facilities such as roads to link them to existing financial centres. In this way, digitalization of financial services has enabled some of the long-term poor segments of the African populations to build up credit histories which can help lenders assess their credit risks when assessing their loan requests.

Hitherto, both IFAs and mobile banking systems have not succeeded in achieving comprehensive financial inclusion due to a number of factors. For example, despite the apparently close-knit social structures that enable informal financial associations to operate, there is still evidence of structural holes that discourage some segments of the population to use them as financial service delivery options (Gugerty, 2007). Structural holes in this context imply the fragmentation of valuable knowledge within and among IFAs. These knowledge gaps must be bridged.

With regard to digital financial transactions, it has been noted that these services have hitherto been used to a lesser degree to finance investments in small rural farming and non-farming businesses (Duncombe, 2012). Furthermore, services such as savings, borrowing and insurance have not as yet been included in the current product portfolio of the mobile phone companies. In addition to this, some important sectors such as health care, education and agriculture have not as yet been covered by mobile phone transactions in Africa (Jack & Suri, 2010). There is therefore a need to extend the technology to these sectors.

A way forward is to consider the potentials of using the advantages provided by digital financial transactions to facilitate the integration of IFAs into the formal financial systems in SSA. One challenge of increasing the membership of IFAs beyond those within a specific local community (and thereby increasing the financial resources that each member can leverage) is the

---

[5]The study covered 18 branchless banking providers with a collective total of more than 50 million customers from such countries as Afghanistan, Brazil, Cambodia, India, Kenya, Pakistan and Tanzania.

uncertainties regarding payments from individual members on stipulated dates. With the digital transfer arrangements, this problem can be solved. It is also conceivable that different IFAs can be brought into networks of financial service associations that further expand their financial resource capacities. Formal financial institutions can serve as bridges (or brokers) in creating linkages between the different associations. The position of a bridge between the associations will allow them to transfer valuable information and knowledge from one association to another (i.e. bridging the structural holes). In addition, financial institutions can combine all the ideas they access from different sources to produce more innovative solutions to common problems. They can do so by virtue of being positioned at crossroads in the flow of information between the associations. In this way they will be able to channel new ideas and best practices between the associations.

Embracing digital financial service delivery in rural communities also means creation of jobs for financial service delivery agents as well as financial technology start-ups, microfinance institutions, retailers and other companies. These jobs and micro-enterprises, by themselves, will enhance the economic development potentials of the communities.

The process of integrating IFAs into a formalized financial system may be gradual, the duration varying from one context or country to another. The transitioning process may start by making some of these IFAs quasi-formal. Candidates may be experimentally chosen on the basis of robustness of the current organization and willingness of the leaders to participate. The first challenge will be to determine whether networks of IFAs can be established for purposes of knowledge generation and sharing of best practices within a given context or between similar contexts.

5. Some Unresolved Issues and Implications for Future Research

The discussions above provide some good promises for designing realistic policies and strategies for achieving inclusive financial sectors in SSA. The discussions have also shown that a number of issues require additional policy and research attention in order to place African countries on a firmer path to poverty reduction.

First, there is the need to understand the nature and requirements for financial capability development among the long-term poor people in African countries. If we accept the view that poverty is more than just lack of income, then the financial capability of poor people implies having both the knowledge to make financial decisions, access to financial services and products as well as the motivation to leverage these resources and use them in creating a pathway out of poverty (Sherraden, 2013). It may therefore be described as a set of variegated competencies that individuals and groups possess that enable them to actively face the challenges of life and to take moderate personal and/or collective risks to achieve what they set out to achieve. Thus, while policies are designed and instruments are fine-tuned to ensure speedy and inclusive delivery of financial resources, it is imperative that efforts are also made to change the mindset of the long-term poor and encourage them to take steps that will pull them out of poverty.

Kane (1987) argues that the long-term poor experience three major interrelated attitudinal constraints that impair their ability to get them out of poverty: (1) motivational deficit (people come to believe that poverty is endemic and actions to reduce it are futile); (2) cognitive interference (people will have difficulty learning that action can produce favourable results in new situations); and (3) an affective reaction (depression or resignation). But perception of helplessness can also be inferred from the environment without direct experience of failure. Under such conditions, having access to finance does not provide the intrinsic motivation to seek funds or undertake the poverty reducing investments that we have identified above.

Second, it has been suggested that poverty is not a static or binary concept and it is not appropriate to assume that the poor constitute a homogeneous group. Previous frameworks (e.g. Baulch & McCouth, 1998) have offered different classifications of the poor. There may be the transiently poor farmers who move in and out of poverty depending on the outcome of their harvests simply because they engage in rain-fed farming practices. There are also those that have the potential for lift off due to unique skills or competences that they have. And then there are the long-term poor. This means inclusion and exclusion into formal financial systems also change over time. This implies that not all the 'financially excluded' may lack the motivational resources to find a pathway out of poverty. However, the heterogeneity among poor households may be unobserved by financial institutions without community-based knowledge and insight. Furthermore, the heterogeneity of the poor should suggest that each one will require a separate set of interventions to facilitate their movement out of poverty. However, we currently lack the research knowledge that can provide reliable profiles of the different groups of poor people in every country as well as insights into what works best for each group.

Third, economists have been accused of a tendency of talking *about* the poor rather than *with* them. This orientation to poverty eradication has proved to be counterproductive and has resulted in biases in conceptualizations as well as governments abandoning policies that could have worked had they given them enough time and support. It has also denied policymakers the opportunity to consider innovative policies that might have worked for some groups of people in some countries. It is important to gain insight into how poor people understand their situations and the options that they examine in their efforts to pull them out of poverty. This calls for new research, since our current level of knowledge is inadequate to guide policy on the issue.

Fourth, in spite of promising developments in digital financial services and informal financial associations in Africa, the field is under-researched. For example, we need a better understanding of the factors that can ensure the rapid adoption of mobile financial transactions in different SSA countries. We also need a better understanding of the group dynamics of informal financial delivery associations and the manner in which these dynamics play out to include or exclude members of different segments of the communities within which they are formed. Such knowledge will provide policy guidelines for the twin and symbiotic development of the digital and informal financial service sector development.

6. Conclusions

The discussions in this chapter highlight the potentials of financial inclusion in helping achieve some of the 17 UN SDG's in SSA countries. The direct contributions of financial inclusion to the attainment of SDGs 1, 2, 5 and 8, in particular, have been highlighted. It has also been noted that financial inclusion will accelerate the pace of enterprise development and job creation in African countries and thereby contribute immensely to economic growth and poverty alleviation. The chapter also provides pointers to some of the challenges that need to be addressed. The arguments favour multi-faceted policy interventions and strategies, rather than an attempt to merely extend the outreach of existing financial institutions since current services are fundamentally flawed in terms of appropriateness to the needs and financial capabilities of the unbanked segments of the populations. This will include interventions that strengthen the poorest individuals' control over their experienced situations as well as beliefs in their personal efficacy to take initiatives that will take them out of poverty.

I have also discussed the role of digital financial service delivery networks and the IFAs in the financial inclusion process. While digitalization has enabled parts of the unbanked segments of populations to engage in transactions seamlessly by breaking the transactions into sizes that are convenient for most of them, the IFAs have provided them with psychological certainty that their temporary savings will not be lost. The two mechanisms, if combined, have the promise of introducing financial services to the poor without overstretching their comfort zones.

References

Aghion, P., & Bolton, P. (1997). A theory of trickle-down growth and development. *The Review of Economic Studies, 64*(2), 151–172.

Allen, F., Demirgüç-Kunt, A., Klapper, L., & Pería, M. S. M. (2016). The foundations of financial inclusion: Understanding ownership and use of formal accounts. *Journal of Financial Intermediation Advance online publication.* https://doi.org/10.1016/j.jfi.2015.12.00.

Andrianaivo, M., & Yartey, C. A. (2009). *Understanding the growth of African financial markets.* Working Paper No. 9/182. International Monetary Fund. available at: www.imf.org/external/pubs/ft/wp/2009/wp09182.pdf.

Asongu, S. A., & De Moor, L. (2015). *Recent advances in finance for inclusive development.* Yaoundé: African Governance and Development Institute. Working Paper No. 15/005.

Aterido, R., Beck, T., & Iacovone, L. (2013). Access to finance in Sub-Saharan Africa: Is there a gender gap? *World Development, 47*, 102–120.

Baulch, B., & McCouth, N. (1998). *Being poor and becoming poor: Poverty status and poverty transitions in rural Pakistan.* Institute of Development Studies at the University of Sussex. IDS Working Paper 79.

Beck, T., Demirgüç-Kunt, A., & Honohan, P. (2009). Access to financial services: Measurement, impact, and policies. *The World Bank Research Observer, 24*(1), 119–145.

Beck, T., Demirgüç-Kunt, A., & Levine, R. (2007). Finance, inequality, and the poor. *Journal of Economic Growth, 12*(1), 27–49.

Beck, T., Maimbo, S. M., Faye, I., & Triki, T. (2011). *Financing Africa through the crisis and beyond.* Washington DC: The World Bank.

Brune, L., Giné, X., Goldberg, J., & Yang, D. (2011). *Commitments to save: A field experiment in rural Malawi.* World Bank Policy Research Working Paper No. 5748. Washington, DC.

Chibba, M. (2009). Financial inclusion, poverty reduction and the millennium development goals. *European Journal of Development Research, 21*(2), 213–230.

Cull, R., Ehrbeck, T., & Holl, N. (2014). *Financial inclusion and development: Recent impact evidence.* Focus Notes No. 92 World Bank Publication Washington, D.C.: CGAP. Available at: http://documents.worldbank.org/curated/en/269601468153288448/pdf/881690BRI0FN920Box385210B000PUBLIC0.pdf.

Demirguc-Kunt, A., Klapper, L., & Singer, D. (2013). *Financial inclusion and legal discrimination against women: Evidence from developing countries*. World Bank Policy Research Paper 6416.

Duncombe, R. (2012). An evidence-based framework for assessing the potential of mobile finance in Sub-Saharan Africa. *The Journal of Modern African Studies, 50*(3), 369–395.

European Investment Bank. (2016). *Banking in Sub-Saharan Africa recent trends and digital financial inclusion*. Available at: http://www.eib.org/attachments/efs/economic_report_banking_africa_digital_financial_inclusion_en.pdf.

Goudie, A., & Ladd, P. (1999). Economic growth, poverty and inequality. *Journal of International Development, 11*, 177–195.

Gugerty, M. K. (2007). You can't save alone: Commitment in rotating savings and credit associations in Kenya. *Economic Development and Cultural Change, 55*(2), 251–282.

Jack, W., & Suri, T. (2010). *The economics of M-PESA*. Available at: http://www.mit.edu/~tavneet/M-PESA.pdf.

Kane, T. J. (1987). Giving back control: Long-term poverty and motivation. *Social Service Review, 61*(3), 405–419.

Karlan, D., Osei-Akoto, I., Osei, R., & Udry, C. (2014). Agricultural decisions after relaxing credit and risk constraints. *Quarterly Journal of Economics, 129*(2), 597–652.

Karlan, D., & Zinman, J. (2010). Expanding credit access: Using randomized supply decisions to estimate the impacts. *Review of Financial Studies, 23*(1), 433.

Kimuyu, P. K. (1999). Rotating saving and credit associations in rural East Africa. *World Development, 27*(7), 1299–1308.

Kirkpatrick, C. (Winter 2000). Financial development, economic growth, and poverty reduction. *The Pakistan Development Review, 39*(4 Part I), 363–388.

Klapper, L., Laeven, L., & Rajan, R. (2006). Entry regulation as a barrier to entrepreneurship. *Journal of Financial Economics, 82*, 591–629.

Kuada, J. (2009). Gender, social networks, and entrepreneurship in Ghana. *Journal of African Business, 10*(1), 85–103.

Kuada, J. (2015). *Private enterprise-led economic development in Sub-Saharan Africa: The human side of growth*. London: Palgrave Macmillan.

Kuada, J. (2016). Financial market performance and growth in Africa. *African Journal of Economic and Management Studies, 7*(2), 3–6.

Leão, P. (2005). Why does the velocity of money move pro-cyclically? *International Review of Applied Economics, 19*(1), 119–131.

Makina, D. (2017). Introduction to the financial services in Africa – special issue. *African Journal of Economic and Management Studies, 8*(1), 2–7.

McKay, C., & Pickens, M. (2010). *Branchless banking 2010: Who's served? At what price? What's next?*. Focus Note 66. Washington, DC: Consultative Group to Assist the Poor.

McLoyd, V. C. (1998). Socioeconomic disadvantage and child development. *American Psychologist, 53*(2), 185–204.

Mullainathan, S., & Shafir, E. (2013). *Scarcity: Why having too little means so much*. New York, NY: Times Books.

Ndikumana, L. (2001). *Financial markets and economic development in Africa*. Working Paper Series No. 17. Amherst, MA: Political Economy Research Institute, University of Massachusetts. available at: http://scholarworks.umass.edu/cgi/viewcontent.cgi?article=1010&context=peri_workingpapers.

Nussbaum, M. C., & Sen, A. K. (1989). Internal criticism and Indian rationalist traditions. In M. Krausz (Ed.), *Relativism, interpretation and confrontation* (pp. 299–325). South Bend: University of Notre Dame Press.

Ramsaran, R. (1992). Factors affecting the income velocity of money in the Commonwealth Caribbean. *Social & Economic Studies, 41*(4), 205–223.

Sanyal, P. (2014). *Credit to capabilities: A Sociological study of microcredit groups in India.* Cambridge: Cambridge University Press.

Shapero, A. (1984). The entrepreneurial event. In C. A. Kent (Ed.), *The environment of entrepreneurship* (pp. 21–40). Lexington: Lexington Books.

Sherraden, M. S. (2013). Building blocks of financial capability. In J. Birkenmaier, M. Sherraden, & J. Curley (Eds.), *Financial capability and asset development: Research education, policy, and practice* (pp. 3–43). New York, NY: Oxford.

Thomas, J. J. (1992). *The informal financial sector – how does it operate and who are the Customers.* London: Regent's College. Overseas Development Institute Working Paper 61.

Tita, A. F., & Aziakpono, M. J. (2017). *The effect of financial inclusion on welfare in sub-Saharan Africa: Evidence from disaggregated data.* Economic Research Southern Africa (ERSA) Working paper 679.

UNICEF. (2000). *Poverty reduction begins with children.* New York: Unicef.

World Bank. (2014). *Global financial development report.* Washington: Financial Inclusion.

13

ALTERNATIVE FINANCING APPROACHES AND REGULATION IN AFRICA

Iwa Salami

Royal Docks School of Business and Law, University of East London, United Kingdom

CHAPTER OUTLINE

Extending Financial Inclusion in Africa. https://doi.org/10.1016/B978-0-12-814164-9.00013-X

1. The Rise in Mobile Financial Services in Africa

The development of mobile financial services, and more specifically mobile payments services as a type of mobile financial Service, has helped advance financial inclusion in many developing countries and granted opportunities to the 'financially excluded' to participate in the benefits of financial services since excluded from the formal financial sector.

Suffice it to mention at the onset that mobile financial services refer to all financial transactions conducted through a mobile device. It therefore encompasses mobile banking, mobile money and mobile payments. Mobile banking by definition involves the performance of actions on a traditional bank account such as obtaining account information and transacting on accounts. Mobile banking is offered by nearly all major banks in developed nations and typically uses a mobile device application, such as a smartphone application, to securely perform bank transactions. Mobile money is a stored value account that is accessed from the user's mobile phone. It is typically operated by the mobile network operator and managed separately to the user's phone account. Mobile money is popular in developing nations where most people do not have regular bank accounts (the unbanked population). The money can be used to pay for goods and services and can be sent from a payer to a recipient. As it bears some similarities with formal bank accounts, mobile money and mobile banking are often used interchangeably. Mobile payments are payment for goods and services using a personal mobile device as the transaction terminal. Mobile payments can use a traditional bank account or a mobile money account. Other services also offered as mobile financial services include insurance and microfinance services.

Due to the growth of the mobile financial services industry, huge percentages of the unbanked in many parts of Africa are now able to access financial services, and there are still huge opportunities for the largely unbanked adult population on the African continent to be included in this way. Previously, the most basic form of financial inclusion was having a bank account; however, advances in financial technology, particularly enabled through the inventions of mobile phones, has led to the creation of mobile money accounts and thus a drastic transitioning from bank account ownership to a digital platform where mobile phones and devices can be used to effect payments. All of this is helping to transform the developing world, including sub-Saharan Africa, to move from cash payment-based societies to digital payment societies characterized by the replacement of payments of wages, fees, utilities and services digitally rather than by cash with the benefit that payments are cheaper, quicker, safer, more transparent and well documented.

This form of payment is also known to provide access to people who would typically not have access to conventional bank accounts because of non-affordability, distance and other requirements. It enables such people to access other financial services including savings, loans and even insurance.

While opportunities for promoting mobile financial services in Africa are huge, issues around the risks that they raise and the regulatory approaches to mitigating these risks—and especially the payments components of this system − continue to emerge.

The risks from mobile payment services originate from the precise model of payment services. As such, the ensuing paragraphs examine the two main models in operation in Africa before then discussing the risks inherent in these.

1.1 Main Models of Mobile Payment Services in Africa

As defined above, mobile payments are payments initiated and transmitted by access devices that are connected to mobile communications networks. Currently, transaction values are small and serve the purpose of purchasing goods or services at the point of sale or remitting funds. Money originates from two major sources, including customer funds located at banks in the form of a deposit account or credit account (including prepaid cards) or customer 'stored-value funds' maintained by mobile network operators (MNOs). In some jurisdictions, such accounts may also take the form of current account, card account, payment account, or transaction account. As such, mobile payments are funded by links to accounts or payment instruments (credit cards are not necessarily linked to an account) and are different in terms of risks. Customers can 'pay in advance' (with a prepaid card, gift card, prepaid deposits with an MNO), 'pay now' (with a debit card or bank account number), or 'pay later' (with a credit card or phone bill). However, the main models of mobile payment services in the African continent are through customer 'stored-value funds' maintained by mobile network operators (the MNO model) and a combination of a bank, MNO or other third party that offers communications and financial transaction services that combine characteristics of both the pure bank and the pure MNO model (the hybrid model).

1.1.1 Mobile Network Operator Model

A pure mobile network operator (MNO) service extends the wireless network messaging functionality to provide payment services that enable customers to send funds to each other that can be settled through the MNO's established agent network. Individual payment transactions occur entirely within the MNO and do not require the service user to have a bank account. The funds in transit − paid in by the sender but not yet withdrawn by the recipient, are in principle on deposit in a segregated account with one or more banks (trust account if under common law) and so are within the formal financial system. Since the service provider is only executing client payment instructions and is not performing the credit evaluation and risk management function of a bank, these services arguably do not constitute 'banking' and do not require the level of regulatory oversight needed for deposits that are used to fund lending. The depository bank is not involved in or responsible for payments through the MNO system. Given the relatively high cost of a bank account (minimum balance, service charges, full KYC requirements, and travel time to a branch) and the easy, low cost and increasingly universal access to mobile phone services, the MNO model arguably is highly effective in bringing informal cash transactions into a form of formal financial system, expanding access to financial services. This is the reason why it has been popular for promoting financial inclusion in the African context.

1.1.2 Hybrid Model

The hybrid model is a combination of a bank, MNO or other third party that offers communications and financial transaction services. This combination hybrid model is referred to as MNO/Bank Model. Under this model, a mobile phone company based payment services that handle payments internally with cash in/out through the MNO's agent network, is linked to formal banking services such as savings, loans and insurance through partnership with a regulated financial institution by enabling communications with the bank and transfers between the user's mobile phone payment account and accounts at the bank. Most mobile financial services are hybrid, drawing on the relative strengths of the partners involved. This thus enables those without formal bank accounts to be able to transact with those with formal bank accounts and through this including them in the formal financial system.

However, as mobile payments services become more widely used, particular attention needs to be drawn to the potential risks associated with their use. The ensuing sections considers the risks that may arise in the operation of mobile payments and considers actions that need to be taken to mitigate such risks so that mobile money and payments can further promote financial inclusion.

1.2 Risks and Legal and Regulatory Challenges With Mobile Payment Services in Africa

The risks associated with the two models of mobile payment services considered above include systemic risk — a risk that could cause collapse of the financial system or a risk which results in adverse public perception, possibly leading to lack of confidence, and in a worst-case scenario, a 'run' on the system; liquidity risk — a risk that lessens the ability of a bank or mobile financial services (MFS) provider/agent to meet cash obligations upon demand; cross-border risk — a systemic risk (as defined above) that could have a cross-border contagion effect; payment systems risk — a risk associated with the two that could result in the failure of payments systems to settle transactions as and when they fall due; operational risk — a risk which damages the ability of one of the stakeholders to effectively operate their business or a risk which results in a direct or indirect loss from failed internal processes, people, systems or external events; and reputation risk — a risk that damages the image of one of the stakeholders, the mobile system, the financial system or of a specific product.

These risks derive from interactions between players in typical mobile payments transactions such as consumers, merchants, agents, account providers (such as MNOs) and financial institutions holding customer funds in transit, and the risks are discussed to the extent that they affect these players.

1.2.1 Liquidity Risk of Agents Preventing Cashing-Out Services and the Rise of Agent Banking

At the moment, liquidity risk — which includes the risk that lessens the ability of an agent to meet cash obligations upon demand—is resulting in delays in cashing-out services. This is one of the most significant challenges facing mobile payments in Africa today.

It is argued that this risk can be mitigated by agent banking, which is a very new financial service targeted to reach the unbanked and which is quite similar to mobile money kiosk operations. An agent bank is a retail or postal outlet contracted by a licensed deposit-taking financial institution or a mobile money operator to provide a range of financial services to customers. In agent banking, the agent is trained to provide banking services according to the standards set by the bank in order to help the customer access fast, convenient and affordable banking and provided with a mobile phone or point-of-sale terminal (Okwii, 2017). Services they provide can include account opening, funds transfer; deposits and withdrawals; bill payment; payment of salaries; balance enquiry; generation and issuance of mini statements; cash disbursement and cash repayment of loans; cash payment of retirement benefits; chequebook request and collection; collection of bank mails for customer; and other activities to be determined and approved by the banking regulator.

As agents in agent banking services must always have enough liquidity to enable users to withdraw funds, they are likely to have the same problems as agents in mobile payments services run by mobile network operators/providers. Since mobile money agents are currently facing this challenge and since agent banking is a similar model, it will in the short run require banks to monitor their agents' liquidities, particularly during special seasons such as national holidays when agents are more likely to operate many cash-out services that need to be balanced with cash input from banks. Although banks are developing mechanisms such as applications to help improve the way agents distribute money, they are still relying on legacy banking infrastructure. The idea, however, is that in the long term, agent banking would facilitate, among the unbanked, the ownership of accounts where account holders can through mobile banking make payments leading to the reduction of the usage of cash by many to settle transactions. The rationale being that with the success of agent banking reaching the unbanked in this way, many people become so used to using digital/mobile payments for all forms of payments. The need then to cash out or cash in is reduced, because as payments are made into the bank accounts of users, they can use their mobile devices/phones to pay merchants and to pay for other services, and the need to use cash is reduced as is the need to have many more agents. Therefore, the increase and success of agent banking enhanced by mobile banking can facilitate a cashless society which, in the long term, solves the liquidity challenges of agent banking and agents of MNO.

For now, however, the success of the system is questioned if customers have to travel miles in search of a liquid agent. Also, as the challenge is quite pervasive across mobile network operators, advising customers to change providers is not a useful solution. There are also hardly effective and speedy legal redress for these types of issues in Africa, so it is of no advantage to advise the customer to seek legal action. Although most customers are willing to wait till agents have liquidity, this may not be sustainable, and operators and regulators would therefore need to come up with a more robust mechanism to address this issue—at least until the gains of a truly digital payment system through agent banking are realized.

1.2.2 Systemic Risks: Insolvency of Bank Holding Customer Funds for MNOs or the Insolvency of MNOs

This is the risk that the customer loses its balance due to the failure of bank holding customer funds in transit. This could also occur where customer funds held by the mobile network operator (MNO) are compromised as a result of the insolvency of the MNO and where the bank accounts holding those funds are not legally segregated from the general pool of bank assets available to satisfy creditors pulled into the bankruptcy process, thus leaving customers without access. This could also occur where − even if these accounts may be technically segregated − no rapid procedure for transferring these funds exists in such a way that they are accessible by customers. All of this would affect the MNO cashing-out service to customers, which could have systemic implications by weakening public confidence in the financial system. This risk can be mitigated by the introduction of law/regulation relating to bank failure or insolvency that ensures the segregation of customer assets/funds (held in MNO accounts including those in transit) from the general pool of assets of the MNO which is subject to the bankruptcy process. Customer accounts including those holding the value of items in transit would be legally segregated from the MNO's own assets in bankruptcy.

A systemic risk from the failure of a bank holding the MNO accounts with customer funds exists if the necessary safety nets for the failure of such banks are not effectively catered for by the financial regulatory regime. In other words, there is a potential systemic risk if, for instance, no adequate deposit guarantee scheme exists to guarantee customer funds held in MNO bank accounts at MNOs who have been adversely affected by the failure of the bank.

As such, the deposit guarantee scheme must be robust enough to provide protection for customer funds held in MNO accounts – in other words, all deposits held in connection with mobile payment services. As most African deposit insurance schemes provide implicit deposit guarantee covers or are – in certain circumstances – non-existent, this should of necessity be an area of regulatory focus in the development of the regulatory landscape for mobile financial services in Africa in the future.

To add to this, the ability for customers to now send and receive funds on a cross-border basis through mobile payments services calls for a coordinated regional approach to regulating these mobile payment services. As seen above, this in particular would involve establishing regional safety nets such as a coordinated regional approach to deposit guarantee schemes for the treatment of customer funds held in financial institutions that are connected to mobile payments services. This should ideally be built into existing regional financial regulatory regimes which, in a significant number of regional economic communities in Africa, are still in rudimentary stages (Salami, 2012).

2. Crowdfunding in Africa

Crowdfunding is a mechanism for raising finance for a cause or business ventures from the public or investors using internet/online platforms.

The four main types of crowdfunding are reward-, donations-, equity- and debt-based. In rewards-based crowdfunding, backers give a small amount of money in exchange for a reward. In donation-based crowdfunding, donors donate a small amount of money in exchange for gratitude and the feeling of supporting a cause they believe in. In equity crowdfunding, investors invest large amounts of money in a company in exchange for a small piece of equity in the company. In debt crowdfunding, lenders make a loan with the expectation to make back their principal plus interest.

Crowdfunding has increased in popularity in Africa over the last decade. However, its use in Africa has been limited in comparison with other regions of the world. According to a World Bank report, in 2015 the African crowdfunding market amounted to about $70 million, accounting for less than 1% of the global crowdfunding market (World Bank, 2015, p. 1) – although a

2013 report estimated that by 2025, crowdfunding will be a $96 billion industry growing at a rate of 300% per year (World Bank, 2013, p. 43). Huge opportunity still exists for crowdfunding to engender financial inclusion and build business and entrepreneurship across the continent; however, the regulatory infrastructure needs to be robust enough to enable this development and should not constitute a barrier to this process.

Crowdfunding platforms are usually structured as follows. An entrepreneur posts a business pitch to a website. These pitches include a fundraising target that the entrepreneur hopes to reach. There are also non-African platforms that allow African entrepreneurs to pitch their businesses and raise capital from funders abroad. However, certain international platforms may use payment systems that restrict contributions originating in lower-income countries. Frequently, funders are members of the entrepreneur's social network, but in many cases funders may be the general public or institutional investors looking for small businesses to support. Most crowdfunding activities in sub-Saharan Africa are donations-based, but there has been some significant early activity around equity-based and debt-based platforms in South Africa, Kenya and Ghana.

2.1 Opportunities

Crowdfunding presents three clear opportunities for entrepreneurs on the African continent.

As seen in the section on mobile financial services, African entrepreneurs' access to credit is often constrained — banks are highly risk-averse and potential borrowers are often too small-scale, or lack the credit history and other data, to qualify for bank loans. By enabling entrepreneurs to appeal directly to supporters or potential customers without onerous inquiries into their creditworthiness, business histories or incomes, more avenues are created for businesses to access capital.

Second, as a purely digital mechanism, African crowdfunding can leverage the increased use of mobile networks to transact business. The rapid expansion of mobile technologies in Africa in the last decade, as discussed earlier, therefore promotes its development, as people across Africa are using phones for transactions ranging from common purchases to peer-to-peer micro-lending. Even though there is less familiarity (and in certain cases, trust) in Africa when it comes to online fundraising as a capital-raising tool, the prevalence of mobile phones could allow for rapid increases in crowdfunding activity in this context.

Third, crowdfunding platforms subsidize the costs of marketing and promotion by typically allowing entrepreneurs to use the platform for free. The platforms themselves have a built-in user base, and most of the platforms that are currently active in Africa have no subscription costs. Listing a venture on a crowdfunding platform not only increases exposure to investors, but it also enables entrepreneurs to benefit from the platform's infrastructure (e.g. online presence) and brand recognition.

2.2 Legal and Regulatory Challenges of Crowdfunding in Africa

Investors and African entrepreneurs who use crowdfunding platforms are operating in an unregulated space, at least in most African countries. The ensuing paragraphs assess the legal and regulatory issues raised by crowdfunding.

First, the absence of regulation means an absence of adequate investor protection. The absence of laws requiring disclosures and data protection which enable contributors to have opportunities for legal redress when violated would, not surprisingly, dissuade investors from funding entrepreneur ventures through this mechanism. By contrast, in the United States, Title III of the Jumpstart Our Business Start-ups Act regulates equity crowdfunding and permits companies to issue securities through crowdfunding platforms. US law requires potential crowdfunders to make substantive disclosures that provide investors with information. Similar disclosure rules in African nations would enable investors to make informed decisions and potentially improve investor confidence.

Another area of regulatory concern is the lack of clarity about the legal status of African crowdfunding organizations, which is a huge concern for international investors. For instance, most equity or debt crowdfunding organizations in Africa are not licensed as financial services companies; as a result, some investors are concerned that they may be violating money laundering and terrorism financing laws by making contributions to these platforms. In order to encourage more crowdfunding, governments need to mitigate these concerns by enacting laws on crowdfunding, which among other things would clarify the status of crowdfunding organisations and allay investor concerns around money laundering.

Some countries are beginning to take steps in this direction; for example, the Financial Services Board in South Africa released a list of potentially applicable existing regulations and encouraged crowdfunders to contact the Board to ensure the lawfulness of their campaigns. There is reason to believe that as the crowd-funding industry grows in African markets, so too will be the push for an adequate regulatory framework. For instance, in 2015, the African Crowdfunding Association was founded with the specific objective of lobbying for clear and simple crowdfunding legislation and harmonization of such legislation across countries (ACA, 2018a). The organization has not succeeded in getting any laws passed but counts among its members the largest African-based crowdfunding organisations including Thundafund and M-Changa (ACA, 2018b).

Since many start-ups solicit financing locally, and access to the internet through mobile phones facilitates this, a regional framework designed around these infrastructures to ensure a coordinated regional regime is needed. This will ensure that a robust regional regulatory regime exists, since the vast majority of crowdfunding platforms available across the continent today are locally-oriented and do not support international payment mechanisms which enable most crowdfunding platforms across the world to attract capital internationally. Raising finance within the region can therefore be a useful channel to facilitate financial inclusion of start-up entrepreneurs who may not be able to access finance through the formal financial sector and thus promote the growth of start-ups and small businesses across the African continent.

3. Cryptocurrencies, Initial Coin Offerings and Access to Finance in Africa

Cryptocurrencies are defined as decentralized convertible virtual currencies. They are decentralized, meaning that they are issued without a central administering authority. They are cryptography-based, distributed open source and function on a peer-to-peer basis. Significantly, the underlying protocols on which most cryptocurrencies are based do not require or provide user identification and verification. Also, the historical transaction records generated on the blockchain (the technology behind bitcoin, which serves as a public ledger of all cryptocurrency transactions) are not necessarily associated with an individual's identity.

Cryptocurrencies are also—by definition—convertible virtual currencies, as they can be exchanged for fiat currency such as pounds, dollars and euros, and this facilitates their use for settling commercial transactions. They are a recent phenomenon, and Bitcoin was the first to gain international reputation as a digital currency that could be used to settle transactions after it was anonymously created in early 2009. Amongst other things, it is believed that they have the potential to facilitate financial inclusion, as they require no central administrating body to coordinate their use and parties that use them can make payments directly on the blockchain on a peer-to-peer basis. By by-passing the sometimes stringent requirements for accessing the formal financial sector and opening a bank account, they can facilitate financial inclusion and enable individuals excluded from the formal financial sector to transact nationally and internationally with parties willing to accept cryptocurrencies for goods and services sold. To that extent, they can facilitate financial inclusion in Africa. However, despite that cryptocurrencies can facilitate financial inclusion in Africa in this way, Salami argues that they raise significant regulatory issues — which are more accentuated in the African context — as they can also be used to facilitate crime, money laundering and terrorism financing (Salami, 2018).

Cryptocurrencies can also be used as financial securities, like stocks. In this context, they can be used by blockchain start-ups as a means to fund projects or business ideas by issuing digital 'tokens' (or new cryptocurrencies) to subscribers who pay using mechanisms including prominent cryptocurrencies—such as bitcoin or ethereum—or through fiat currency in order to acquire proprietary interests in the business or project.

Some firms have used this as a mechanism to raise finance to start businesses. These start-ups would have found it almost impossible to raise finance through the traditional initial public offering (IPO) method due to regulatory requirements they would not have been able to fulfil.

Under an IPO, companies need to be listed on a domestic stock exchange and, to do so, are required to fulfil prospectus requirements including disclosure of their accounts. This method is designed to protect retail investors and preserve market integrity.

By bypassing any requirement to access financing from the public through exchanges or intermediaries, it becomes cheaper, quicker and easier for new companies to raise funds to finance their business. Blockchain start-ups have raised over US$1.5 billion in funding through ICOs (initial coin offerings) since the start of 2017. A few African start-ups have also benefitted from raising finance through ICOs, such as SureRemit, which raised $7 million through an ICO in 2018 (Ayuga, 2018). However, suffice it to mention that the global regulatory framework for ICOs is still very confused and so is the case in the African context. This position is much unlike the detailed regulatory framework for IPOs in countries with advanced capital markets. So, for example, a firm seeking financing via an ICO is only expected to circulate a white paper setting out the basic objectives of the business, the cost of setting it up and how this would be done. Also, as the business is a blockchain company and the issuing is done on that digital ledger of transactions, the identities of those subscribing to tokens are hidden. The true identity of the issuing company may also be disguised regardless of statements in the white paper—which also poses a potential threat to subscribers.

As the true identities of parties are largely unknown, and as regulation within this space is sparse in most countries, firms seeking funding in this way currently are usually not obliged to know their subscribers under, for example, anti-money laundering (AML) requirements, which makes these platforms easy targets for miscreants. Given the weak financial regulatory framework in numerous African countries, this presents a huge problem for both investor protection and the monitoring of AML and terrorism financing. So, although ICOs can benefit African entrepreneurs/SMEs, they raise the same regulatory issues and concerns as those raised in the case of equity crowdfunding. Although a global regulatory approach to regulating ICOs is very needful for the financing of businesses internationally − as noted above, they can be described as a type of equity crowdfunding or very similar to this − attracting investor interest predominantly on the basis of their network, which, as seen above, is predominantly national and regional—d therefore calls for a coordinated regional regulatory approach for their operation across the continent.

4. Financial Integration With These Recent Financial Developments

The new financial developments on the African continent discussed above—mobile financial services, crowdfunding and cryptocurrencies—have significant regional implications calling for a coordinated regional approach to regulating these financial developments. This is significant for these developments to promote financial inclusion within a stable, safe and fair environment that does not stifle financial innovations.

The achievement of a coordinated financial regulatory framework can be done within the context of existing regional economic communities (RECs) which are enshrined in the African Union and the African Economic Community agenda to achieve monetary union for the whole of Africa by 2028 in six stages (AEC Treaty, 1991, Art 6(2)). An integral part of this plan includes the achievement of financial harmonization, first among RECs (AEC Treaty, 1991, Art 6(2), stage 2) and then across the entire continent (AEC Treaty, 1991, Art 6(2), stages 5 and 6). However, for an effective regional regulatory framework to be achieved, certain requirements need to be in place. These are discussed in the ensuing paragraphs.

4.1 Strengthening Existing Regional Cooperation on Mobile Financial Services Among African Member States

The Alliance for Financial Inclusion (AFI) is the world's leading organisation on financial inclusion policy and regulation. It promotes and develops evidence based policy solutions that improve the lives of the poor through the power of financial inclusion. It comprises central banks and other financial regulatory institutions from over 90 developing countries. Its vision is making financial services more accessible to the world's unbanked by empowering policymakers to increase access to quality financial services for the poorest population. It has also developed a more harmonized approach in the regulatory reporting of mobile payments for central banks and banking supervisors.

The African Mobile Phone Financial Services Policy Initiation (AMPI) is one of the initiatives of the AFI, which was created in February 2013 to be a platform for AFI member institutions (mainly central banks and financial regulatory authorities) in Africa to provide high-level leadership in the overall development of MFS policy and regulatory frameworks and to coordinate efforts of regional peer learning (AFI, 2009).

However, for this group to make a significant positive contribution to the development of mobile financial services in Africa, their work would need to be plugged into the regional regulatory framework characterized by close collaboration with RECs. Such work — for example, of the AMPI in the development of MFS policy and regulatory frameworks — can inform the regional financial regulatory framework (Salami, 2012). This regulatory framework would necessarily require stronger levels of harmonization from African states and much more commitment to the overall goals of mobile financial services.

4.2 Devising Regional Standards Tailored to the Stage of Mobile Payments/Financial Services Development of African RECs

A way forward to achieve financial harmonization of mobile financial services among African RECs would be to devise regional standards relevant to the stages of mobile financial services development on the continent. As African states are at different stages in this process, one way to proceed would be to adopt regional standards and mechanisms for the different groups at the same stages of development. Another alternative would be to integrate only those Member States within RECs that have attained a certain level of mobile financial services development and progressively increase the numbers as the mobile financial services of more Member States develop. Taking a 'one-size-fits all' approach would achieve only minimal if any success, and the AMPI should bear this in mind as it pushes forward its agenda. So, for example, in the case of a regional approach to regulating mobile financial services this should seek to integrate states within a sub-region which have achieved similar degrees of development such as Kenya, Tanzania and Uganda—who can be said to have achieved almost similar growth in mobile financial services development in the East African community.

Another alternative would be to use the financial regulatory framework of a regional success story, such as the Kenyan Central Bank's regulation of M-Pesa, as the model for the single regional regulatory framework for all the RECs. As member states' mobile financial services develop, they can begin to join this regional framework.

4.3 Instituting a Regional Regulatory Regime for Crowdfunding

As seen above that crowdfunding presents huge opportunities for raising finance for business ventures and causes but with hardly any regulation of this activity in Africa, there is first a need for the introduction of national regulation on crowdfunding by African governments, and second, following the former, regional coordination of the activities of the regulatory authorities concerned. This would ensure financial stability, investor protection and the institution of anti-money laundering and terrorism-financing procedures. As such, it would necessarily involve the coordination of the activities of national financial services authorities; financial intelligence units/agencies — if these exist within the countries.

4.4 Preparing for a Robust Regional Framework for Regulating the Use of Cryptocurrencies

As stated above, the global regulatory regime for checking the money laundering and terrorism financing implications of cryptocurrencies is still under discussion (Salami, 2018). The regional approach for regulating cryptocurrencies can be aligned with the global framework when instituted. In the meantime, however, African states can start to prepare for this by concentrating their efforts on tackling money laundering. This can be achieved by harmonizing their domestic provisions on the identification of suspicious transactions, investigation of such transactions, and the prosecution and conviction of those involved in money laundering activities (Salami, 2017). The largely incompatible legal and regulatory approaches that currently exist for money laundering and terrorism financing are unlikely to enable the achievement of a future robust regional regulatory regime for cryptocurrencies, which then threatens both financial stability and regional and international security (Salami, 2017).

The harmonization of regional regulation of money laundering and terrorism financing can be based on the application of international standards as set out by the Financial Action Task Force recommendations (FATF, 2012). This would facilitate tracking and prosecuting money laundering and terrorism financing activities generally within financial institutions. This would require harmonization of information sharing among regulatory authorities in order to track illicit cross-border transactions as geographic borders diminish in importance, the ability also for law enforcement entities and regulators to work collaboratively is critical. The absence of regional harmonization in this context would make it even more difficult to achieve any form of harmonization for the even more regulatory challenging cryptocurrency payment mechanism.

Regional harmonization can be achieved in this context through regional economic communities (RECs). RECs wishing cryptocurrencies to be used to facilitate further financial inclusion would need to be prepared to harmonize their legal and regulatory frameworks.

4.5 Strong Domestic Financial Regulation and Financial Regulatory Authorities

The increase in the use of mobile payment services which still necessitate customer funds and funds in transit to be held in banks and require that banks are effectively regulated for deposits/funds they hold to be safeguarded. Also, as discussed above, provisions concerning deposit insurance would need to be strengthened and built in − in the case of mobile payment services. The domestic financial regulatory regime, for all participating member states of the regional regulatory framework of mobile financial services therefore needs to be strong. This would be necessary to avoid any systemic risks resulting from the operation of mobile payment services. As such, financial regulation in African states needs to be strengthened. Areas of focus would include strengthening the accounting and disclosure standards for financial institutions and companies as well as their corporate governance provisions. Also useful would be the strengthening of financial regulatory authorities' enforcement powers in order that they are able to effectively perform oversight functions.

4.6 Effective Co-ordination Among National Supervisors

Supervisory authorities would need to be able to coordinate their activities within the robust REC framework. Coordination would be required with respect to mobile payment services for the following areas: coordination through information sharing among authorities including financial regulatory authorities, financial intelligence units and crime investigations agencies; coordinating anti-money laundering and countering terrorism financing approaches; and coordination with respect to treatment of customers, standards for mobile network operators, protection of customer funds stored in bank accounts and coordination of approach to be taken for a possible deposit guarantee scheme for protecting such funds within the financial system. A good example of the latter is seen in the operation of EU fund safeguarding provisions for mobile payment systems which is provided for in the Payment Services Directive. Article 10 of this directive, among other things, provides for member states' treatment of funds derived through mobile financial services. This provision covers aspects discussed above such as ensuring the safeguarding of such funds through prohibitions to co-mingling; insulation against claims of from creditors upon insolvency of MNO or financial institution; and their coverage by the deposit guarantee scheme for financial institution (Directive, 2015).

The implementation of this provision in EU member states is enabled through the supranational structure that characterizes the governance framework for EU generally, and more specifically EU financial services. Since national central banks are used to operating within the European System of Central Banks as branches of the ECB, it is not surprising to see the coordination of member states' regulatory authority to ensure that mobile payment systems funds are effectively safeguarded through the requirements to comply with this directive that is binding on all states.

As the governance framework of African RECs is not as robust as that of the EU — not embracing the concept of supranationalism — Salami argues (Salami, 2008) that this makes submission to a regional financial regulatory authority more of a challenge, especially where African states are likely to have different approaches for the treatment of customer funds held in bank accounts.

4.7 Strengthening the General Legal Environment as a Foundation for Robust Financial and Payment Systems Regime in Africa

Reforming African legal and judicial systems is essential in order to support any form of financial systems development (Salami, 2011a,b). As such, the slow and inefficient manner in which contract, property, insolvency and criminal laws are enforced should be improved in order to enhance financial inclusion through mobile payments, crowdfunding and the use of cryptocurrencies.

5. Conclusion

The recent development in the world of finance in Africa including the growth of mobile payment services, agent banking, crowdfunding and the use of cryptocurrencies to facilitate financial inclusion all come at a cost to regional financial stability and international and regional security. It is therefore essential — as discussed in this chapter — that a strong regional regulatory regime be instituted to further enhance financial inclusion through these developments but not at the expense of regional financial stability and international and regional security.

References

African Crowdfunding Association. (2018a). *About*. http://africancrowd.org/about/.

African Crowdfunding Association. (2018b). *Directory of members*. http://africancrowd.org/membership/directory-of-members/.

African Economic Community Treaty. (1991). *AEC treaty*. Available from: https://au.int/sites/default/files/treaties/7775-treaty-0016_-_treaty_establishing_the_african_economic_community_e.pdf.

Alliance for Financial Inclusion. (2009). *African financial inclusion policy initiative*. http://www.afi-global.org/initiatives/african-mobile-phone-financial-services-policy-initiative-ampi.

Ayugi, W. (2018). *Nigerian blockchain startup SureRemit raises $7 million in biggest African ICO to date*. http://bitcoinafrica.io/2018/02/16/sureremit-ico/.

Directive (EU) 2015/2366 of the European Parliament and the Council of 25 November 2015 on payment services in the internal market. Available from: https://eur-lex.europa.eu/legal-content/EN/TXT/PDF/?uri=CELEX:32015L2366&from=EN (Payment System Directive).

Financial Action Task Force (FATF). (2012). *International standards on combatting money laundering and the financing of terrorisms*. Available from: http://www.fatf-gafi.org/media/fatf/documents/recommendations/pdfs/FATF_Recommendations.pdf.

Okwii, D. (2017). *The banks are about to go after mobile money with agency banking*. Available from: http://www.dignited.com/25154/banks-going-mobile-money-agency-banking/.

Salami, I. (2008). Devising a governance structure for the African union. *African Journal of International and Comparative Law, 16*(2), 262–273.

Salami, I. (2011a). African financial markets – going global or staying at home? *Journal of International Banking Law and Regulation, 26*(11), 35–44.

Salami, I. (2011b). Financial regulation in African frontier markets – can the EU approach work? *Law and Financial Markets Review, 5*(5), 380–387.

Salami, I. (2012). *Financial regulation in Africa: An assessment of financial integration arrangements in african emerging and frontier markets*. Farnham Surrey: Ashgate.

Salami, I. (2017). Terrorism financing with virtual currencies - Can RegTech help combat this? *Studies in Conflict and Terrorism*. Available from: https://www.tandfonline.com/doi/abs/10.1080/1057610X.2017.1365464.

Salami, I. (2018). *Cryptocurrencies – cross-border regulatory dimensions*. European Financial Review. April – May issue. Available from: http://www.europeanfinancialreview.com/?p=23432.

World Bank. (2013). *Crowdfunding's potential for the developing world*. Available from: https://www.infodev.org/infodev-files/wb_crowdfundingreport-v12.pdf.

World Bank. (2015). *Crowdfunding in emerging markets: Lessons from Eastern Africa start-ups*. Available from: https://www.infodev.org/infodev-files/crowdfunding-in-east-africa.pdf.

14

THE POTENTIAL OF FINTECH IN ENABLING FINANCIAL INCLUSION

Daniel Makina
Department of Finance, Risk Management and Banking, University of South Africa, Pretoria, South Africa

1. Introduction

FinTech, a portmanteau for financial technology, is the new buzzword that summarizes the use of technology to deliver financial services, often referred to as alternative finance. According to the UK Alternative Finance Industry Report (2014), alternative finance covers a variety of new financing models emerging outside the traditional financial system, which utilize online platforms or websites to connect fundraisers directly with funders and investors; in other words, they utilize digital technology to

Extending Financial Inclusion in Africa. https://doi.org/10.1016/B978-0-12-814164-9.00014-1

deliver financial services. Such models include digital payment systems, crowdfunding, peer-to-peer (P2P) consumer lending, peer-to-peer business lending, and invoice trading. Alternative finance has made a significant impact on the consumer and small business lending environments and is rapidly changing the financial inclusion landscape.

From a theoretical perspective, alternative financing models are driven by the need to address the asymmetric information problem inherent in a financing decision. The ability of these models to match funders and fundraisers in a transparent manner goes a long way in reducing asymmetric information among market participants. From another angle, financial innovations are driving reduction in transaction costs. The transaction cost innovative theory is one theory, among others, which underlies such developments in transactions technology (Niehaus, 1983). Advances in technology are resulting in the reduction of transaction costs enabling efficient coordination, management and use of information. These developments have reinforced technology acceptance and its diffusion in delivering financial services.

According to the technology acceptance model (TAM) developed by Davis (1989), a person's actual use of a technology is influenced directly or indirectly by the user's behavioural intentions, attitude towards using the technology, its perceived usefulness (PU) and its perceived ease of use (PEOU). PU and PEOU are two cognitive concepts that underpin TAM. External factors affect intention and actual use through mediated effects on PU and PEOU. Thus, TAM provides a basis upon which to track how external variables influence belief, attitude and intention to use technology. The use of technology in finance is of course not new—but a step change is now expected with the novel application of a number of technologies in combination, notably involving blockchain, the 'Internet of things' and artificial intelligence (AI). This novel application of a number of technologies in combination makes the current wave of disruption different from others we have seen before in finance. FinTech innovations promise a more efficient, accessible and less vulnerable financial system. While some FinTech start-ups or companies are partnering or collaborating with traditional banks, others are offering financial services as standalone institutions. The provision of financial services is no longer the domain of the regulated financial sector alone.

FinTech's ability to reduce information asymmetries and transaction costs makes it a potent weapon for deepening financial inclusion. Both profit-driven private entrepreneurial players and policymakers have taken note of opportunities offered by technology. Two products of FinTech that are having or promising the most profound impact on financial inclusion in Africa, the least banked region of the world, are mobile money and crowdfunding. Mobile money, facilitated by mobile technology, is bringing millions of previously unbanked people into the category of those who own a formal financial account. For many, it is the first stepping-stone into the formal financial system. The World Bank reports that in Africa, more people have a mobile money account than purely have an account with a financial institution. Crowdfunding, which is being spurred by Web 2.0 technologies, has potential to extend financial access for entrepreneurial and innovative small businesses that are financially constrained.

The objective of this chapter is to assess the potential of FinTech in extending financial inclusion in Africa. The rest of the chapter is structured as follows. Section 2 examines the growth of FinTech and its influence on financial services provision in general. Section 3 discusses global efforts underway to promote digital financial inclusion. Section 4 explores the evolution of FinTech in Africa and its impacts. Section 5 examines the emergence of crowdfunding and its prospects in mitigating the SME funding gap in Africa. Section 6 discusses challenges besetting FinTech proliferation in Africa. Finally, the chapter concludes by making some predictions about the future.

2. The Growth of FinTech and Its Influence on Financial Services

The history of FinTech can be traced as far back as 1838 when Samuel Morse introduced the electric telegraph system. This subsequently led to the invention of the first transatlantic cable in 1866, which provided the infrastructure for financial globalization. Developments in FinTech since then have included credit cards in the 1950s, ATMs in the 1960s, electronic stock trading in the 1970s, bank mainframe computers in the 1990s, and internet and e-commerce business models in the 1990s. These developments did not actually threaten the existence of traditional banks but rather aided their operations. In support of this view, Desai (2015) observes that Federal Deposit Insurance Corporation data for 1950–2014 showed that the number of bank branches in the USA increased from approximately 18,000 to over 82,000.

However, the new era of FinTech since 2008 is not defined by the financial products and services delivered but by who digitally delivers them. It is a technological development led by FinTech start-ups, which are not simply enhancing financial services but competing with traditional banks or even replacing them in the provision of financial services. Today financial services are being delivered via mobile wallets, payment apps, cryptography, robo-advisors (use of algorithms and surveys to enable investors to build portfolios) and crowdfunding using Web 2.0 technologies. FinTech is revolutionizing the provision of digital financial services and creating new markets that are attracting the unbanked as bankable clients. The Consultative Group to Assist the Poor has observed that digital financial services have a 'significant potential to provide a range of affordable, convenient and secure banking services to poor people in developing countries'.

According to the International Finance Corporation (IFC) (2017), the FinTech sector has exponentially grown, attracting $19 billion from investors in 2016 as compared with $12.2 billion in 2014. FinTech companies are influencing the financial industry in at least three significant ways. First, they are promoting efficiency in the provision of financial services through digitalization of services delivery. Second, FinTechs are providing the flexibility needed to provide cheap and accessible products and services, which flexibility is absent in traditional banks. Third, they are offering bank-like services but are not regulated as traditional banks.

PwC's *Global FinTech Report* 2017 provides some insights regarding FinTech's growing influence on financial services. The report observes that FinTech is a major disruptor to traditional financial institutions, as an increasing number of consumers are planning to increase usage of non-traditional financial services providers. Furthermore, it observes that in response to this threat, traditional financial institutions are embracing the disruptive nature of FinTech by significantly increasing their internal efforts to innovate. They hope to achieve this feat through collaborating and integrating with FinTech companies. 'We learn from innovative FinTech firms, partner with them, and give them projects to deliver for us. It is a symbiotic relationship', is the general response the traditional financial institutions give, so the PwC *Global FinTech Report* says. Table 14.1 provides a list of the Top 10 FinTech companies in 2016 as surveyed by H2 Ventures and KPMG (2016).

It is noteworthy that China, an emerging economy, dominates the FinTech industry, having the largest number of the top FinTech firms in the world in 2016. For the developing world, Arner, Barberis, and Buckley (2015) observe that FinTech is spurred by characteristics such as a growing and young digitally well-informed population that utilizes mobile devices, a fast-growing middle class, and inefficient financial and capital markets. China as well as other developing countries possess these characteristics. While about two billion people out of the world's seven

Table 14.1 Top 10 FinTech Companies in 2016.

Name of FinTech	Year Founded	Location	Nature of Business
Ant Financial	2004	China	Open ecosystem providing inclusive financial services to small and micro-enterprises and individual consumers
Qudian	2014	China	Operates two main business platforms — a consumer finance platform and a micro-credit lending platform
Oscar	2013	USA	Health insurance employing technology, design, and data to humanize health care
Lufax	2011	China	Internet based lending and wealth management platform
ZhongAn	2013	China	Internet insurance company that utilizes mobile internet, cloud computing, big data, etc
Atom Bank	2014	UK	Branchless app based bank that utilizes biometric security: face and voice recognition
Kreditech	2012	Germany	Utilizes machine learning to provide access to better credit and higher convenience for digital banking services
Avant	2012	USA	Online lending platform that utilizes big data and machine-learning algorithms to mitigate default risk and fraud
SoFi	2011	USA	Assists early stage professionals accelerate their success with student loan refinancing, mortgages, mortgage refinancing, and personal loans
JD Finance	2013	China	Engages in seven lines of business: supply chain finance, consumer finance, crowd-funding, wealth management, payment services, insurance and securities services

H2 Ventures, KPMG. (2016). FINTECH100: Leading global FinTech innovators. *2016 FINTECH100 Report.*

billion population are estimated to have no access to financial services, one billion of them are in Asia of which two-thirds are in China and India. According to the *Peking University Digital Inclusive Finance Index* (2011–15), China has experienced an increasing digital dividend as mobile payment users in the country exceeded 520 million.

Indeed, digital technology is revolutionizing access to finance in the developing world. FinTech innovations overlap and feed off each other, which complementarities have the potential to provide disruptive financial services. He et al. (2017) have observed that the adoption of new applications can grow non-linearly. Several notable technologies are transforming financial services:

1. AI and big data, which have enabled innovations such as machine learning and predictive analytics; these innovations are being used in investment advice, credit solutions, regulation technology (Regtech), fraud detection and asset trading
2. distributed computing, which has enabled distributed ledger and blockchain innovations that are being used for settling payments, business-to-business payments, back-office recording, and digital currencies
3. cryptography, which has facilitated innovations such as smart contracts and biometrics being used for automatic transactions, security and identity protection
4. mobile access and the internet, which have enabled innovations such APIs and digital wallets being used for finance dashboards, crowdfunding, peer-to-peer lending, interoperability and scalability

What is evident is that FinTech is pervasive in all aspects of financial services — payment systems, regulation, back-office operations, savings, credit, risk management and the provision of financial advice. He et al. (2017) have further observed that FinTech companies though relatively small to reflect their knowledge-based business models, have attracted substantial investment, increasing from $9 billion in 2010 to over $25 billion by 2016 globally.

Research by the McKinsey Global Institute (2016) shows FinTech's economic impacts and offers some predictions of these by the year 2025:

- GDP in the developing world is forecast to rise by 6%, or $3.7 trillion in monetary terms. Low-income countries such as Ethiopia, India, and Nigeria, with low levels of financial inclusion, would have the greatest potential and would add 10% −12% to their GDPs.
- The additional GDP is forecast to create an estimated 95 million new jobs spread across all sectors of developing economies.
- An estimated 1.6 billion unbanked people, more than half of them women, are forecast to become financially included.
- Digital technology is forecast to revolutionize credit risk assessment so that an additional $2.1 trillion could be sustainably lent out to individuals and small businesses of the developing world.
- Financial services providers are forecast to save $400 billion annually in direct costs, and an estimated $4.2 trillion of new deposits would be attracted, creating revenue opportunities.
- Digital technology would enable governments to save $110 billion by reducing leakage in spending and tax revenue.

3. Global Efforts to Promote Digital Financial Inclusion

The Global Partnership for Financial Inclusion (GPFI) Report (2016, p. 3), titled *Global Standard-Setting Bodies Financial Inclusion: The Evolving Landscape*, states: '"Digital financial inclusion" refers broadly to the use of digital financial services to advance financial inclusion. It involves the deployment of digital means to reach financially excluded and underserved populations with a range of formal financial services suited to their needs, delivered responsibly at a cost affordable to customers and sustainable for providers'. The GPFI summarizes the four key elements of a digital financial inclusion model aimed at offering financially excluded and underserved customers a range of financial services in Box 14.1.

Policymakers have since recognized that digital financial inclusion provides an opportunity to accelerate inclusive growth. Hence, global efforts are now ongoing to promote digital financial inclusion through the setting of standards that would assist countries in formulating national strategies and action plans. At its Toronto Summit in 2010, the Group of 20 (G20) endorsed nine Principles for Innovative Financial Inclusion that reflected the experiences and lessons learned from policymakers worldwide, viz leadership, diversity, innovation, protection, empowerment,

Box 14.1 Four Key Elements of a Digital Financial Inclusion Model.

- a digital device: either a mobile phone or a payment card plus a points of sale device that transmits and receives transaction data;
- agents: individuals, retail stores or outlets, or automated teller machines where customers can put cash in (that is, convert cash into digitally stored value or make a digital payment or transfer) and take cash out (for example, withdrawing from a digital stored-value account or receiving a digital remittance or other transfer or payment);
- a digital transactional platform which (1) enables payments, transfers and value storage through the use of the digital device and (2) connects to an account with a bank or non-bank permitted to store electronic value; and
- the offer of additional financial products and services through the combination of banks and non-banks (including potentially non-financial institutions), leveraging digital transactional platforms.

The Global Partnership for Financial Inclusion (GPFI) report (2016). *Global standard-setting Bodies financial inclusion: The Evolving landscape.* https://www.gpfi.org/sites/default/files/documents/GPFI_WhitePaper_Mar2016.pdf.

cooperation, knowledge, proportionality and framework. These formed the basis of the Financial Inclusion Action Plan. Building on these nine principles and recognizing the potential of digital technology to foster financial inclusion, the G20 published eight High-Level Principles for Digital Financial Inclusion in 2016 to drive the adoption of digital approaches to achieve financial inclusion and inclusive growth goals as well as to increase women's economic participation.

High-Level Principle 1 – Promote a Digital Approach to Financial Inclusion

This high-level principle builds on Principles 1, 'Leadership', and 6, 'Cooperation', of the 2010 G20 Principles. It encourages countries to embrace digital technology as one means to develop inclusive financial systems. This should be achievable through mainstreaming the technology in their national strategies and action plans in a coordinated and monitored manner.

High-Level Principle 2 – Balance Innovation and Risk to Achieve Digital Financial Inclusion

This high-level principle builds on Principles 1, 'Leadership', 'Innovation', and 4, 'Protection', of the 2010 G20 Principles. There are risks involved in adopting financial technology including cybersecurity, system failures and regulatory risks. It is therefore necessary to identify, assess, monitor and manage these risks.

High-Level Principle 3 – Provide an Enabling and Proportionate Legal and Regulatory Framework for Digital Financial Inclusion

This high-level principle builds on Principles 4, 'Protection', 8, 'Proportionality', and 9, 'Framework', of the 2010 G20 Principles. Financial technology has developed in an environment of 'light touch regulation'; that is, a regulatory framework supportive of innovation and competition that at the same time protects consumers. Hence, an appropriate approach is one that does not stifle innovation but always embracing international standards and best practices.

High-Level Principle 4 – Expand the Digital Financial Services Infrastructure Ecosystem

This high-level principle builds on Principle 9, 'Framework', of the 2010 G20 Principles. The majority of the financially excluded in the developing world live in rural areas where basic infrastructure such as roads, electricity, telecommunications and internet access are in short supply. Such infrastructure needs to be upgraded to reach the marginalized segments of the population.

High-Level Principle 5 – Establish Responsible Digital Financial Practices to Protect Consumers

This high-level principle builds on Principles 4, 'Protection', and 5, 'Empowerment', of the 2010 G20 Principles. Largely, it requires integration of two regulatory principles – know your customer and know your data. By providing equal weight to the two principles, consumer and data protection issues are given due attention.

High-Level Principle 6 – Strengthen Digital and Financial Literacy and Awareness

This high-level principle builds on Principle 5, 'Empowerment', of the 2010 G20 Principles. One severe barrier to financial inclusion is lack of technological and financial education. It is thus necessary to support initiatives that enhance both digital and financial literacy.

High-Level Principle 7 – Facilitate Customer Identification for Digital Financial Services

This high-level principle builds on Principles 1, 'Leadership', and 6, 'Cooperation', of the 2010 G20 Principles. One of the barriers to financial inclusion is lack of identity documentation. Digital technology that facilitates biological recognition is providing a risk-based approach to customer due diligence to break this barrier.

High-Level Principle 8 – Track Digital Financial Inclusion Progress

This high-level principle builds on Principle 7, 'Knowledge', of the 2010 G20 Principles. Since progress should be measurable, a system capable of analysing and monitoring the supply of and demand for digital financial services should be put in place.

4. The Emergence of FinTech in Africa

4.1 The Emergence of Mobile Money

In Africa, telecommunications companies have led FinTech developments, the most successful being mobile money – M-Pesa – launched in East Africa, which is the provision of payment services using e-money recorded on a mobile phone. In 2014, World Bank's Findex Database noted that while globally, 1% of adults reported having both a financial institution account and a mobile account, in sub-Saharan Africa (SSA), 12% of adults reported having a mobile money account, and half of them were not customers of conventional financial institutions.

According to the GSMA, there were more than four billion mobile phone handsets in the world by the end of 2016. It reports that in 2016 there were more than 500 million registered mobile money accounts around the world, with SSA accounting for 277 million accounts. SSA is the fastest growing mobile market, with 420 million unique mobile subscribers as at the end of 2016 representing a penetration rate of 43%. SIM connections alone reached 731 million and are estimated to rise to about a billion by 2020. The forecast trend of the mobile industry in SSA over the period 2016–20 is shown in Table 14.2. Though SSA accounts for about a 10th of the global mobile subscriber base, it is predicted to be the fastest-growing region over the 5-year period from 2016 to 2020. This is expected to have a significant impact on economic growth, since the World Bank estimates that an extra 10 phones per 100 people can boost GDP growth by 0.8 in a typical developing country (The Economist, 2009).

Mobile technology, which is spurring mobile money, is one technology that has satisfied the main constructs of the TAM, viz PU and PEOU, and hence the widespread acceptance of mobile money in Africa. Studies in Kenya and Somalia by Ahmed (2017) indicate that PEOU, convenience and technology fit had a significant impact on consumers' perception of mobile money. Tobbin and Kuwornu (2011) reported similar results for Ghana. A study by Oliveira and others (2014) conducted in Portugal, a country with the highest mobile phone adoption in the European Union, found that initial trust, performance expectancy,

Table 14.2 Sub-Saharan Africa Mobile Industry Statistics.

	Position in 2016	Estimate for 2020
Unique mobile subscribers	420 million	535 million
Sim connections	731 million	942 million
Smart phones	198 million	498 million
Mobile internet penetration	26%	38%
Mobile industry contribution to GDP	7.7%	8.6%
Employment (direct jobs)	1.1 million	1.3 million

Extracted from https://www.gsma.com/mobileeconomy/sub-saharan-africa-2017/.

technology characteristics, and task technology fit have an effect on the behavioural intentions to use mobile banking.

In Africa, mobile money originated in Kenya in 2007, where it was termed M-Pesa, which means mobile money in Swahili. It was launched by two private mobile telecommunications companies — Vodacom and Safaricom. M-Pesa is a simple technology, as anyone with a basic phone can use it. It uses SMS and there is no data capability required. A user does not need to have a bank account. The mobile money account can easily get a top-up, and cash is withdrawn via a network of agents. It is personalized, as it is operated with a secret PIN so that money remains secure even if the phone is lost. Thus, M-Pesa satisfies both the attributes of PEOU and PU. In 2008, 1 year after launch, M-Pesa surpassed one million active accounts. In the same year, another mobile operator, Orange Cote d'Ivoire, launched mobile money called Orange Money in West Africa, while Vodacom launched another M-Pesa service in Tanzania. By 2010, MTN Mobile Money was live across seven SSA markets: Benin, Cameroon, Côte d'Ivoire, Ghana, Guinea-Bissau, Rwanda and Uganda.

In 2016 there were more than 100 million active users of mobile money in SSA, with seven countries having more than 40% of the adult population using the service, viz Gabon, Ghana, Kenya, Namibia, Tanzania, Uganda and Zimbabwe. The GSMA (2016) reports that between 2011 and 2016, the number of active mobile money accounts in West Africa increased from 1.5 million to 29 million. Compared with other emerging regions, financial inclusion brought about by mobile money in SSA has been more inclusive, as the gender gap in mobile money usage, at 19.5%, is about half the average for all low- and middle-income countries. Notwithstanding the better gender gap, more than 225 million women in SSA are still without a mobile money account.

From inception, the dominant use of mobile has been person-to-person transfers within the same country and airtime top-ups. However, by 2016 the mobile money ecosystem transactions had expanded to include bill payments, bulk payments, international remittances (especially in the East African and West African corridors) and merchant payments. Other mobile money services such as credit, savings and insurance have also been rolled out. The GSMA (2015) reports that mobile-money-enabled credit services have risen in SSA from six services in Kenya in 2011 to 39 services in 11 countries by 2016. The uptake of credit has been phenomenal in mature mobile money markets such as Kenya and Tanzania. As of June 2016, the mobile credit service in Kenya, M-Shwari, had 15 million accounts, whereas the mobile credit service in Tanzania, M-Pawa, had about 5 million accounts, only having been launched in 2014. In Kenya, mobile money services are even venturing into capital markets. Box 14.2 provides an example of a mobile money bond issue launched in 2017.

Mobile money is now serving other sectors of the economy such as water and sanitation, education, energy and agriculture. In 2009, Tanzania's Dar es Salaam Water and Sewage Corporation (DAWASCO) partnered with Vodacom Tanzania to digitize bill payments, a technological development that resulted in savings of 1 billion Tanzanian shillings per month within 4 years and increased revenue by 38% in 2013. In East Africa, households are accessing energy through pay-as-you-go solar home systems that are integrated with mobile money payments. During the period 2015−16, 99% of secondary school students in Cote d'Ivoire paid their school fees via mobile money. In Liberia, teachers save 15% of the cost of receiving their salaries if they are paid via mobile money. The saved costs include the cost of bank fees and the cost of taking a bus to the nearest town with a bank.

4.2 Crowdfunding

Crowdfunding is a financial innovation that describes alternative financing models that are transforming how start-ups and small businesses are being funded. According to Mollick (2014, p. 2), 'crowdfunding refers to the efforts by entrepreneurial individuals and groups − cultural, social, and for-profit−− to fund their ventures by drawing on relatively small contributions from a

Box 14.2 Mobile Money Bond Launched in Kenya

In an effort to promote a savings culture, on 30 June 2017 the government launched the M-Akiba (Akiba means savings in Swahili), the first sovereign bond sold exclusively through mobile platforms. The bond is designed for small investors with only a mobile money account. The minimum amount that could be invested was 3000 shillings ($29) which was far less than the minimum of 50,000 shillings required for other bonds. The first sovereign mobile money bond was for 3 years with a coupon rate of 10%, about 3% above the deposit rate of commercial banks. The coupon payments would be made through mobile money. The issue was intended to raise 5 billion shillings for infrastructure projects. Though a tiny fraction of the 269 billion shillings the government intends to raise in 2017 for infrastructure projects, it opened opportunities for the future of mobile money.

The Economist. (2017). *Kenya's sovereign debt.* July 1st, 2017.

relatively large number of individuals using the internet, without standard financial intermediaries'. In essence, crowdfunding utilizes Web 2.0 technologies and existing online payment systems to facilitate transactions between creators or entrepreneurs (funds deficit units) and funders (surplus units) (Gerber and others, 2012).

Though crowdfunding can exist in many forms, there are four main models, viz (1) donations-based, (2) reward-based, (3) peer-to-peer (P2P) lending and (4) equity crowdfunding. Donations-based crowdfunding is where the funds are raised from many individuals for a specific noble cause without expectation of compensation, whereas in reward-based crowdfunding the funders would be expecting some token gift. P2P lending connects individuals or businesses looking for small loans and people willing to lend money in small amounts. An equity crowdfunding platform is where investors purchase equity in private companies in small amounts. The platform has two networks— one of investors and one of entrepreneurs. Crowdfunding is facilitated by social media such as Facebook, Twitter and the like because of their ability to enable the creation and exchange of user-generated content.

In recent years, the global crowdfunding market has grown significantly. According to Massolution (2015), crowdfunding platforms raised $16.2 billion in 2014, an amount that was a 167% increase over the amount raised in 2013, and the global crowdfunding market grew to $34.4 billion in 2015, more than doubling the 2014 figure. When market share is analysed by region, North America accounts for more than half (50.1%) of the crowdfunding market, followed by Asia (30.6%), Europe (18.8%) and other regions (0.5%), which include South America, Oceania and Africa. Notwithstanding the low market share for Africa, crowdfunding in the region is growing fast, as it achieved an annual growth rate of 101% in 2014.

Afristart (2016) reports that crowdfunding is a recent phenomenon in Africa, with only a little over 75 crowdfunding platforms, prototypes and pilot crowdfunding platforms having been launched since 2012. In 2015 there were 57 listed crowdfunding platforms founded and headquartered in Africa spread throughout the continent as per Table 14.3, which also shows internet and Facebook penetration. Notably, with regard to crowdfunding platforms, South Africa is the market leader followed by Nigeria in West Africa and Egypt in North Africa. This is also reflected in volumes raised through crowdfunding in 2015 — South Africa having raised $30.8 million, Egypt $862,000 and Nigeria $314,445.

Table 14.3 African Crowdfunding Platforms, Internet and Facebook Penetration.

Country	Number of Crowdfunding Platforms (2015)	Internet Penetration (% Population) 30 June 2017	Facebook Penetration (% Population) 30 June 2017
Algeria	2	45.2%	43.8%
Egypt	5	39.2%	34.7%
Ghana	2	34.7%	14.0%
Kenya	2	89.4%	12.8%
Ivory Coast	2	26.5%	10.1%
Morocco	4	58.3%	34.1%
Nigeria	9	47.7%	8.3%
Senegal	2	25.7%	14.3%
South Africa	21	54.0%	28.9%
Togo	2	13.0%	4.4%
Tunisia	2	50.9%	50.5%
Uganda	2	45.6%	5.3%
Zimbabwe	2	41.1%	5.2%

Afrikstart. (2016): Crowdfunding in Africa. Report by Afrikstart Crowdfunding Africa. http://afrikstart.com/report/wp-content/uploads/2016/09/Afrikstart-Crowdfunding-In-Africa-Report.pdf; https://www.internetworldstats.com/stats1.htm.

Considering that crowdfunding platforms are internet-based, internet penetration is critical, and Africa happens to have the least penetration in the world, hence presenting a huge constraint. According to *Internet World Stats*, as at 30 June 2017, internet penetration as a percentage of the population in Africa was 31.2% compared with a 55.8% average for the rest of the world. Social media usage, which also plays a critical role in facilitating crowdfunding, is lagging in Africa, as only slightly over 160 million people out of a population of over one billion were Facebook users in 2017.

Notwithstanding internet penetration challenges and slow adoption of social media, crowdfunding is set to be a significant funding mechanism for SMEs. Platforms that have sprouted in Africa are donation-based, rewards-based, equity-based, peer-to- lending and hybrid types. Equity-based crowdfunding platforms are being used to fund start-ups, SMEs and investment in residential and commercial properties, while peer-to-peer lending platforms are sector focused − fundraising for business and entrepreneurship projects.

Afristart (2016) reports that overall, an estimated $32.3 million was raised through crowdfunding in Africa during the year 2015 in a market projected by the World Bank-infoDev to grow and reach $2.5 billion by 2025. An estimated $17.5 million was raised through peer-to-peer business lending and $13.9 million in equity-based crowdfunding platforms for start-ups and SMEs. Most crowdfunding platforms are clustered in South Africa. For instance, the South African peer-to-peer lending platform Rainfin accounted for over 95% of total business loans to local start-ups and SMEs; Lendico, another South African peer-to-peer lending platform, accounted for the remainder. On the other hand, Afineety, a Moroccan equity crowdfunding platform, is becoming more Pan-African, raising equity capital for start-ups and small businesses in Cote D'Ivoire, Tunisia, Algeria, Gabon, Cameroon, Ghana and Kenya.

Though still in its infancy, the potential for equity crowdfunding in filling the funding gap for start-ups and SMEs in Africa is great. Research done by Estrin and Khavul (2016) on the UK equity crowdfunding platform − Crowdcube− demonstrates its potential as an alternative form of entrepreneurial finance. Their evidence shows that investors do not follow the herd to invest irrationally in equity crowdfunding. Rather they find that the pitching process, whereby investors and entrepreneurs share information transparently, reduces the biases and location limits on funding typical of entrepreneurial finance in early stages. The use of Web 2.0 technologies brings entrepreneurial finance into the digital space where wider networks of entrepreneurs and investors can engage each other, exploiting increasing network effects and facilitating low transaction costs. Therefore, once constraints preventing the proliferation of technology-enabled equity crowdfunding are addressed in Africa, the market failure in funding start-ups and SMEs will be significantly addressed.

4.3 A Survey of FinTech Companies Enabling Financial Inclusion in Africa

Africa is increasingly attracting FinTech start-ups that are changing the landscape of financial services. These FinTech start-ups, driven by profit motives, are at the same time enabling financial inclusion. Friendsvow (2017) identifies

Table 14.4 Selected FinTech Companies in Africa.

Name of FinTech	Year Launched	Country of Origin	Nature of Business
RainFin	2012	South Africa	Online lending marketplace that connects borrowers with lenders
22Seven	2012	South Africa	Budgeting & investing app
Bankymoon	2014	South Africa	Builds blockchain-based solutions
Bitsoko	2014	Kenya	Mobile money payment platform that uses blockchain technology
Cellulant	2004	Kenya	Provide mobile payments across 11 African countries
ExpenZA	2011	South Africa	Assist budgeting by automatically keeping track of transactions
GetBucks	2011	South Africa	Online lender that manages credit profiles and budgets
Gust Pay	2012	South Africa	An app that facilitates smart mobile payments
IMB		South Africa	Online payment platform
InterSwitch	2002	Nigeria	Africa-focused integrated digital payment commerce solutions
InVenture	2012	Kenya	Provides a credit scoring and real-time credit
Kobocoin	2014	UK	Digital currency and payment system similar to Bitcoin
Lendico	2013	Germany	Loan marketplace- connect borrowers with investors directly
Microcred	2005	France	Digital finance for micro & SMEs and mass market
M-Pesa	2007	Kenya	Mobile money transfer and micro financing services
Musoni	2009	Kenya	Microfinance leveraging ICT and mobile technology
Nomanini	2011	South Africa	Enable transactions in the cash-based informal retail sector
Paga	2009	Nigeria	Delivers universal access to financial services across Africa
Zoona	2009	South Africa	Provide money transfer and other services to unbanked consumers

Freindsvow. (2017). 22 FinTech companies enabling financial inclusion in Africa. http://www.friendsvow.com/22-fintech-companies-enabling-financial-inclusion-in-africa/.

selected FinTech start-ups as shown in Table 14.4, offering financial services to SMEs and the mass market in Africa.

5. Challenges in Unlocking the Full Potential of Mobile Technology

The GSMA estimates that if mobile money providers in SSA can achieve a 40% activity rate across their existing GSM base, they could increase their active user base by 118 million, doubling the present active user base. It further observes that so far, mobile money providers have only captured 17% of the rural markets in SSA. However, for mobile money providers to realize their potential, Raithatha (2017) outlines the following challenges that must be addressed in order to expand access:

- high levels of investment amidst long payback periods;
- financial infrastructure that accelerates interoperability and facilitate cross-border remittances; and
- a proportionate risk-based regulatory framework that attracts investments from banks and non-banks.

Interoperability among mobile money providers has been actively pursued in East and West African markets to facilitate cross-border remittance transfers. In Southern Africa, the SADC Bankers Association is involved in an initiative that will create a mobile money central transaction hub to allow users to transact across 15 markets in the region.

The importance of having an enabling regulatory environment cannot be underestimated. By 2017, 30 countries in SSA had enabling regulatory frameworks for mobile money. Research by the GSMA shows that the total mobile money transaction value was 5.4% higher in markets with enabling regulation than in markets without enabling regulation.

Digital financial solutions also create some challenges for central bank supervision. The many small loans offered by various mobile phone providers are not recorded on central banks' credit registers. Therefore, as more business activities move to mobile channels, the more the risk of fraud, hacking, data compromise and other cyber vulnerabilities. Central banks are lagging behind in the development of digital technical capacity to be able to supervise a digital financial services ecosystem.

The other major barriers to digital financial inclusion in Africa are, broadly, lack of basic infrastructure (especially energy) and low internet connectivity. Some FinTech applications require a lot of energy, which is a scarce commodity in Africa. According to Afrobarometer (2016), across 36 African countries only 4 in 10 people have a reliable supply of electricity. The International Energy Agency further observes that whilst Africa is rich in energy resources, 625 million people in SSA are without power, representing 68% of the total population. With regard to internet connectivity, the core platform on which FinTech runs, Africa, has the lowest internet penetration in the world.

6. Looking Ahead

FinTech is indeed changing the landscape of financial services. One of its significant impacts is that it is blurring the boundaries among financial institutions, markets, and new service providers that are non-financial institutions. In addition to improving the quality and range of financial services, FinTech is accelerating the financial inclusion agenda. While formal financial institutions find rural areas to be unprofitable for extending branch networks, FinTech services such as mobile money and e-wallets are offering low-cost financial services in many remote parts of Africa. Banks may eventually lose relevance in rural places of Africa; in any case, they have more mobile money accounts than formal bank accounts.

One area in which FinTech will have a significant impact in Africa going forward is its ability to reduce the costs of international remittance transfers. Within regions, interoperability among mobile money providers is already facilitating cross-border remittance transfers at a cheaper cost. Beyond African borders, blockchain technology is a very promising technology that will facilitate cheaper international remittance transfers.

References

Afrikstart. (2016). *Crowdfunding in Africa*. Report by Afrikstart Crowdfunding Africa. http://afrikstart.com/report/wp-content/uploads/2016/09/Afrikstart-Crowdfunding-In-Africa-Report.pdf

Afrobarometer. (2016). *Off-grid or 'off-on': Lack of access, unreliable electricity supply still plagues majority of Africans*. Afrobarometer Round 6: New data from 36 African countries, Dispatch No. 75, 14 March 2016.

Ahmed, I. S. Y. (2017). Determinants of continuance intention to use mobile money transfer: An integrated model. *Journal of Internet Banking and Commerce, 22*(S7), 1–24.

Arner, D., Barberis, J., & Buckley, R. (2015). *The evolution of FinTech: A new post-crisis paradigm*. University of Hong Kong Faculty of Law. Research Paper No. 2015/047.

Davis, F. D. (1989). Perceived usefulness, perceived ease of use, and user acceptance of information technology. *MIS Quarterly, 13*(3), 319–339.

Desai, F. (2015). The evolution of Fintech. *Forbes Magazine*. December 13, 2015, available at: https://www.forbes.com/sites/falgunidesai/2015/12/13/the-evolution-of-fintech/#301334d57175.

Estrin, S., & Khavul, S. (2016). *Equity crowdfunding: A new model for financing entrepreneurship? CentrePiece Winter 2015/2016*. LSE: University of London.

Freindsvow. (2017). *22 FinTech companies enabling financial inclusion in Africa*. http://www.friendsvow.com/22-fintech-companies-enabling-financial-inclusion-in-africa/.

GSMA. (2015). *Mobile money crosses borders: New remittance models in West Africa*. GSMA.

GSMA. (2016). *The state of mobile money in Western Africa*. GSMA.

H2 Ventures, & KPMG. (2016). *FINTECH100: Leading global FinTech innovators*, 2016 FINTECH100 Report.

He, D., Leckow, R., Haksar, V., Mancini-Griffoli, T., Jenkinson, N., Kashima, M., et al. (2017). *Fintech and financial services: Initial considerations*. IMF Staff Discussion Note SDN/17/05, Washington, DC.

IFC. (2017). *How FinTech is reaching the poor in Africa and Asia: A start-up perspective*. Washington, DC: World Bank Group. Note 34 March 2017, International Finance Corporation.

MGI. (2016). *Digital finance for all: Powering inclusive growth in emerging economies*. McKinsey Global Institute, McKinsey & Company.

Niehaus, J. (1983). Financial innovation, multinational banking and monetary policy. *Journal of Banking & Finance, 7*(4), 537–551.

Oliveira, T., Faria, M., Thomas, M. A., & Popovič, A. (2014). Extending the understanding of mobile banking adoption: When UTAUT meets TTF and ITM. *International Journal of Information Management, 34*, 689–703.

PwC. (2017). *Redrawing the lines: FinTech's growing influence on financial services*. PwC Global FinTech Report 2017.

Raithatha, R. (2017). *The future of mobile money in Sub-Saharan Africa*. A foundation for greater financial inclusion. https://www.gsma.com/mobilefordevelopment/programme/mobile-money/future-mobile-money-sub-saharan-africa-foundation-greater-financial-inclusion.

The Economist. (2009). Mobile phones have transformed lives in the poor world. *The Economist*. September 24, 2009.

The Economist. (2017). *Kenya's sovereign debt*. July 1st, 2017.

The Global Partnership for Financial Inclusion (GPFI) report. (2016). *Global standard-setting Bodies financial inclusion: The evolving landscape*. https://www.gpfi.org/sites/default/files/documents/GPFI_WhitePaper_Mar2016.pdf.

Tobbin, P., & Kuwornu, J. K. M. (2011). Adoption of mobile money transfer technology: Structural Equation Modelling approach. *European Journal of Business and Management, 3*, 59–78.

Further Reading

AlliedCrowds. (2015). *Developing world crowdfunding-sustainability through crowdfunding*. Q2 2015 Report, London, U.K.

AlliedCrowds. (2016). *Crowdfunding annual report January 2016*. London, U.K.

Baeck, P., Collins, L., & Zhang, B. (2014). *Understanding alternative finance*. NESTA and University of Cambridge. The UK Alternative Finance Industry Report 2014.

Demirguc-Kunt, A., Klapper, L., Singer, D., & Van Oudheusden, P. (2015). *The global Findex database 2014: Measuring financial inclusion around the world*. World Bank Group Policy Research Working Paper 7255, Washington, DC.

G20. (2016). *G20 High level principles for digital financial inclusion*. Global Partnership for Financial Inclusion.

GeoPoll, & World Wide Worx. (2015). *The Mobile Africa 2015 study, conducted by mobile surveying company*. Available at: http://www.itnewsafrica.com/2015/04/study-reveals-african-mobile-phone-usage-stats/.

GSMA. (2013). *The mobile economy Asia pacific 2013*. prepared by the Boston Consulting Group.

Kim, C., Mirusmonov, M., & Lee, I. (2010). An empirical examination of the factors influencing the intention to use mobile payment. *Computers in Human Behavior, 26*(3), 310–322.

Makina, D. (2017). The role of social media in crowdfunding. In *Proceedings of the 4th European conference on social media*. Vilnius, Lithuania: Mykolas Romeris University, 3–4 July 2017.

Mugambe, P. (2017). UTAUT model in explaining the adoption of mobile money usage by MSMEs' customers in Uganda. *Advances in Economics and Business, 5*(3), 129–136.

Peng, R., Zhao, M., & Wang, L. (2014). Financial inclusion in the people's Republic of China: Achievements and challenges. In Asian Development Bank Institute (Ed.), *Financial inclusion in Asia: Country surveys*. Japan: Asian Development Bank Institute (2014).

World Bank. (2013). *Crowdfunding's potential for the developing world*. Washington, DC: World Bank Infodev, Finance and Private Sector Development Department.

World Bank. (2015). *Crowdfunding in emerging markets: Lessons from East African start-ups*. Washington, DC: World Bank.

INDEX